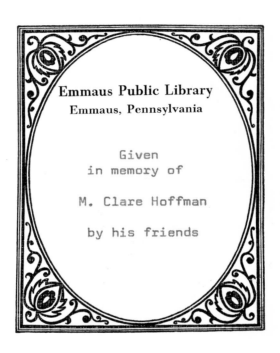

The
Pennsylvania
Antiwar Movement, 1861–1865

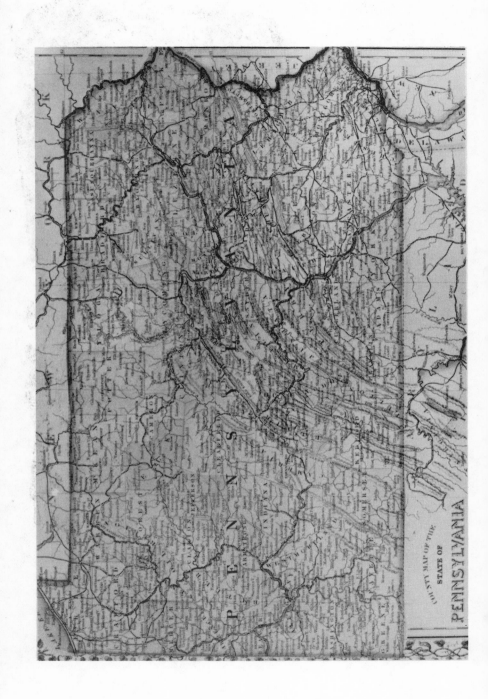

COUNTY MAP OF THE
STATE OF
PENNSYLVANIA

The Pennsylvania Antiwar Movement, 1861–1865

Arnold M. Shankman

Rutherford • Madison • Teaneck
Fairleigh Dickinson University Press
London and Toronto: Associated University Presses

Associated University Presses, Inc.
Cranbury, New Jersey 08512

Associated University Presses
Magdalen House
136-148 Tooley Street
London SE1 2TT, England

Associated University Presses
Toronto M5E 1A7, Canada

Library of Congress Cataloging in Publication Data

Shankman, Arnold M   1945-
    The Pennsylvania antiwar movement, 1861-1865.

    Bibliography: p.
    Includes index.
    1. Pennsylvania—Politics and government—Civil
War, 1861-1865.   2. United States—History—Civil
War, 1861-1865—Protest movements—Pennsylvania.
I. Title.
E527.S52   973.7'12'09748   78-75186
ISBN 0-8386-2228-3

Printed in the United States of America

For My Mother
and *In Memory of My Father*

Contents

Acknowledgments

In the nine years I have been studying antiwar sentiment in Civil War Pennsylvania I have become indebted to numerous individuals. First and foremost is my debt to Bell Irvin Wiley. Professor Wiley, who personifies the gentleman scholar, supervised the dissertation upon which this book is based. He provided wise counsel, made available his extensive note collection on Civil War soldiers, wrote letters to facilitate my use of archival collections, and, when necessary, used his red pencil to improve my style and to refine my arguments. Also, he and Professor John L. Stipp of Knox College helped teach me tolerance of the copperheads, men and women whose racial prejudices are diametrically opposed to my own thinking on the subject and that of Professors Wiley and Stipp. The antiwar leaders' ideas on race were backward, but their concerns for civil liberties deserve to be remembered.

Others who read all or parts of the manuscript, corrected errors, and offered suggestions and moral support include Professors James Harvey Young, James Z. Rabun, and John T. Juricek, all of Emory University, Dr. George R. Lamplugh of the Westminster School in Atlanta, Sue Culp Garrett, Dr. Rose Begemann of Georgia College, Dr. Michael B. Dougan of Arkansas State University, Steve Livengood, Dr. Eleanor F. Straub, Thomas S. Pearce, Dr. Mark K. Bauman of Atlanta Junior College, Margaret Gail

Stephenson, Dr. Michael B. Chesson of the University of Massachusetts, Boston campus, Dr. Adelynne H. Whitaker of the University of Maryland, University College—European Division, Dr. Frederick M. Heath of Winthrop College, Dr. Rodney O. Davis of Knox College, Dr. Thomas Keene of Kennesaw College, and Dr. Charles F. Hobson, editor of the Papers of John Marshall. Dr. Hobson made available the papers of Colonel Charles F. Taylor, and Professor Keene xeroxed letters of William Cairnes and of W.H. Logan, which are in the possession of his mother. Professor Harold Cox of Wilkes College arranged for me to obtain copies of pertinent letters from the Charles Buckalew Papers deposited at his college. Professor Joel Silbey of Cornell University and Professor Michael F. Holt commented on a paper presented at the Organization of American Historians meeting in Boston in 1975 that concerned the antiwar movement in Pennsylvania.

Librarians and archivists facilitated my research in many ways. I am grateful to the librarians at the Robert Woodruff Library of Emory University, Ida Dacus Library of Winthrop College, the Pennsylvania State Library, George Williams College Library, the University of Pennsylvania Library, the Harvard University Libraries, and the Cleveland Public Library. Archivists were helpful at the Historical Society of Pennsylvania, the Western Reserve Historical Society, the Pennsylvania Historical and Museum Commission, the National Archives, the Library of Congress Manuscripts Division, and the Presbyterian Historical Society. In particular I would like to thank Irwin Simpkins, Ruth Walling, William Orth, Adelaide Williams, Patricia Ridgeway, and Carolyn H. Sung.

Other assistance came from Joel Nichols, Winthrop College photographer, Anne Rhodes, a Winthrop art student who helped with the preparation of maps, and from my expert typists, Jo Shaw and Judy Carter Faile. Anne Hebenstreit and her helpers at the Associated University Presses were gracious and patient with me whenever I sought to make "last minute" revisions in the manuscript. The Historical Society of Pennsylvania, the Library of

Congress, and Wilkes College provided material for several of the photographs used in this volume.

I am grateful to the Historical Society of Pennsylvania for permission to quote from the many manuscripts I used from their collections and from the diary of Sidney George Fisher, which Nicholas Wainwright edited so expertly. Mr. Wainwright gave permission to use in this book the material in chapter 7, the bulk of which appeared as "Draft Resistance in Civil War Pennsylvania," *The Pennsylvania Magazine of History and Biography* 101 (1977): 190–204.

Finally, but most importantly, I am of course, responsible for any errors of fact or interpretation that appear in this book.

Arnold Shankman
Winthrop College
June 1979

Introduction

Despite the presence of a veritable mountain of books and articles relating to the Civil War, there are many aspects of the conflict yet to be examined. More than a century after Lee's surrender at Appomattox, one can find few good studies of Northern politics on the state level.[1] Perhaps it is more glamorous to write about the exploits of generals, the quarrels of congressmen, or the activities of diplomats, but to achieve a proper understanding of the Civil War it is necessary also to look at life on the home front.

This study seeks to examine peace sentiment in Pennsylvania, a state in which most historians have concluded that such sentiment was inconsequential. My findings, however, dispute this commonly held view. I argue that opposition to the war in the Keystone State was as intense as it was in Ohio, Illinois, or New York, states traditionally associated with peace sentiment. From the spring of 1862 until the fall of 1864 at least a quarter of the Pennsylvania electorate favored a nonmilitary solution to the conflict. War critics nominated and elected candidates to state and congressional offices, and in 1863 they nearly sent one of their number to the executive mansion in Harrisburg. Thus, it is fair to conclude that peace sentiment in the commonwealth was both a reality and a significant political force. And it is a subject worthy of study.

Unfortunately it is impossible to be precise when discussing the

composition of Pennsylvania's antiwar factions. In many cases
sentiments about the conflict changed with the times. News of a
Union army defeat, of the scheduling of a new draft lottery, of the
arrest of a local editor, or of the employment of Negro strikebreakers at a nearby factory doubtless would promote increased
resentment toward the war. On the other hand, stories about the
successful routing of Johnny Rebs, the capture of Southern blockade runners, the bread riots in Richmond, or the rise of Unionist
sentiment in Dixie would serve to reinforce Pennsylvanians'
desire to seek a martial solution to the nation's troubles.

Basically, there were two antiwar factions in Pennsylvania.[2]
Both were associated with the state Democratic party, for peace
men were persuaded that, if the Democracy controlled the legislature and governorship and dominated the state's congressional
delegation, it would promote a speedy and pacific end to the war.

The smaller and more radical of the two factions constituted the
"peace at any price" men. These individuals championed peace
even if this could only be had by permanently dividing the Union.
Some, in fact, thought Pennsylvania should join the Confederacy.
This faction was composed of several diverse elements and it
never numbered more than ten percent of the state's voters. It
included several prominent members of Philadelphia's aristocracy, men such as Pierce Butler, Joshua Francis Fisher, Charles
Ingersoll and his brothers, Harry and Edward, and William B.
Reed. With the exception of Reed, these were men with familial
and financial ties to Dixie. Resentful of crass Yankee commercial-
ism, they strongly feared that the intemperate spirit of New
England puritanism was descending upon the state. Particularly
upsetting to them was the rise of abolitionism, which they blamed
for the needless disruption of the Union.

George W. Woodward and Francis W. Hughes were probably
the most celebrated non-Philadelphians associated with this faction. Both were Pennsylvania natives, defenders of state rights,
and critics of abolitionism. Echoing the sentiments of Hughes and
Woodward were several newspaper editors. Intense hostility to

the war was evident on the editorial pages of the Selinsgrove *Times*, the Johnstown *Democrat*, the Kittanning *Mentor*, the West Chester *Jeffersonian*, the Bedford *Gazette*, the Greensburg *Argus*, and the Bellefonte *Democratic Watchman*. Unfortunately we know little about the background of these editors. Like most other Pennsylvania war critics, they, with good reason, destroyed their personal papers after 1865. The only two factors which most consistently mark the extreme peace faction are (1) support for John C. Breckinridge in the 1860 presidential election and (2) intense hatred of the abolitionist movement and of all efforts to promote Negro equality.

The second faction of the Pennsylvania peace movement was composed of men who were more moderate than the Ingersolls, Reeds, and Woodwards. To avoid repetitive use of the words "peace Democrat," I have also called them "antiwar Democrats" and "Copperheads." Like Frank L. Klement, Richard Curry, and Nicholas B. Wainwright, I consider "Copperhead" an appropriate term for the loyal opposition to the Lincoln administration. I consciously join the ranks of those revisionist historians who reject "the traditional stereotype of the Copperhead as traitor."[3]

Peace Democrats in Pennsylvania included many small farmers, German and Irish immigrants, laborers, coal miners, and factory workers. These people opposed the war for a variety of reasons. First, before the firing on Fort Sumter they tended not to be politically aware or sophisticated. The sectional struggles between the North and South of the 1850s had been unintelligible to them. It was easy in the 1860s to persuade them that the war was a nefarious abolitionist plot to free the blacks and encourage them to migrate to Pennsylvania, where they would compete with poor whites for jobs and housing. Moreover, they disliked the abolitionists. Anti-slaverymen, they thought, were pious hypocrites, "do-gooders" with nothing but contempt for lower-middle-class and poor whites. Immigrants, in particular, seemed to sense that abolitionists disliked them. Surprisingly, these same immigrants were willing to get along with the Philadelphia antiwar aristocrats, who despised the masses but nonetheless recognized the necessity of wooing their votes.

The ranks of the peace men were swelled by those who considered the conflict a rich man's war, but a poor man's fight. These people cared little about the economic necessity for raising new sources of revenue to pay for the expenses of suppressing the rebellion. Most did not understand financial statements, and few could have interpreted ledger sheets. They did, however, comprehend the fact that substitutes cost a lot of money and that commutation fees were beyond the reach of the common laborers. Statistically it now can be shown that the draft laws were less onerous than once believed, but Pennsylvanians in 1863 were not aware of this. Hostility to the draft promoted hostility to the war and receptivity to peace sentiment.

Pennsylvania Copperheads may not have been politically aware before 1861, but during the war they showed increased sensitivity to efforts to deprive them of civil liberties. True, some cared little for abstract discussions of state rights, but they resented the suppression of newspapers, the suspension of the writ of habeas corpus, and the arbitrary arrests of war critics. Abstract speeches about the 1798 Virginia and Kentucky Resolutions may have confounded the masses, but the arrest of a nearby farmer or county editor disturbed many a Pennsylvania farmer and promoted peace sentiment.

To those weary of war, a peaceable solution to the conflict seemed desirable and attainable. In county after county during the winters of 1862–63 and 1863–64, Democrats staged meetings and passed resolutions calling for an armistice. Many Pensylvanians seriously believed that a convention of the states was the best way to end the war. There had been compromises in 1820 and 1850, they reasoned, why not one in 1863?

It is not easy to pinpoint centers of Copperhead strength. Nonetheless, it seems fair to conclude that peace sentiment was most evident in counties that voted Democratic in the 1850s, the 1862 state, 1863 gubernatorial, and 1864 presidential elections.

About thirty counties, mainly in northeastern, central, and southern Pennsylvania, fit these specifications.[4]

Mention needs to be made of war Democrats.[5] This element of the Democracy insisted that the war was just and that the South had to be defeated. More tolerant of arbitrary arrests, newspaper suppressions, and conscription laws than peace men, they thought it was unwise to call for an armistice. After 1862, this faction seems to have lost control over the Pennsylvania Democracy. Perhaps this was because it lacked effective leadership. One potential leader, Hendrick B. Wright, a member of Congress until 1863, was unpopular in several sections of the commonwealth. James Buchanan, who was not a peace Democrat, spent most of the war at Wheatland and he exercised little control over the state's Democracy. A third likely leader, John Cessna, was so outraged the party refused to nominate him for U.S. senator or governor in 1863 that he eventually joined the Unionists.

The most effective men in the Pennsylvania Democratic party during the war were former Senator William Bigler, Senator Charles Buckalew, Cyrus Ward, Morrow B. Lowry, Charles John Biddle, Jeremiah Sullivan Black, Francis W. Hughes, Justice George W. Woodward, and Jehu Glancy Jones. To be sure, not every one of these men was a Copperhead, but all sympathized somewhat with the opponents of the war.

As I have already made clear, I do not consider the Copperheads to have been disloyal. Joel Silbey aptly titled his study of the Democratic party in the Civil War *A Respectable Minority*. There was no chapter of the Knights of the Golden Circle in Pennsylvania; neither were there lodges of the Order of American Knights or the Sons of Liberty.[6] Very few Pennsylvanians committed treason as defined by the Constitution, but that was because they were conservatives, not revolutionaries. Consistently they preached that redress of all grievances would have to come at the ballot box. In the end, all they really wanted was "the Constitution as it is and the Union as it was."

CENTERS OF PEACE SENTIMENT IN CIVIL WAR PENNSYLVANIA

Centers of Peace Sentiment

NOTES

1. In their introduction to the second volume of *Civil War Books: A Critical Bibliography* (Baton Rouge, La., 1969), Allan Nevins, James Robertson, Jr., and Bell Wiley noted there were "disappointingly few studies in the areas of government and politics, North and South."

2. The most important study of the Democratic party in the 1860s is Joel Silbey, *A Respectable Minority: The Democratic Party in the Civil War Era, 1860-1868* (New York, 1977). Silbey's book came into print after this volume was accepted for publication. In Silbey's study peace Democrats are classified as Purists. Unlike Silbey, I divide the Purists, the subject of my book, into two groupings.

3. See Richard Curry, "The Union As It Was: A Critique of Recent Interpretations of the 'Copperheads,'" *Civil War History* 13 (1967): 25-39; Eric J. Cardinal, "Disloyalty or Dissent: The Case of the Copperheads," *The Midwest Quarterly* 19 (1977): 24-35.

4. These counties were Adams, Bedford, Berks, Bucks, Cambria, Carbon, Centre, Clarion, Clearfield, Clinton, Columbia, Cumberland, Elk, Fayette, Fulton, Greene, Juniata, Lehigh, Luzerne, Lycoming, Monroe, Montgomery, Montour, Northampton, Northumberland, Pike, Schuylkill, Sullivan, Wayne, Westmoreland, Wyoming, and York.

5. In Silbey's book the group I refer to as "war Democrats" are called "Legitimists." The war Democrats in Silbey's study were so much in favor of the Civil War that after 1862 they, in many cases, became members of the Unionist party of Abraham Lincoln. John Cessna is an example of a Pennsylvanian who would fit into Silbey's categorization of war Democrats.

6. A very perceptive article on the myth of the Knights of the Golden Circle, the Sons of Liberty, and other allegedly traitorous organizations is Frank L. Klement, "Civil War Politics, Nationalism, and Postwar Myths," *The Historian* 38 (1976): 419-38. An important article on the peace movement that concentrates on the Midwest see Robert H. Abzug, "The Copperheads: Historical Approaches to Civil War Dissent in the Middle West," *Indiana Magazine of History* 66 (1970): 40-55.

The
Pennsylvania
Antiwar Movement, 1861–1865

1

"We Were Foredoomed to Defeat"

"These are times that try the fidelity and courage of men"*

"[Abolitionists] have just as good a right to force free-love upon Pennsylvania as free labor upon Virginia."**

On November 6, 1860, Pennsylvania voters overwhelmingly cast their ballots for Abraham Lincoln, the Republican presidential candidate. To some Pennsylvania Democrats the election of a "black" Republican president represented the logical—albeit the undesirable—result of tolerating thirty years of "fanatical" New England abolitionist agitation. The antislavery leaders, these Democrats believed, were disunionists, for they preached hatred of the South and its peculiar institution and they argued that the Union could not—and should not—exist with nearly half of its member states sanctioning slavery. Less than a year before the election, Charles Jared Ingersoll, one of the leaders of Philadelphia society and a prominent Democratic politician, dismissed the abolitionist orators as enemies of mankind and Christianity "upon whom summary punishment ought to be ruthlessly in flicted." He sarcastically suggested that the ideal solution of the

*Harrisburg *Patriot and Union,* July 13, 1860.

**Jeremiah S. Black to George W. Woodward, November 24, 1860, Black MSS, Library of Congress (LC), hereafter cited as Black MSS.

23

nation's sectional problems would be to dissolve the Union; that is, he proposed that New England, New York, and British North America form another republic. "If they c[ould] no longer endure the slave communion," he concluded, he hoped they would part in peace; there was "room enough for all."[1]

Although Ingersoll's proposal was drastic, his low opinion of the antislavery leaders was hardly unique. A sizable number of Pennsylvanians, some of whose families, like Ingersoll's, were of New England origin,[2] argued that the abolitionists were deliberately and unjustly promoting sectional antagonism. Unless this was checked and Southerners were allowed to bring their property into the territories, they insisted, the slave states would be forced to secede, and the United States would be permanently divided. Then what they considered to be the greatest nation man had ever created would be no more. And for what? All for the Negro, who most Democrats and many Republicans thought was innately inferior to the white man. Freeing the black man, many declared, would ruin the Southern economy, promote the immigration of former slaves to the North, where they would compete with white laborers for jobs, and lead to the amalgamation of the races.

Sentiment against free Negroes was quite unconcealed throughout the state. Citizens from all corners of the commonwealth petitioned the legislature to prohibit the future immigration of free blacks into Pennsylvania. Anti-black riots erupted in Philadelphia in 1834, 1848, 1842, and 1849; and its Afro-American residents had good reason to doubt that they lived in the city of brotherly love. In Pittsburgh blacks were second-class citizens, and Republican politicians were less likely to complain about the evils of slavery than about the disproportionate power Southerners wielded in national affairs.[3] Under the 1838 Pennsylvania Constitution Afro-Americans had been disfranchised and declared ineligible for citizenship, but some whites continued to call upon the legislature to deprive the blacks of their few remaining civil rights and to adopt a slave code. According to their petitions, free Negroes represented a burden to the poor fund, for "owing to their great indolence and dissipation they have filled our prisons, thus increasing our taxes to an enormous extent."[4]

Charles Jared Ingersoll was a prominent Philadelphian. An outspoken foe of
the abolitionist movement, he proposed in 1860 that New England and New
York secede from the Union and join with British North America to form
another republic. Charles Jared Ingersoll's son Charles was arrested in 1862
for expressing criticism of the government. Three years later Edward, another
of Charles Jared Ingersoll's sons, was jailed after he expressed sympathy for
the South and tried to attack a veteran who quarreled with him. *(Courtesy
Historical Society of Pennsylvania.)*

It would be a mistake to suppose that all of these Pennsylvanians envied the South for keeping slaves; probably most were pleased that they lived in a free state. Charles Jared Ingersoll's son, Charles, noted in November 1860 that he never returned from Dixie to his home in Philadelphia without congratulating himself that his "lot was not cast in the planting country, cultivated by slave labor, with a meagre population, [and] a lower civilization."[5] But neither he nor those sharing his political philosophy and racial prejudices thought that owning slaves was in itself evil or that the North had any right to interfere with the domestic institutions of the slave states. As late as October 1860, a Pennsylvanian confidently—if inaccurately—wrote that no more than one thousand residents of Philadelphia held "extreme opinions on the subject of slavery. As a general rule they are profoundly indifferent about it." Admittedly this estimate was low, but abolitionists were unpopular in the city. Many Philadelphians argued that Jesus never condemned slavery and that bondage exposed the blacks to Christianity and the other blessings of civilization.[6] A Philadelphia religious organ maintained that free blacks were "more cut off and oppressed than slaves," and it condemned the abolitionists for ignoring the plight of Northern Negroes. Attorney General Jeremiah S. Black denounced the antislavery leaders for doing "mischief like monkeys for the mere sake of mischief" and expected that next they would organize "a war against the institution of marriage."[7]

Undoubtedly the greatest mistake of Black and his friends was their failure to realize that, although there were hypocrites in the ranks of the abolitionists, there were also idealists, men who sincerely believed that blacks and whites were entitled to the same political and social privileges.

For decades Southerners had complained that Yankees hoped to promote slave insurrections in Dixie, which, they stated, would result in a bloodbath and economic chaos. John Brown's ill-fated raid confirmed the worst of their suspicions about the goals of the antislavery crusade. A significant number of Pennsylvanians were also upset about the possibility of whites leading a racial insurrection in the slave states. For example, James Alexander Fulton of Kittanning wrote Governor Henry Wise of Virginia to express his concern over Brown's raid and to assure the people of Virginia that in the Keystone State all Democrats and many Republicans were devoted to the Union. He asked Wise how to end the sectional strife that was threatening to sunder the country. The governor responded that all difficulties coud easily be solved if the North would no longer "nullify the laws of the Union."[8]

Far more impressive than this exchange of letters was a huge rally held at Jayne's Hall in Philadelphia on December 7, 1859. Tens of thousands of people came to the meeting, and organizers had to rent a nearby hotel to accommodate the overflow crowd. The Philadelphians had assembled to voice their approval of the hanging of John Brown, "the treason plotter"; some carried banners proclaiming, "Down with ALL TRAITORS, FAC- TIONALISTS, AND DISUNIONISTS."[9] William Bradford Reed, who had served as President James Buchanan's minister to China, authored the resolutions adopted at the meeting. These called for the enforcement of the Fugitive Slave Law, the prompt denunciation of all attempts to excite slave revolts, and the noninterference of all Americans with the domestic institutions of the states. A copy of the resolutions was sent to Governor Wise.[10] Though the audience was representative of Philadelphia society as a whole, those in charge of the gathering included members of the city's "best families."

It was hoped that news of the meeting would soothe the feelings of Southerners, but, alas, few non-Pennsylvania papers bothered to mention it in their columns. Reed was angry, for he insisted that only if slaveholders realized that Pennsylvanians shunned abolitionism would there be peace.[11]

Reed's fears seemed to be confirmed when, to protest John Brown's raid, hundreds of Southern medical students left the state. The former diplomat considered the "stampede" to be unfortunate and thought that the exodus had been instigated by members of the Richmond Medical College.[12] Lest this departure be dismissed as an incident of concern only to keepers of boardinghouses and professors, it should be noted that a very high percentage—if not a majority—of practicing Southern physicians in 1859 had been trained in Pennsylvania. Of 1,950 medical students graduating from the University of Pennsylvania during the first quarter of the nineteenth century, nearly 1,000 came from south of the Mason-Dixon Line. "Over and over again," noted one historian, "more students came from Virginia or even Georgia than from any northern state." In 1836, for example, the state's colleges and universities had more graduates from Virginia than from Pennsylvania.[13] Despite the departure of so many medical students from Dixie, over half of the men enrolled at Jefferson Medical College in Philadelphia in 1860 were from the South. Other schools also had large numbers of students from the slave states. As late as 1859 Dickinson College reported that 74 of its 164 students were from Dixie; 81 of the remainder were Pennsylvanians.[14]

Many Pennsylvanians wanted to promote friendly relations between the North and the South, and they thought that this could best be effected by electing a Democratic successor to Buchanan. This was easier said than done, for the president's handling of the difficulties in Kansas had helped split the state's Democracy into pro-administration and anti-Lecompton factions and had been a major factor in the Republican victories of 1858. To win the October and November elections the two wings of the party would have to cooperate and support one set of candidates. At first it seemed as though defeating Republicans was more important than feuding, and at their state convention, which was held at Reading on February 29, 1860, the Democrats appeared to have forgotten their factional quarrels. There they selected Henry C. Foster to be their gubernatorial candidate and they avoided expressing any preference for any of the presidential candidates.[15] Since Pennsylvania traditionally voted Democratic, it was generally believed that Foster would be able to defeat his opponent, Andrew Gregg Curtin. To remind would-be defectors to stick with the party the Ebensburg *Democrat and Sentinel* warned, "This is no time for the Democracy to wrangle and quarrel among themselves about mere abstractions. The Disunionists must be defeated next fall."[16]

When the Democrats split at Baltimore, the chances for victory in the fall all but disappeared. Both Breckinridge and Douglas had sizable followings in the Keystone State, and the presence of four presidential candidates would work to Lincoln's advantage.

William Welsh, the manager of the Democratic campaign in Pennsylvania, thought that, if the Breckinridge and Douglas supporters agreed to a fusion ticket, the Republicans could still be defeated. Therefore he scheduled a meeting of the Democratic state committee to propose a compromise acceptable to both factions, and this was held in Philadelphia on July 2. Only about two-thirds of those invited attended the gathering, and the overwhelming majority of these men favored the election of Breckinridge. Without much difficulty they promised to support Foster and all local candidates. On the presidential question they were pragmatic and agreed to a fusion ticket. If the Democrats won in November, the party electors would vote for Douglas provided that their support would secure his election as president; but if their ballots could not elect him and could insure the selection of Breckinridge as president, they would then be cast for the Kentuckian. In the event that neither man could become president with Pennsylvania's help, the electors could split their votes.[17]

Most Douglas supporters would not agree to the compromise, and their candidate urged his friends to spurn any deals and to conduct their own campaign. His supporters alleged that only he was the regular party nominee and therefore to accept Welsh's compromise would be to support fraud and corruption. Richard Vaux, one of the Democratic electors, informed Welsh that he considered the July 2 meeting to be illegal and he would vote for Douglas only. If this was unacceptable to the party, he would resign and a new elector could be appointed in his place.[18] J. R. Crawford, another elector, wrote a letter similar to that of Welsh.[19]

Breckinridge men, who expected that the compromise would

work to their advantage, professed to be shocked at the action of Vaux, the former mayor of Philadelphia and a former Whig. "These are times that try the fidelity and courage of men," declared the Harrisburg *Patriot and Union* on July 13, 1860, "and it is not surprising that some should fail, and that the Hon. Richard Vaux should be the first man to desert the cause of a united Democracy to enlist under the banner of disunion." Welsh urged Vaux to support the compromise, warning that failure to do so would suggest a preference for "the success of the opposition candidates."[20] The two continued their correspondence, which was published in party newspapers, but neither man persuaded the other to abandon his position.

Pro-Douglas Democrats acted as though the election of Breckinridge would be as disastrous as that of Lincoln, and Welsh feared that, unless he did something to promote harmony, Republicans would sweep local, state, and national contests. So he scheduled another meeting, at Cresson on August 9. At this assembly delegates approved of another compromise, which, they hoped, would satisfy the Douglas faction and still keep a fusion ticket. This provided for a Democratic electoral ticket on which the voter could express his preference for Douglas or Breckinridge. In the event of a Democratic victory, if the greater number of popular ballots had been cast for Douglas, he would get the state's electoral votes; if, on the other hand, Breckinridge had a majority, he would receive the twenty-seven electoral votes. But if the twenty-seven votes could not elect the candidate with a majority of the popular votes and could "elect any man running for the office of President of the United States claiming to be a Democrat," that candidate was to receive the ballots.[21]

Nearly all of the party faithful agreed to abide by the "Cresson Compromise." Senator William Bigler thought that it was an ingenious solution to the problem, for technically it was "no compromise or fusion." Breckinridge and Douglas men continued to support their candidates but now their votes counted against Lincoln. The Pittsburgh *Post,* a Douglas organ, considered the agreement to be "conciliatory," and the Bedford *Gazette,* which also favored the "Little Giant," said that the "motto of the Democracy should be 'Any Democrat in preference to Lincoln.'" In Wilkes-Barre the Douglas Democratic Club endorsed the "Cresson Compromise" as the best way to elect Douglas.[22]

Yet some Douglasites and the senator himself would not agree to the compromise. A number of them, including Hendrick B. Wright, retired from the campaign; others reluctantly decided to vote for Lincoln or Bell.[23] Newspapers representing this point of view denounced "the Cresson treason" as an "UNCONSTITU-TIONAL . . . double headed swindle."[24] One group of Douglas backers met in Harrisburg on August 15 to select electors pledged only to the "Little Giant" and to plan the formation of a Douglas electoral ticket. When Douglas toured the state in September, he opposed fusion, thereby alienating some of his friends who had committed themselves to the "Cresson Compromise." Richard Vaux suggested that he not visit Philadelphia because many of his supporters there had become *"weak-kneed"* and no longer stood by the Democratic nominations.[25]

Throughout the campaign Democrats continued to hope to win the October elections, and the Blairsville *Record* reminded its readers that no matter whom they supported for president, there was "no good or valid reason why any dissention or division should prevail in reference to the Gubernatorial question."[26] At Democratic rallies speakers in behalf of the state ticket were careful to speak of national politics only in general terms and to avoid mentioning Breckinridge or Douglas by name.[27]

Most voters thought that a higher duty on foreign goods was necessary to Pennsylvania's continued prosperity, and therefore the tariff question was a key election issue.[28] Neither Douglas nor Breckinridge was identified with the efforts to boost tariff rates, and, mindful of Southern hostility to an increase in duties, neither could afford to champion a protective tariff during the campaign and expect to win the electoral votes of the slave states. Democrats lamely commented that a desirable tariff was more likely to be passed if they were victorious than if Lincoln won, but voters were unconvinced. Astute politicians knew that hundreds of votes in each county would be cast for Republicans because the Chicago platform called for higher tariff duties.[29]

By October it was apparent that Andrew Curtin, the Republican candidate, would win by a sizable margin. James Alexander Fulton, a veteran Democratic campaigner, noted that the meetings in 1860 lacked enthusiasm and the speakers were unusually dull. "We all felt we were foredoomed to defeat," he recalled. "It was the most gloomy campaign I ever passed." Over 32,000 votes separated Foster from the victorious Curtin, and Democrats realized that Lincoln would almost certainly carry the state in November.[30]

On October 12, Welsh, not yet willing to acknowledge defeat in November, convened another meeting of Democrats, and a new fusion ticket was formulated. In the event of a Democratic victory, each elector was to agree to vote as the state committee directed; this decision would not be made until November 20. Considering the chances that this would happen to be remote, even most Douglas holdouts gave their assent. John Forney, however, who preferred Lincoln to Breckinridge, helped organize a separate Douglas ticket. Almost no one would agree to endorse this faction. Voters were told that "every straight Douglas vote" would help only Lincoln.[31]

The fusion campaign presented a gloomy picture of the likely results of a Lincoln victory. A Republican president, the Democrats said, would allow New England to govern the nation, and slaveowners would prefer disunion to existing in a nation under the control of abolitionists.[32] "If the South can by secession escape the doom threatened by Helper, and Seward, and John Quincy Adams," asked the Pittsburgh *Post* on October 30, 1860, "would it be strange if they should do so?"

The electorate, however, ignored these arguments. Pennsylvanians did not believe that voting Republican would lead to dissolving the Union, and they were more interested in tariff hikes than in protecting Southern rights in the territories. There was no way to prevent the state from going "for Lincoln by a very large majority."[33]

PENNSYLVANIA DEMOCRATS AND THE 1860 ELECTIONS

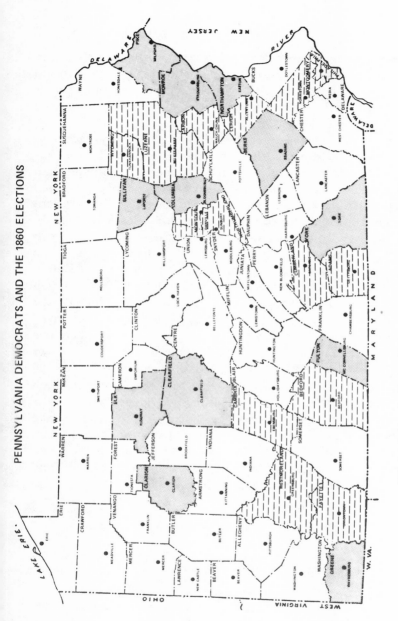

[░] Carried by the Fusion Ticket in November and by Foster in October

[▨] Carried by Lincoln in November but by Foster in October

[ ] Carried by Lincoln in November and by Curtin in October

In fact, the November elections were so anticlimactic that voter turnout was below the October level. To no one's surprise Lincoln swept the state, capturing fifty-three of the commonwealth's sixty-five counties, and a margin of nearly 90,000 votes separated him from the fusion ticket.[34]

Several things help explain Lincoln's large majority. Factionalism within the Democracy had promoted ill will and disorganization. Contributions to the party coffers were lower than anticipated, and some Douglas men refused to support a fusion ticket even though they knew fusion was the only way to prevent Lincoln from winning the commonwealth's electoral votes. In fact, the Democrats spent so much time quarreling among themselves that they had little time to deal with the issues of the campaign. Instead of countering Republican claims that Democrats were hostile to a protective tariff, the Democracy found itself forced to schedule meetings to bind party wounds. Not only did these conferences fail to promote harmony, but they tended to disgust the party faithful who sensed defeat in November. The vote cast for Lincoln was a mere 6,000 more than that won by Curtin. Foster, on the other hand, had garnered more than 20,000 votes above the combined total for the three non-Republican candidates. In other words, 16,000 Pennsylvanians voted in the October gubernatorial election but failed to cast ballots in the more important November presidential contest. Factionalism and voter apathy in November cost the Democrats fourteen counties they had carried in October.[35] Thus, party disunity and the tariff issue had been fatal to the Democracy.

NOTES

1. Charles Jared Ingersoll to Tammany Society of New York, January 3, 1860, quoted in Smethport *McKean County Democrat,* February 9, 1860.

2. Despite their origin, members of the Ingersoll family gladly castigated New Englanders. Charles Ingersoll wished that the Puritans—or, as he called them, "Impuritans"—had "never left their native shores." Had they remained in England, he mused, Americans might "never have heard of the attempted abolition of the hereditary order of negro slavery in America." Charles Ingersoll, *A Brief View of Constitutional Powers,*

Showing that the Union Consisted of Independent States United (Philadelphia, 1864), p. 4, hereafter cited as *Brief View;* see also William Taylor, *Cavalier and Yankee* (New York, 1961), *passim.*

3. To woo nativists and former Whigs, the Republicans campaigned for office under the banner of the People's party. To avoid confusion, they will be referred to as Republicans. Elizabeth Geffen, "Violence in Philadelphia in the 1840's and 1850's," *Pennsylvania History* 36 (1969): 383–88; Leon Litwack, *North of Slavery* (Chicago, 1961), pp. 21, 100–104; Michael F. Holt, *Forging a Majority: The Formation of the Republican Party in Pittsburgh, 1848-60* (New Haven, 1969), p. 4; Michael Feldberg, *The Philadelphia Riots of 1844* (Westport, Conn., 1975), *passim.*

4. *The National Crisis* (New York, Philadelphia, and Washington), May 15, 1860; see also Carlisle (Pa.) *Democrat,* n.d., quoted in *Democratic Expositor* (Washington, D.C.), July 4, 1860; Bedford *Inquirer,* December 14, 1860. The black population of Pennsylvania in 1860 was 56,949; the total population of the state was 2,906,215. *The United States on the Eve of the Civil War* (Washington, 1963), pp. 61, 63.

5. Charles Ingersoll, *Civil War Speeches, 1860-64* (Philadelphia, 1865?), p. 306.

6. William B. Reed, *The Last Appeal* (Philadelphia, 1860), pp. 1–2; Harrisburg *Patriot and Union,* December 15, 1860. Arnold Shankman, "William B. Reed and the Civil War," *Pennsylvania History* 39 (1972): 458.

7. *Christian Observer and Presbyterian Witness* (Philadelphia), February 21, 1861, hereafter cited as *Christian Observer;* Black to George W. Woodward, November 24, 1860, Black MSS; see also [anonymous], *The Ides of March* (Philadelphia, 1861) pp. 17, 22–23; *The End of the Irrepressible Conflict by a Merchant of Philadelphia* (Philadelphia, 1860), pp. 7–14, 35–37.

8. Fulton to Wise, December 15, 1859; Wise to Fulton, December 20, 1859, Fulton MSS, Pennsylvania Historical and Museum Commission (PHMC).

9. *Fanaticism Rebuked, the Philadelphia Meeting of December 7, 1859* (n.p., n.d.), pp. 6, 10–11; Ellis Oberholtzer, *Philadelphia* (Philadelphia, 1912), 2: 354.

10. Reed to Buchanan, December 6, 9, 1859, Buchanan MSS, Historical Society of Pennsylvania (HSP), hereafter cited as Buchanan MSS.

11. Reed to Jeremiah Black, December 14, 1859, Black MSS.

12. Reed to Buchanan, December 23, 1859, Buchanan MSS; Clement Eaton, *Freedom of Thought in the Old South* (New York, 1951), pp. 209–10; December 22, 1859 entry in Nicholas B. Wainwright, Jr., ed., *A Philadelphia Perspective: The Diary of Sidney George Fisher* (Philadelphia, 1967), p. 342, hereafter cited as *Fisher Diary.*

13. Edward Cheyney, *History of the University of Pennsylvania* (Philadelphia, 1940), p. 209; see also Edward Ingle, *Southern Sidelights* (New York, 1896), p. 144.

14. Philadelphia *Evening Bulletin,* May 18, 1859, February 17, 1860.

15. Francis W. Hughes to William Bigler, March 2, 1860, Bigler MSS, HSP, hereafter cited as Bigler MSS; York *Gazette,* March 6, 1860; Lock Haven *Clinton Democrat,* March 9, 1860.

16. As used in this study, the term "Democracy" refers to the Democratic party. Ebensburg *Democrat and Sentinel,* March 7, 1860; Stroudsburg *Jeffersonian,* March 8, 1860; Franklin *Venango Spectator,* October 3, 1860.

17. Stanton Davis, *Pennsylvania Politics, 1860-63* (Cleveland, 1935), pp. 107–108; John Coleman, *The Disruption of the Pennsylvania Democracy* (Harrisburg, 1975), pp. 126–27.

18. J. B. Baker to Black, July 2, 1860, Black MSS; Philadelphia *Press,* n.d., quoted in Pottsville *Miners' Journal,* July 7, 1860; Pittsburgh *Post,* July 31, 1860.

19. Easton *Argus,* July 19, 1860; Bedford *Gazette,* July 26, 1860; Pittsburg[h] *Dispatch,* July 12, 1860.

20. York *Gazette,* July 17, 1860; Welsh to Black, July 26, 1860, Black MSS; Pittsburgh *Post,* July 27, 1860; Lock Haven *Clinton Democrat,* August 17, 1860.

21. Davis, *Pennsylvania Politics,* p. 111; Lock Haven *Clinton Democrat,* August 17, 1860; Coleman, *The Disruption of the Pennsylvania Democracy,* p. 127.

22. Bigler to Buchanan, August 14, 1860, Buchanan MSS; Bedford *Gazette,* August 17, 1860; Pittsburgh *Post,* August 24, 1860; Erie *Observer,* August 25, 1860.

23. John Campbell to Simon Cameron, August 14, 1860, Cameron MSS, Historical Society of Dauphin County, hereafter cited as Cameron MSS, DC; Daniel Curran, "Hendrick B. Wright" (Ph.d. diss., Fordham University, 1962), p. 212.

24. Greensburg *Argus,* n.d., quoted in Pittsburg[h] *Dispatch,* September 12, 1860; Harrisburg *Sentinel,* n.d., quoted in *ibid.,* August 31, 1860. The word order in the second quotation has been inverted.

25. Wilkes-Barre *Luzerne Union,* September 5, 1860; Easton *Sentinel,* September 13, 1860; Carlisle *American Volunteer,* September 20, 1860; Vaux to Douglas, September 5, 1860, Douglas MSS, Chicago Historical Society.

26. Pennsylvania held its state election in October and its presidential election in November. Blairsville *Record,* n.d., quoted in Lock Haven *Clinton Democrat,* July 26, 1860; William Welsh to Bigler, August 30, 1860, Bigler MSS.

27. Thomas McDowell to Bigler, September 17, 1860, Bigler MSS.

28. The tariff was especially important in the eastern, southern, and central counties of the commonwealth; in western and northern counties slavery was emphasized.

29. *Speech of the Hon. William B. Reed on the Presidential Question, Delivered Before the National Democratic Association, Philadelphia* (Philadelphia, 1860), pp. 11–13; Henry Acker to Bigler, May 24, 1860, Bigler MSS; William Russell, "A Biography of Alexander K. McClure" (Ph.d. diss., University of Wisconsin, 1953), pp. 168, 171–72.

30. Fulton, "It Happened in Western Pennsylvania, 1822–65," ed. Cecil Fulton (MSS typescript, copy in PHMC), p. 83, hereafter cited as "Western Pennsylvania."

31. Pittsburgh *Post,* October 22, 1860; Bedford *Gazette,* October 26, 1860; Easton *Sentinel,* October 25, 1860; York *Gazette,* November 6, 1860; William Dusinberre, *Civil War Issues in Philadelphia, 1856–65* (Philadelphia, 1965), p. 99, hereafter cited as *Civil War Issues.*

32. Ebensburg *Democrat and Sentinel,* October 24, 1860; Lock Haven *Clinton Democrat,* October 19, 1860.

33. James Campbell to Franklin Pierce, October 22, 1860, Pierce MSS, LC.

34. Foster had carried twenty-seven counties. The final vote was Lincoln, 268,030; fusion, 178,871; Douglas, 16,765; Bell, 12,776. *The Tribune Almanac for 1861* (New York, 1861), p. 47. The fusion ticket carried Berks, Clarion, Clearfield, Columbia, Elk, Fulton, Greene, Monroe, Northampton, Pike, Sullivan, and York Counties. A recent analysis of Schuylkill County shows that in 1860 Lincoln did poorly in Irish Catholic districts but carried urban areas. He also won a majority of the ballots of those German voters who were assimilated, commercially oriented, and evangelical in religious orientation. In 1860, 35 percent of the county's residents were German, 35 percent were English and Welsh, and 25 percent were Irish. See William Gudelunas and William Shade, *Before the Molly Maguires:*

The Emergence of the Ethno-Religious Factor in the Politics of the Lower Anthracite Region, 1844–1872 (New York, 1976), pp. 19, 80.

35. These fourteen counties were Adams, Bedford, Cambria, Carbon, Cumberland, Fayette, Lehigh, Luzerne, Montour, Montgomery, Northumberland, Philadelphia, Westmoreland, and Wyoming.

2

"No Civil War. Justice to the South"

"Nullification of Mr. Lincoln's election . . . seems necessary for the public good at this time."*

"[I trust] soon to hear of the disruption and overthrow of the Lincoln Government, as it at present represents only the mob. Each state would then rest upon its own sovereignty, and in the course of time the interests of Pennsylvania, New Jersey, and other States will cause them to seek admission into the Southern Confederacy."**

Few Pennsylvanians in November 1860 realized that civil war was imminent. Most residents of the state saw no reason to encourage sectional animosities, for it would have been most unwise for citizens of the commonwealth to alienate their best customers. Each year they imported Southern cotton, lumber, and turpentine and sold finished goods to the slave states. Figures on the volume of this business do not exist, but it certainly totaled many millions of dollars each year. Census records for 1860 provide valuable economic data for the Keystone State. According to government figures, there were 140,433 manufacturing establishments in the nation in 1860 producing $1,885,862,000 worth of goods each year

*The Ides of March (Philadelphia, 1861), p. 28.
**George McHenry, The African Race in America (London, 1861), p. 13

and annually paying their workers $378,879,000. No fewer than 22,363 of the firms were in Pennsylvania, turning out $290,121,000 worth of merchandise and paying their workers $60,369,000. Nearly twenty percent of all capital invested in American business was concentrated in Pennsylvania. The annual total value of manufactured products in the 102 leading industrial centers amounted to $874,934,827. Philadelphia alone contributed nearly $136,000,000 toward this sum and Pittsburgh, Reading, Lancaster, and Harrisburg supplied an additional $18,000,000. In contrast, Savannah, Georgia, produced a mere $2,000,000 and New Orleans only $11,000,000 per year.[1] (See table 1.)

Tonnage rates between Philadelphia and the slave states were lower than those from New York or Boston, and consequently each year large quantities of iron, coal, machinery, clothing, locomotives, books, and other goods were sold to residents of Dixie. Over 100,000 Philadelphians earned their living in the city's factories, and they feared that they would be unemployed if the Southern trade were halted.[2]

Some Pennsylvanians also invested in the South. Charles Jared Ingersoll's son, John, purchased a large plantation in Mississippi and moved there before the outbreak of war. Frances W. Hughes of Pottsville bought 2,900 acres of Georgia forest land on which he planned to harvest timber for the construction of ships. One of his brothers managed the tract; another was a doctor in New Bern, North Carolina. A prominent officer of the Pennsylvania Militia, Robert Patterson, owned sugar and cotton plantations in Louisiana. Certainly these men had a stake in promoting friendly intercourse between the two sections.

Not all ties between Pennsylvania and Dixie were economic. According to the 1860 census, thousands of Pennsylvanians were natives of the slave states. Many of these transplanted Southerners were prominent in civic and political affairs, and they plainly countered the abolitionist image of Dixie's ruling class as uncultured, immoral, and inhuman. A remarkable number of Philadelphia's most socially acceptable families included natives of the South. On a single block of elegant Walnut Street lived no fewer than twenty-two families with at least one member who was a native of Dixie. Was it any wonder then that some New Englanders considered Philadelphia to be a Southern rather than a Northern city?[3]

Talk of secession greatly scared Philadelphians. Even James Harvey, a prominent Republican newspaperman who had been born in Charleston, South Carolina, became upset that his native state was about to secede. Harvey blamed Southern demagogues for creating false alarms about the menace of Lincoln's victory. Nonetheless he still believed that most Pennsylvanians sympathized neither with abolition nor with secession and should therefore take the lead in promoting conciliation. Businessmen also were worried. Some became panicky and had misgivings about having voted for Lincoln. Convinced that the South was serious about leaving the Union, they began to sell their stocks, dispose of their surplus goods, and dismiss a large number of their employees. On November 22, 1860, Philadelphia banks suspended specie payments.[4]

Talk of massive unemployment prompted Mayor Alexander Henry of Philadelphia to call for an assembly of all citizens at Independence Hall on December 13, 1860, to discuss methods of averting disunion. On that day businesses closed, the courts adjourned, and even the navy yard shut down its operations. Thousands listened to speakers who called for the repeal of Pennsylvania's personal-liberty laws and for the strict enforcement of the Fugitive Slave Law. One speaker, Judge George Washington Woodward, a justice of the state supreme court, insisted that "human bondage and property in man is divinely sanctioned, if not ordained" and that "Negro slavery has been an incalculable blessing to us."[5]

Philadelphia's sentiments were not unique, for at a union rally in Reading on December 14, speakers called for compromise with the South. Resolutions were passed condemning "all interference by men of the North with the domestic and social relations of citizens of the South." Similar meetings were held in Easton on December 14, in Germantown on December 15, and in Williamsport on December 18.[6]

TABLE 1: Philadelphia as a Manufacturing Center (1861)

Classes of Manufactures	Number of establishments	Capital	Raw material value	Operatives		Value of annual product
				Male	Female	
Textile fabrics in Philadelphia	525	$8,795,226	$12,584,440	9,670	9,731	$23,561,568
Textile fabrics in Delaware, Chester, and Montgomery counties, &c., owned and run by Philadelphians		5,038,040	3,226,869	3,564	3,309	6,777,349
Manufactures of iron and steel	106	10,290,125	6,350,329	10,917	56	14,775,213
Wagons, carriages, and carts	649	1,743,550	929,711	2,284	—	2,542,957
Implements & instruments	145	217,500	110,158	245	—	387,776
Iron—manufactories near Philadelphia	45	3,044,610	1,663,003	2,430	—	3,888,151
Manufactures of clothing and apparel	34	7,951,877	8,162,648	7,645	14,452	16,085,864
Hosiery and shawls, &c	821	2,379,400	2,000,260	1,671	278	2,342,845
Gold and silver manufactures	139					4,030,380
Manufactures of wood	592	4,278,652	2,457,954	4,855	15	6,153,715
Glass, and glass manufactures	16	712,000	408,250	928	—	1,244,800
Bricks and pottery	68	1,318,100	125,522	2,067	—	1,395,106
Paper and manufactures of paper	57	1,385,400	1,115,590	727	575	2,190,110
Printing, publishing, binding, and blank books	206	4,129,500	2,303,202	2,933	943	6,441,403
Liquors and products of distillation	116	3,015,900	2,718,524	805	3	4,384,974
Leather, and manufactures of leather, except boots and shoes	184	2,368,620	3,008,182	1,981	229	5,028,552
Boots and shoes	701	1,730,815	1,912,657	6,497	1,937	5,329,887
Soaps, candles, and oils	78	1,902,500	2,723,552	609	43	4,261,916
Chemicals, &c	44	2,851,900	2,146,206	853	35	3,685,554
Manufactures associated with chemicals	42	1,386,000	1,246,215	470	124	2,228,904
Metal manufactures, brass, lead, and copper	148	1,576,600	1,072,759	1,231	24	2,358,287
Marble and fine stone manufactures	67	855,800	399,070	787	—	1,075,125
Drugs and medicines	48	614,600	645,155	263	88	1,421,350
Sugar refineries and manufactures	97	1,780,400	5,785,363	720	58	6,907,950
Cigars and manufactures of tobacco	231	499,200	522,740	1,140	175	1,868,400
Flour and meal	30	614,860	2,648,645	198	—	3,098,328
Cured meats and provisions	23	1,145,500	3,510,415	238	—	4,575,807
Gas-works	3	3,956,248	586,200	863	—	1,837,500
Unclassified manufactures	1,249	6,055,579	7,119,740	8,944	1,937	12,474,597
Total in Philadelphia	6,314	$73,087,852	$72,333,805	69,388	29,609	$141,048,658
Total, including vicinity	6,467	81,608,502	77,473,677	75,535	32,996	152,355,318

Source: Data furnished by Lorin Blodget, secretary of the Philadelphia Board of Trade to The National Almanac and Annual Record for 1863 (Philadelphia, 1863), p. 444.

On December 14, a prominent New York abolitionist, Henry Curtis, was to have spoken in Philadelphia, but Mayor Henry warned that it would be dangerous and "unwise" for him to deliver his oration. The owner of the hall in which the address was to have been given was persuaded to cancel the speech.[7]

With each passing week demonstrations increased in number and in willingness to appease the South. The biggest and most radical meeting of all was held at Philadelphia's National Hall on January 16, 1861, with an estimated attendance of 4,000. The overflow crowd spilled out onto the streets, where men less willing to conciliate Dixie also assembled. A number of police attended as a safeguard against rioting. Typical of the banners displayed was one bearing the caption "NO CIVIL WAR. JUSTICE TO THE SOUTH. EQUAL RIGHTS IN THE TERRITORIES." Bands played patriotic airs, but cynics sarcastically noted that there was an absence of American flags.[8]

Among the speakers was William B. Reed, who denounced the "senseless clamor" for coercion of the South and who called for the repeal of Pennsylvania's personal-liberty law. The climax of his speech came when he asked, "If this goodly fabric fails, what shall Pennsylvania do?" Spontaneously several spectators shouted that the state should go with the South, forcing him to respond quickly that such a proposal was "an eventuality" he did not wish to consider. "But," he added, "this I may safely say, that Pennsylvania will, whether she be detached or not—whether she is compelled for a time to go with the North or South, or stand by herself—she will . . . be always ready to pacificate."

Another orator, George Miflin Wharton, was as pro-Southern as Reed. He made his position clear when he declared: "Our interests are with the South—mine are at any rate. The South and the West are our best friends and if there is to be a breaking up, we shall have a word to say as to which we shall go with. We can't be brought up by Boston and New York."

Resolutions adopted at the meeting accorded generally with sentiments expressed by the speakers. These called for strict adherence to the Constitution, the Virginia and Kentucky Resolutions, and the Crittenden Compromise. They blamed sectional differences on the agitation of the abolitionists and advocated the summoning of a convention to amend the Constitution. The most memorable resolution was the twelfth, which Reed had written. It declared:

> Resolved, That in the deliberate judgement of the Democracy of Philadelphia, and, so far as we know it, of Pennsylvania, the dissolution of the Union by the separation of the whole South, a result we shall most sincerely lament, may release this Commonwealth from the bonds which now connect her with the Confederacy except so far as for temporary convenience she chooses to submit to them, and would authorize and require her citizens through a Convention to be assembled for that purpose, to determine with whom her lot should be cast, whether with the North and East, whose fanaticism has precipitated this misery upon us, or with her brethren of the South, whose wrongs we feel as our own, or whether Pennsylvania should stand by herself, as a distinct community ready when occasion offers to bind together the broken Union, and resume her place of loyalty and devotion.[9]

Not all Democrats could sustain such a position. James Van Dyke, who was to have addressed the meeting, read the resolutions in advance and then wrote a letter disassociating himself from their text, which, he thought, lacked practical sense. Other letters read at the gathering, however, were as radical as the resolutions.[10]

Hardly anyone was foolish enough to think that a series of Pennsylvania demonstrations and resolutions by themselves could arrest the secession crisis. To persuade the Southerners that their destiny lay in the Union, compromises of some sort would be necessary. It seemed most appropriate to start with a reexamination of the commonwealth's personal-liberty law. Though it is now believed that such statutes "did not prevent even one slave from being returned to the South where the claim was legitimate,"[11] their importance in 1861 was more symbolic than real. After some free blacks had been kidnapped from their homes in the North and had been enslaved, the Pennsylvania legislature made it a criminal offense to kidnap a free Negro and remove him from the state. Furthermore, it was illegal for any justice of the peace to take cognizance of any case involving a fugitive slave. Naturally these laws were denounced in Dixie for nullifying the Fugitive Slave Law.

Joshua Francis Fisher, a leader of Philadelphia society and the husband of a Southerner, suggested that Pennsylvania adopt a series of compromises he had devised to protect free blacks and facilitate the return of fugitives. He called for the repeal of the personal liberty law and the passage of legislation requiring the government of a county in which a slave was rescued to reimburse the slaveowner for the his loss. To protect free Negroes, he suggested a five-year statute of limitations on the extradition of fugitives. Alleged slaves were to be given jury trials in the county from which they had supposedly escaped. Realizing that cynics would insist that no such trial would be held, or, if held, would be unfair, he proposed that the claimant and two Northerners post a $2,000 bond to insure that the accused would be returned to his home at no personal expense if the Southern jury did not unanimously decide he was a slave. A suspected fugitive was to be given free legal counsel.[12]

Fisher was not the only one to call for the repeal of the personal-liberty law; meetings calling upon the legislature to rescind the "obnoxious" legislation from the statute books were held in Philadelphia, Dauphin, Beaver, Bedford, Fayette, Fulton, and York counties. Moreover, at a convention of state Democratic leaders pleas were made to purge the lawbooks of all statutes offensive to Dixie. Delegates at this gathering threatened to prevent Republicans from waging "any armed aggression upon the Southern States . . . so long as laws contravening their rights shall remain unrepealed on the Statute books of Northern States." Furthermore, several state legislatures were deluged with petitions requesting them to act on this matter; one displayed a scroll bearing the signature of 11,000 Philadelphia voters to his colleagues in Harrisburg.[13] It should not be assumed that only

To the Honorable the Members of the Senate and House of
Representatives of the State of Pennsylvania.

Your Memorialists, Citizens of Philadelphia,

Respectfully represent—

THAT in their opinion the provisions of the 95th and 96th Sections of the Revised Penal Code, so far as the same relate to Fugitives from labor or servitude, are not needed for the protection of the rights of the Citizens of Pennsylvania, and may be regarded by the Citizens of other States as unfriendly in their purport, and therefore they pray your honorable body to enact the repeal of such provisions.

ALEXANDER HENRY,	EDWARD KING,	GEORGE SHARSWOOD,	JOSEPH ALLISON,
JOSEPH R. INGERSOLL,	JOHN A. BROWN,	OSWALD THOMPSON,	JAMES R. LUDLOW,
JOHN B. MYERS,	THEODORE CUYLER,	DAVID JAYNE,	SAMUEL C. MORTON,
CHARLES B. TREGO,	A. WHITNEY,	WM. H. DRAYTON,	STEPHEN BENTON,
S. V. MERRICK,	JAMES DUNDAS,	CALEB COPE,	W. C. KIDERLEN,
RICHARD PRICE,	JOHN C. BULLITT,	J. G. FELL,	ELI K. PRICE,
CHARLES E. LEX,	JAMES MARTIN,	PETER McCALL,	GEORGE ERETY,
JOSEPH RIPKA,	JOHN O. JAMES,	JAMES CAMPBELL,	DANIEL DOUGHERTY,
RICHARD D. WOOD,	B. GERHARD,	A. J. LEWIS,	MARK MUNDY,
JOHN WELSH,	C. J. INGERSOLL,	THOMAS ROBINS,	A. J. DREXEL,
GUSTAVUS REMAK,	WILLIAM DEVINE,	CHARLES HENRY FISHER,	DANIEL HADDOCK, JR.,
DAVID S. BROWN,	RICHARD C. DALE,	J. P. STEINER,	ANDREW MILLER,
S. A. MERCER,	WM. L. HIRST,	WILLIAM STRUTHERS,	S. W. DE COURSEY,
JAMES PAGE,	STACEY B. BARCROFT,	JAMES R. CAMPBELL,	JAMES P. SMITH,
J. B. LIPPINCOTT,	STEPHEN COLWELL,	THOMAS S. NEWLIN,	DAVID WEBSTER,
RICHARD NORRIS,	WILLIAM WELSH,	WM. C. LUDWIG,	JAMES C. HAND,
EDWARD C. BIDDLE,	F. H. FRENCH,	JOHN MURPHY,	WM. C. ALLISON,
ROBERT SELLRIDGE,	P. B. SAVERY,	GEORGE W. PAGE,	THOMAS DRAKE,
BENJAMIN MARSHALL,	L. C. CASSIDY,	M. S. SHAPLEIGH,	JAMES W. PAUL,
A. McBURNEY.	JOHN TUCKER.	ROBERT J. MERCER.	J. W. BACON, M.D.

Petition of prominent Philadelphians asking that the state legislature repeal
Pennsylvania's personal liberty laws. The first name on the petition is that of
Alexander Henry, mayor of Philadelphia. *(Courtesy Library of Congress.)*

Democrats signed such remonstrances, for Mayor Henry was among those to lend his support to the movement.[14] Outgoing Governor William F. Packer urged the legislature to revise the penal code and asked for the passage of a bill enabling visiting Southerners to bring their slaves into the commonwealth without losing the right of their services. On January 23, 1861, the Philadelphia *Inquirer* reported that Rhode Island had abolished her personal liberty law and warned that "Pennsylvania must not be laggard with her peace offering."

Even incoming Governor Andrew Curtin favored concilation. In his inaugural address, he stated that "if we have any laws upon our statute books which infringe upon the rights of the people of any of the States or contravene any law of the Federal Government . . . they ought to be repealed."[15]

For a while it seemed reasonable to expect that the legislature would respond favorably to requests for conciliation. On January 2, 1861, Representative Robert Randall of Philadelphia introduced a resolution in the Pennsylvania House to repeal the personal-liberty law. His measure was referred to the judiciary committee, and the House was never given an opportunity to vote on it.[16]

While the legislature was pondering repeal of the personal-liberty law, considerable sentiment was being voiced in favor of the Crittenden Compromise as a panacea for Union.[17] Because Senator John Jordan Crittenden was known to favor a political solution for the sectional difficulties of the nation, many Pennsylvanians sent him their suggestions for an acceptable compromise; these ranged from dividing the territories into slave and nonslave regions, to requiring all blacks to move south of the 35° parallel, to dividing the nation into two confederacies, each with a separate chief and governmental bureaucracy but with one common president possessing "very limited powers." Even after Crittenden made his proposals, residents of the Keystone State continued to devise new methods of preserving the Union. One Philadelphian wanted a convention of judges to settle the secession crisis, and a man from Easton proposed that the governors of the states decide what part—if any—of new territory the United States acquired should be open to slavery.[18] However unworkable these ideas were, they were signs of antiwar feeling in the second most populous state.

Nearly all Pennsylvania Democrats enthusiastically endorsed the Crittenden Compromise as the "most practical, the most probable, and the most fortunate plan" to save the Union. In all parts of the state concerned citizens staged demonstrations in favor of the enactment into law of this "just and honorable remedy for our present threatening problems." In January and February 1861, meetings in its behalf were held in Adams, Bedford, Centre, Cumberland, Dauphin, Fayette, Fulton, Luzerne, and York counties.[19]

The most impressive gatherings were those of unemployed workers. In Philadelphia, where over 20,000 had lost their jobs since the election, the jobless believed that securing employment was dependent upon the restoration of friendship between the North and South. Therefore they deluged Senators William Bigler and Simon Cameron with memorials urging approval of Crittenden's plan, and they held meetings impressive in both size and enthusiasm to convince the public to support the proposal. Despite snow, 6,000 persons participated in a mass meeting of Philadelphia workers at Independence Square on January 26. Harrisburg workers also favored conciliation, and they passed resolutions in favor of the Crittenden Compromise, sending copies to newspapers and legislators.[20]

With the exception of the Kentucky senator himself, no one more wholeheartedly endorsed the Crittenden proposals than William Bigler. Pennsylvania's senior senator, a loyal friend of Buchanan, had long argued that the Union could easily exist half slave and half free—if only the abolitionists would let it—and he believed that the courts should be allowed to determine the status of slavery in the territories. After serving on the ill-fated Committee of Thirteen in December 1860, he modified his views and concluded that Crittenden's proposal was the proper way to save the Union. Mail from his constituents strengthened his belief that this was the best method of thwarting the secession of the South.[21]

Bigler made his views known in Washington, but Congress ignored him, and he feared that the compromise was doomed. Discouraged, he wrote a friend that adoption of the Crittenden Compromise would give the North 900,000 square miles of free land and the South only 280,000 square miles for slavery—and some of this territory was unsuitable for the peculiar institution. The plan was honorable, he said, for "no umpire could award the South less. . . . The Republicans ought to have accepted this adjustment long ago."[22]

Bigler also proposed that a popular referendum be held to determine national sentiment on the compromise. Constituents assured him that "if these Resolutions could be submitted to the people of Va. and Western Pa. to-morrow, they would carry ninety nine out of every hundred votes." No referendum was held though, and Bigler watched helplessly as secession sentiment grew more intense in the slave states.[23]

The secession crisis provided Pennsylvania's junior senator with a unique dilemma. In ability to manipulate men and to amass wealth and power, Simon Cameron was without peer in Pennsylvania. Yet, depite his shrewdness, he had allowed himself to become embroiled in a bitter feud with Governor Andrew Curtin, and this split the state Republican party into two factions, one loyal to him and one faithful to the governor. At the Chicago convention Cameron had received assurances that he would be appointed to the Lincoln cabinet. After the election, however, Curtin's friends urged the incoming president to ignore the promise made Cameron. The senator, who was no abolitionist and who counted Southerners among his friends, had to decide whether to favor conciliation, which was the desire of many of his constituents and quite probably his own preference, or to oppose the Crittenden Compromise as Lincoln was urging Republicans to do.

Cameron shrewdly decided to play both sides of the fence; that is, he indicated his desire to support an honorable compromise with the South, but if he received a cabinet post, he planned to vote against the Crittenden resolutions. The strategy was sound,

and individuals both for and against a peaceful settlement considered him to be a moderate whom they might swing over to their
side. Once he was assured of becoming secretary of war, he
demonstrated increasingly less interest in compromise and he
refused to vote for the proposal when it finally came up before the
Senate.[24]

To those in favor of conciliation the lethargy of Congress and
the state legislatures was disgraceful. Instead of trying to save the
Union, elected public officials seemed to be more interested in
denouncing their political opponents and shutting their eyes to
the ever-worsening crisis that was imperiling the Union. Some
thought that the solution was to require all congressmen to resign
and to hold a special election to choose new representatives more
amenable to the wishes of their constituents and therefore favorable to compromise measures. Others, despairing of any initiative
from Congress, lent their support to the Washington Peace
Conference, which first met on February 4. Since Governor Curtin
had named only Republicans to the Pennsylvania delegation,
Democrats feared that the conference was doomed to failure.
Admittedly it would have been better to have a bipartisan delegation represent the state, but not all of the Republican members
were hostile to compromise. Former Governor James Pollock
attended the conference sessions convinced that they represented
the last opportunity to save the country. Despite much quarreling,
the conference approved of seven constitutional amendments,
which were markedly similar to the Crittenden Compromise.[25]
These amendments won the endorsement of the Philadelphia
Inquirer, an independent journal, which stated on February 15,
1861: "If they furnish the means of restoring peace to the country,
they should receive cordial support." But just as the Crittenden
resolutions failed to be adopted, so too were these amendments
destined to be rejected. It seemed as though fate was thwarting
every attempt to keep the country together.

Largely ignored were the Union-saving proposals of private
individuals. In addition to his suggestions to modify the Fugitive
Slave Law, Joshua Francis Fisher devised a number of other

proposals for conciliating the South. Among these were laws to reduce the tariff, to allow each town to elect its own postmaster and thereby prevent Republicans from building up an abolition party in the South, and to require that all Supreme Court cases involving slavery be decided by a court composed of an equal number of Northern and Southern justices.[26]

Charles Jared Ingersoll, on the other hand, was convinced that the best way to avert disunion was to arrange for a conference of the five living former presidents. These men, he thought, would rise above partisan politics and devise an equitable alternative to dividing the nation into two confederacies. Even after the war began, he refused to abandon his plan; in fact, he drew up one of the first proposals—if not the first—to end the war by concilia-tion. His friend Benjamin Patton explained his views as follows: no later than May 1, the five men would meet and use their prestige to force President Lincoln to call for a one-year armistice. In return, the Confederates would have to suspend their customs and postal laws for the year. During the armistice a national convention composed of representatives from each congressional district would meet until they formulated a compromise accept-able to two-thirds of the delegates. That compromise would be binding upon all of the states. Ingersoll thought the scheme was foolproof, but the former presidents were so skeptical of its practicality that they ignored it.[27]

A third Philadelphian, William B. Reed, thought that only a friendly foreign power could impartially arbitrate the quarrel between North and South. Why not let England "pacificate" the quarrel?, he asked. The former diplomat alleged that Britain believed that the preservation of the Union was in her own best interests. Since she was the best customer of the South, slaveowners "would listen to such intercession tho' deaf to all else. Cotton is the king of [their] heart even when inflamed." Reed's suggestion proved to be as unpopular as Ingersoll's.[28]

A final compromise idea, which may not have ever been made public, involved amending the Constitution. Charles Rollin Buck-alew, the American minister to Ecuador, thought that only a plan involving a change of power could bring about an "enduring peace." Therefore he suggested that the man receiving the second highest number of electoral votes in a presidential election become president of the Senate and be allowed to exercise the veto power. Under this system, he argued, minority rights would be protected, secession would be prevented, and extreme sectionalism would be averted. It is not known whether Buckalew ever realized that what he proposed was unworkable; his plan would have promoted a weak presidency and inefficient government.[29]

For various reasons some thought that there should be no effort either to compromise or to coerce the South. The Towanda *Bradford Reporter* of January 3, 1861, declared: "If South Carolina will not return unless 'conciliated,' let her go in peace. It will be less a loss than to lose our honor and self-respect [by making more compromises]." One month earlier, on December 6, 1860, the Bellefonte *Central Press* had professed to be delighted that the Palmetto State was leaving the Union and taking with her "all her cotton, debts, and negroes." It added that she should not be coerced, for she was "of no earthly advantage" to the nation. David Salomon of Philadelphia thought that it was too late to pass compromises to prevent what was already a *fait accompli*. He hoped that the border states would join the Confederacy, for when the question of reconstruction was discussed, they would be able to promote the reunion of the divided republic. More radical was Henry Dieffenbach, a Lock Haven editor, who expressed the view that there was no point in seeking reunion unless New England was expelled from the United States; otherwise it was best to consider separation as "Providential."[30]

When Pennsylvania Democrats met in Harrisburg on February 22, 1861, they declared that peaceable separation was preferable to coercion. "The idea of fighting for the preservation of the Union in its present circumstances is simply preposterous," thundered the Reverend John W. Nevin of Lancaster, for "no victory in such a war could deserve to be considered a triumph." Other delegates also warned that they would "by all proper and legitimate means, oppose, discountenance, and prevent any attempt on the part of

Quito, Ecuador,
April 16, 1861.

Dear Sir:—

Suppose the following Proposition of Constitutional Amendment be adopted in place of those heretofore proposed, whenever the subject of Amendment comes to be considered in a popular Convention?

In elections of President the Candidate second highest in electoral votes, to be President of the Senate and possess the Veto. This is not sectional and yet it gives protection to minorities, & would always prevent decession & revolution. The Protective or Minority Veto, as this might be called, would be a powerful weapon for defence but not for aggression. It would be a conservative power, rarely interposed, but effective to produce a sense of security in the country against the violence or injustice

The first page of Charles R. Buckalew's proposal to save the Union. Buckalew, then the outgoing minister to Ecuador, was preparing to return to Pennsylvania. In 1863 he was elected to the United States Senate. (*Courtesy Wilkes College.*)

the Republicans in power to make any armed aggression upon the Southern States" until the personal-liberty laws had been repealed.[31]

Residents of the Keystone State urged Buchanan, Pennsylvania members of his cabinet, Senator Bigler, and even Abraham Lincoln to avoid coercion and bloodshed. One correspondent wrote Jeremiah Black, "if there must be civil war, let the Black Republicans begin it." Vincent Bradford, a leading Philadelphia Democrat, hoped that Buchanan would recognize the independence of the South and negotiate a "most favored" nation contract with the Confederacy so that the two sections could soon resume their trade relations. According to his argument, the two countries should live together in amity and at some future date when "under the pressure of . . . foreign aggression" might decide to reunite. Few worked as hard and with such sincerity to prevent bloodshed at Fort Sumter as James Harvey. Unlike Vincent, Harvey, a Republican, did not want the United States to recognize the Confederacy. Rather he favored ignoring the activities of the seceding cotton states, believing "the people who have been deceived and betrayed [in the South] will soon rise up in their might to crush out the treason and seek a return to the Union, in which their prosperity and protection were so well received."[32]

Why was there such fierce opposition to coercion? In part, this was because many conservatives believed that the Union was a voluntary compact and that its members were free to depart if they thought that independence was in their best interests. Some argued that the history of the Constitution furnished ample proof that the Founding Fathers "never intended that the military and naval powers of the Federal Government should be called out to force *States,* against their will, to remain in the Union." Coercion, therefore, would destroy the government "formed by our fathers." Others thought that until the North repealed its "unjust" personal liberty laws it had no right to order the South to remain in the Union.[33]

Some opponents of coercion insisted that, however bad secession was, war would even be worse. A conflict would demoralize the people, destroy property, create widows and orphans, and bankrupt the national coffers. On February 23, 1861, the Easton *Argus* stated: "Who wants to go to war with his own countrymen? That would be worse than disunion itself." Others claimed that even if the Yankees did defeat the Confederates, the old Union, which was based on mutual interest and affection, would not be restored. "We cannot whip the South into loving the Union," stated the Harrisburg *Patriot and Union* on January 7, 1861. "We cannot force them to regard us with affection." Less than four weeks later, on January 30, 1861, the Ebensburg *Democrat and Sentinel* reasoned that Southerners would be too proud to admit defeat if vanquished and would bide their time, waiting until they had another chance to seek freedom. Thus, for a variety of reasons, there were Pennsylvanians who thought that a technical military triumph over the South would be more detrimental to the nation than peaceable separation.

Of those who thought that separation would be permanent a small number wanted the Keystone State to join the Confederacy. Believing that because of its fanaticism and manufacturing interests, New England was a greater menace to the state than the South, these people thought that the interests of the Keystone State were with the Confederacy. "If we must fight," one man wrote, "let it be against the Abolitionist [rather] than the Secessionist—[let us strike at] the cause and not the effect."[34] Of those taking this position for whom biographical data are extant, some were natives of the South and others had relatives and property there; most surprising of all, there were a few of New England ancestry who were second to none in their hatred of "Yankee fanaticism." Apparently the only thing common to these men was support of Breckinridge for president in 1860. Though the goal they sought was radical, they considered themselves to be conservatives and patriots. Among those who seriously discussed adherence to the Confederacy were Justice George W. Woodward, William B. Reed, Francis W. Hughes, and Robert Tyler.

Woodward, an admirer of Calhoun, had neither relatives nor financial holdings in the South; in fact, his ancestors had migrated to Pennsylvania from Connecticut. Lincoln's victory profoundly disturbed him, but since the leading Democratic candidate in the North had been Douglas, he was not surprised at the outcome of the election. Even before the Baltimore convention he had predicted that the Illinois senator would not carry a single state in the North or in the South. In Woodward's opinion, the selection of an abolitionist president made it inevitable that the Southern states would secede, and believing that the old Union was dead, his only regret was that Pennsylvania could not go with the departing slave states. His private letters were much more radical than his public orations.[35]

William B. Reed, like Woodward, had no close personal ties with the South, though he had good friends in South Carolina. Not until January 1861 did he think that it would be necessary for Pennsylvania to leave the Union, but once he had decided this was necessary, he authored the infamous twelfth resolution for the January 16 meeting of Philadelphia Democrats. At the start of the war mobs visited his house and he did not again make known his views on politics until 1862.[36]

Perhaps no politician in the state was so reckless about publicizing his view that Pennsylvania should join the Confederacy as Francis W. Hughes. Though a native of the commonwealth, the Pottsville lawyer had familial and financial ties to Dixie. During the secession crisis he announced at a rally that "cotton was king and he was glad of it," and he privately expressed fears that in the event of disunion, Pennsylvania would lose her position as a trading and manufacturing center. In February 1861, he authored a resolution so extreme in tone that relatives and friends persuaded him not to make it public. It declared that, if the Union were divided, Pennsylvanians would have to decide whether to take their "place in some Northern fragment of a once-glorious Union" and lose their customers and profits or join the Southern Confederacy and "become the great manufacturing workshop for a people now consuming annually $300,000,000 worth of products." If they joined the South, he predicted, their cities would become the greatest commercial depots in the continent. Although he suppressed the resolution until 1862, he allegedly told an acquaintance that it was both "the duty as well as the interest" of Pennsylvania to unite with the slave states and he offered to run for public office "on such a platform." After the war started he found it prudent to contribute to soldier relief funds.[37]

Robert Tyler, a son of the former president, had moved from Virginia to Philadelphia in 1836, and had become a Democratic politician. Because of his many ties with the South, he had nothing but scorn for abolitionists, whom he considered to be trouble-makers. After the election of Lincoln he predicted that within a year Pennsylvania would probably secede from the Union.[38]

At times Tyler called for compromise, but he feared that the adoption of a seemingly conciliatory constitutional amendment would merely mislead the South and place it more firmly "under the domination of squatterism and abolitionism." The only fair solution, he thought, was for the United States to adopt the Confederate Constitution.[39] Mobs compelled him to flee Phila-delphia in April 1861.

In varying degrees some Philadelphia newspapers were recep-tive to the idea of merger with the South. On January 3, 1861, the *Christian Observer* set up an office in Richmond, and henceforth the newspaper masthead listed both cities as the places of publica-tion. This continued until the summer of 1861, when authorities suppressed the paper, and its sixty-six-year-old editor, Amasa Converse, moved to Richmond. Once in the South, Converse openly endorsed the secession of the South. Admittedly he had never publicly called for secession of Pennsylvania when in Philadelphia, but his conciliatory editorials made him receptive to the idea.[40]

Even though the Philadelphia *Pennsylvanian* did not itself call for union with the South, it printed articles and letters favoring this course of action and it endorsed "peace at any price." Articles published in the paper claimed that Jefferson Davis's election was no more sectional than Lincoln's, argued that the United States should no longer collect customs revenue in the South, and declared that the North should adopt the Confederate Constitution. One piece insisted that the Yankees should meet every demand of the Southerners, for once disunion was permanent, Dixie would never rejoin the United States unless it received terms even more favorable than those it then sought. By April 2, 1861, the *Pennsylvanian* was bankrupt and forced to suspend publication.[41]

Most explicit of the pro-Confederate newspapers was the *Palmetto Flag,* which started publication on March 30. Fated only to turn out three issues before angry citizens nearly destroyed his office, editor Henry Brent announced that his purpose was "to overthrow the faction now in possession of the Government of the so-called United States" and "to advocate the recognition of the Southern Confederacy by the Government at Washington and by Governments elsewhere. To afford our Southern friends a zealous medium for the expression of their views, placing them in close contact with a Northern auditory." Had the paper been published in Charleston, it could not have been more favorable to Dixie. It tried to prove that coercion was futile and that it was in Pennsylvania's economic interest to become the keystone of the Confederate States. "Can Philadelphia with the South cut off," it asked, "compete with New York in ships, in trade, and other branches of enterprise? We opine not."[42]

Reaction to the *Palmetto Flag* was almost uniformly hostile. Some editors suggested that Brent be hanged and warned that mobs would soon destroy his printing office. The Philadelphia *North American* claimed that the "impudence of establishing such a sheet in this city could only be equalled by issuing in Charleston a paper advocating the insurrection of the slaves." But it thought that Brent was hypocritical since his office also printed the *Stars and the Stripes.* At any rate, violence forced the permanent suspension of the paper before it printed its fourth number.[43]

Despite the various pleas in the commonwealth for compromise and against coercion, there was no conciliation; Pennsylvania espoused war in April 1861. Why? One answer was that on a key point, the tariff, she disagreed with the South. Because they were so heavily dependent upon others for finished goods, residents of the slave states favored low tariff duties. On the other hand, Pennsylvanians believed that, unless import duties were raised, the nation would be flooded with European products that would be sold for less than it would cost to manufacture similar goods in Philadelphia, Reading, or Pittsburgh. On this question even the most conciliatory Pennsylvania congressmen would not agree that their best customers were right. When Congress adopted the Morrill Tariff in 1861, every Pennsylvania representative and both of her senators voted for its passage. In fact, Senator Bigler was the only Democrat in the Senate to vote affirmatively.[44] Certainly Confederates did not relish the thought of reentering a union in which they would have to pay higher prices for manufactured products.

Naturally the refusal of Pennsylvanians to repeal their personal-liberty laws or to persuade Congress to adopt the Crittenden Compromise was crucial. Mainly, the responsibility lay with Republicans, who completely controlled the two branches of the state legislature and who dominated the congressional delegation.[45] Such champions of compromise as William Bigler and Thomas Florence[46] were hampered in their effectiveness by their "lame duck" status. For every speech a Pennsylvanian made in Congress in favor of conciliation, Thaddeus Stevens, Elijah Babbitt, or Samuel Blair would deliver one that condemned the South.

Furthermore, not all in the Keystone State were willing to believe that the North and South were equally responsible for the nation's problems. Republican leader Thomas Williams of Allegheny County, for example, refused to admit that he had sinned. "I find nothing in our statute books," he said, "that I would be willing to sacrifice as a peace offering to this insatiable spirit [of secession]." Similarly several other politicians and a number of newspapers in the commonwealth refused to ascribe the guilt for the nation's woes to the North; if the South wanted enforcement of the laws, slaveowners should allow all Yankee papers and political pamphlets to circulate freely in Dixie.[47]

Some were belligerent. D. Phelps of Kittanning declared that he would not agree to compromise with traitors. If the Southerners sought concessions, he added, they would have to appeal to the government as loyal subjects rather than as aggressors. F. S. Stumbaugh warned that his neighbors would rather furnish one hundred men "to defend the Union, the constitution, & the laws" than to make agreements with slaveowners that would require them to sacrifice their principles. Some insisted that after concessions were made, the South would demand even more. Therefore, by avoiding the "true issues" in 1861, Northerners were merely gaining a little time before they would have to face up to Dixie. Instead of "damming up the waters a little higher preparatory for a more devastating flood a few years hence," wrote a resident of Crawford County, it would be more "manly" to meet the crisis at once and win the respect of the world.[48] "Our advice to every Northern man," boldly proclaimed the Ebensburg *Alleghanian* on January 10, 1861, "is arm yourself at once. If you have a gun, get it ready for use; if you do not own one, get one as soon as possible."

The relative percentage of voters in favor of war, concession, or union with the Confederacy cannot be precisely ascertained. Nor is it possible to determine exactly what number of Pennsylvanians were apathetic to the secession crisis. Nonetheless, contemporary newspaper accounts, letters preserved in the papers of Senators Bigler, Cameron, and Crittenden, and records of political meetings do furnish some indication of the sentiment of residents of the Keystone State. A subjective judgment based on a critical perusal of this information would suggest that not less than five percent favored Pennsylvania's joining the South; a much larger number, at least a third of the electorate, approved of the Crittenden Compromise and were willing to make other minor concessions to Dixie. Slightly under one-third of the voters were prepared to fight rather than to give in to the demands of the slave states, but their number was greatly augmented after the fighting began at Fort Sumter.

Of those who spoke of refusing to make further compromises in January and February, certainly not all expected war. Erskine Hazard of Philadelphia spoke for many people when he wrote that Southerners would not really leave the Union; they were merely "bluffing off the northern dough-faces." When James Alexander Fulton wrote his memoirs, he noted that during the winter of 1860–1861 his neighbors refused to believe that war would really soon erupt; they sincerely thought that the slave states were blustering and would soon "back down."[49] After all, Southern customers continued to buy Pennsylvania goods, and not realizing that war was imminent, on March 18, 1861, Philadelphia banks resumed specie payments. Many persons predicted war, but others expected peace; until the very end too few realized the reality of secession.

NOTES

1. *Statistics of the United States in 1860, Compiled from the Original Returns of the Eighth Census* (Washington, 1866), pp. xviii, 292, 295, 311; Philadelphia *Public Ledger,* September 19, 1861.

2. Frank Taylor, *Philadelphia in the Civil War* (Philadelphia, 1913), pp. 9–10.

3. *Ibid.,* p. 13; Philadelphia *Sunday Dispatch,* April 14, 1861; Christopher Dell, *Lincoln and the War Democrats* (Rutherford, N.J., 1975), p. 54. Evidence of the familial ties between the Philadelphia elite and the South are quite evident in Fanny Kemble Wister, ed., "Sarah Butler Wister's Civil War Diary," *The Pennsylvania Magazine of History and Biography,* 102 (1978): 271–327, hereafter cited as "Wister's Diary."

4. Easton *Sentinel,* November 22, 1860; Philadelphia *Inquirer,* November 23, 1860; Daniel Crofts, "James E. Harvey and the Secession Crisis," *The Pennsylvania Magazine of History and Biography,* 103 (1979): 180–82.

5. Easton *Sentinel,* November 22, 1860; Philadelphia *Inquirer,* November 23, 1860.

6. Ibid., December 17, 1860; Muncy *Luminary,* December 25, 1860; Thomas Meredith, "The Copperheads of Pennsylvania" (master's thesis, Lehigh University, 1947), pp. 46–47, hereafter cited as "Copperheads"; Benjamin Fryer, *Congressional History of Berks District* (Reading, Pa., 1939), p. 190.

7. Franklin *Venango Spectator,* December 19, 1860.

8. Philadelphia *Evening Bulletin,* January 17, 1861.

9. Philadelphia *Inquirer,* January 17, 1861.

10. Philadelphia *Pennsylvanian,* January 17, 1861.

11. Stanley Campbell, *The Slave Catchers* (Chapel Hill, N.C., 1970), p. viii.

12. Joshua Francis Fisher, *Concessions and Compromises* (Philadelphia, 1860), *passim.*

13. Uniontown *Genius of Liberty,* February 28, 1861; Ebensburg *Alleghanian,* March 7, 1861; George Bergner, comp., *The Legislative Record, Containing the Debates and Proceedings of the Pennsylvania Legislature for the Session of 1861* (Harrisburg, 1861), p. 29, hereafter cited as *L.R.*

14. A petition bearing Henry's signature can be found in Pennsylvania MSS Miscellaneous Box 1314, LC.

15. George Reed, comp., *Pennsylvania Archives,* 4th series (Harrisburg, 1902), 8:327–35.

16. Steubenville (Ohio) *Weekly Herald,* January 9, 1861; Alexander F. McClure to Edward McPherson, February 19, 1861, McPherson MSS, LC.

17. In brief, Crittenden's plan proposed to extend the Missouri Compromise line to the Pacific, to compensate slaveowners for fugitive slaves not recovered, and to promise that Congress would not interfere with slavery in states where it existed or in the District of Columbia.

18. William Whiting to Crittenden, December 8, 1860; Francis Marsh to Crittenden, December 31, 1860; William Elder to Crittenden, January 19, 1861, Crittenden MSS, LC; see also David Landreth, *A Plea for Compromise* (Bloomsdale, Pa.?, 1861), pp. 2–3.

19. Pennsylvania Congressman James Hale sympathized with these meetings and proposed a modification of the Crittenden Compromise. Under his plan slavery would be prohibited north of the Missouri Compromise line, but neither Congress nor a territorial legislature could pass any law for or against slavery south of that line. Pittsburgh *Post,* January 31, 1861; York *Gazette,* January 15, 1861; Gettysburg *Compiler,* January 21, February 4, 1861; Bedford *Gazette,* February 15, 1861; Uniontown *Genius of Liberty,* February 7, 14, 21, 1861; Crofts, "James E. Harvey," p. 182.

20. Pittsburgh *Gazette,* January 28, 1861; David Potter, *Lincoln and His Party in the Secession Crisis* (New Haven, Conn., 1942), p. 192.

21. W. Jack to Bigler, December 22, 1860, Bigler MSS.

22. Easton *Argus,* January 31, 1861.

23. Ebensburg *Democrat and Sentinel,* January 30, 1861; William Bigler, *The State of the Union* (Washington, 1861), *passim.*

24. A Caldwell to Cameron, January 22, 1861, Cameron MSS, DC; Gilbert Glover, *Immediate Pre-Civil War Compromise Efforts* (Nashville, Tenn., 1934), pp. 61–62.

25. James Pollock to Eli Slifer, February 13, 1861, Slifer-Dill MSS, Dickinson College, hereafter cited as Slifer-Dill MSS.

26. Fisher, *Concessions and Compromises, passim.*

27. Benjamin Patton to Van Buren, April 17, 1861; Franklin Pierce to Van Buren, April 16, 1861; Van Buren to Pierce, April 20, 1861; Van Buren to Ingersoll, April 27, 1861, Van Buren MSS, LC; Patton to Buchanan, April 17, 1861; Buchanan to Patton, April 24, 1861, Buchanan MSS.

28. Shankman, "Reed," p. 459.

29. Drafts of letters to unidentified correspondents, March 20, April 16, 1861, Buckalew MSS, Wilkes College, hereafter cited as Buckalew MSS.

30. Dieffenbach to Bigler, December 19, 1860; Salomon to Bigler, January 28, February 1, 1861, Bigler MSS; Salomon to Buchanan, January 11, 1861, Buchanan MSS.

31. Gettysburg *Compiler,* March 18, 1861; Uniontown *Genius of Liberty,* February 28, 1861.

32. A. V. Parsons to Black, January 15, 1861, Black MSS (word order of quotation modified slightly); Vincent Bradford to Buchanan, January 3, 1861, Buchanan MSS; John T. Hubbell, "Jeremiah Sullivan Black and the Great Secession Winter," *Western Pennsylvania Historical Magazine* 57 (1974); 273; Crofts, "James E. Harvey," p. 184.

33. Philadelphia *Pennsylvanian,* January 18, 1861; Landreth, *A Plea for Compromise,* p. 4.

34. Col. James Page, quoted in Philadelphia *Pennsylvanian*, January 18, 1861.

35. See the writer's sketch of Woodward in James I. Robertson, Jr., and Richard McMurry, *Rank and File: Civil War Essays in Honor of Bell Irvin Wiley* (San Rafael, Calif., 1976), pp. 93–111.

36. Arnold Shankman, "William B. Reed and the Civil War," *Pennsylvania History* 39 (1972): *passim*.

37. [Christopher Loeser,] *To the People of Pennsylvania and to the Legislature Now in Session* (Philadelphia, 1863), *passim;* Charlemagne Tower to Simon Cameron, January 9, 1863, Cameron MSS, LC; William Gudelunas and William Shade, *Before the Molly Maguires* (New York, 1976), pp. 98–100.

38. Smethport *McKean County Democrat*, March 29, 1861; Philip Auchampaugh, *Robert Tyler* (Duluth, 1934), p. 119.

39. Philadelphia *Pennsylvanian*, March 20, 1861; see also "Wister's Diary," pp. 274–75.

40. For more on Converse see Arnold Shankman, "Converse, *The Christian Observer* and Civil War Censorship," *The Journal of Presbyterian History* 52 (1974): 227–44.

41. Philadelphia *Pennsylvanian*, February 22, March 16, 18, 21, 1861.

42. *Palmetto Flag*, March 30, April 6, 13, 1861.

43. Philadelphia *North American*, April 16, 1861; Warren *Mail*, April 13, 1861; "Wister's Diary," p. 275.

44. *Congressional Globe*, Thirty-sixth Congress, 2nd session, February 20, 1861, p. 1065.

45. Only five of the twenty-five Congressmen elected in 1860 from Pennsylvania were Democrats. In the legislature Republicans outnumbered Democrats in the House by 71-29 and in the Senate by 27-6.

46. For information about Florence see *Congressional Globe*, Thirty-sixth Congress, 2nd session, January 15, 28, February 1, 1861, pp. 378, 598–99, 692; *Appendix*, February 27, 1861, pp. 302–304.

47. *L.R.*, January 14, 1861, pp. 250–54.

48. Phelps to Slifer, February 21, 1861, Slifer-Dill MSS; Stumbaugh to Cameron, January 5, 1861, Cameron MSS, Dauphin County Historical Society; William Morris Davis to Henry Brown, February 7, 1861, Davis MSS, HSP; John Blodgett to Cameron, February 1, 1861, Cameron MSS, LC.

49. Hazard to Cameron, January 22, 1861, Cameron MSS, Dauphin County Historical Society; Fulton, "Western Pennsylvania," p. 84.

3

"Few . . . Advocate Submission to the South"

"The Country is in a very miserably contition."[*]

"We are opposed to Secession and Coercion. If the former is unconstitutional, so is the latter."[**]

As soon as news of the exchange of hostile fire at Fort Sumter on April 12 was made public, it became unpatriotic to defend the South or to call for a peaceable solution to the sectional crisis. Even those newspapers which had previously argued that war would be futile reversed themselves and insisted that it was the duty of all patriotic citizens to suppress the rebellion. The secessionists had insulted the integrity of the nation, they said, and until the disunionists were properly punished, Pennsylvanians should sustain the federal government in its hour of peril. Readers were warned to avoid party quarrels and to work with Republicans to defeat their common enemies. "However much we may deprecate the political causes which have driven the South into this insane madness," insisted the April 15, 1861, Pittsburgh *Post,* it was "too late" to speak about the past; it was the duty of all to defend "the glorious stars and stripes."

[*]R. Wolfarth to Charles Buckalew, September 5, 1861, Buckalew MSS. No effort has been made to correct Wolfarth's spelling.
[**]Montrose *Democrat,* August 22, 1861.

63

The overwhelming majority of Pennsylvania's Democrats echoed these sentiments, and thousands responded to Lincoln's call for 75,000 volunteers. Those few who had misgivings about the war found it increasingly dangerous to voice their opinions publicly. In January, February, or March, men who expressed sympathy for the South might be greeted with hisses or be forced to flee public gatherings[1]; in April or May, however, a man suspected of supporting the Confederacy was more likely to be tarred and feathered, to be forced to wave the flag, or to be compelled to take a loyalty oath.[2]

Nowhere was this patriotic fervor more in evidence than in Philadelphia. On April 15, a mob estimated as numbering in the thousands marched to the office of the *Palmetto Flag* and began shouting crude epithets. They ordered Editor Brent to display an American flag lest he place his life and property in jeopardy. As several policemen and Mayor Henry arrived on the scene, Brent finally located a flag and waved it from the window. This temporarily quieted the crowd, and Mayor Henry, holding another flag in his hands, urged the people to avoid violence. He was cheered only when he promised that no treason would be tolerated in the city.[3]

Later rowdies visited other newspapers, a post office, several stores, and the home of Josiah Reed. At the American Hotel a scuffle nearly broke out because a flag fluttering from a post was upside down. The error was hastily corrected. Next the mob visited the home of William B. Reed and demanded that a flag be placed in front of the house. Reed was away at court, but a Negro servant located the required symbol of patriotism and the rowdies left. Late that night another group assembled near Major General Robert Patterson's home and insisted that he too display the Stars and Stripes. Not only did the general willingly comply with their request, but he also promised to lead the men to battle.[4] The message was clear: Philadelphians had decided that the war was just and they would no longer tolerate any dissenting viewpoints.

Private individuals who had the courage—or stupidity—to utter treasonable statements found themselves the target of angry crowds. Some fled when they saw rowdies, others were forced to cheer for the Union, and a few were physically assaulted. These incidents horrified responsible citizens. The April 16, 1861, issue of the Philadelphia *Evening Bulletin* warned that unless the mobs could be controlled, there was likely to be a serious riot in the city and, if one did occur, "the innocent were quite as likely to suffer as the guilty." Flags, it added, were scarce, and they were not displayed in front of some homes because merchants had none to sell. On May 1, 1861, the Philadelphia *Inquirer* urged its readers not to form vigilante committees, assuring them that the mayor and the police were well able to handle disloyal citizens.

Eventually it became a serious liability to be anything less than a staunch Union man. On May 7, Senator James Bayard of Delaware and his two daughters came to Philadelphia on a train. Hecklers, convinced that the senator had just returned from Dixie, surrounded the coach, and it was necessary for police to rescue him and his family and escort them to their destination. The visitors cut short their trip, and the May 7, 1861, *Bulletin* again urged citizens to maintain order. "The cause of the Union," it asserted, "is damaged rather than strengthened by [such] acts of lawlessness."

Among those forced to flee Philadelphia was Robert Tyler, who had planned to stay in the city after the war started, but, in his own words, he was "forcibly expelled." The expulsion took the form of a meeting held in Independence Square on April 17. One man told the assembly that Tyler had always defended the South, and this statement was greeted with cries that the "traitor" be lynched. Later an effigy of Tyler was hanged, and fearing that his life was in danger, the accused asked Mayor Henry for police protection. Henry suggested that he leave the city for a few days until tempers cooled. Tyler took this advice. When he returned to Philadelphia, he wrote, "While I live in Pennsylvania I shall never raise my hand against the State or the flag she shall follow." But only a few days later he fled to Richmond and took a position in the Confederate government. Philadelphians did not lament the loss; some sarcastically noted that he left owing the state treasury $960.12.[5]

GENERAL ROBERT PATTERSON.

Mobs visited the home of Robert Patterson in April 1861 and demanded that he display the Stars and Stripes. Patterson, who had many ties with the South, willingly complied and promised to lead the men to battle. Illustration from J. Thomas Scharf and Thompson Westcott, "History of Philadelphia, 1609–1884" (Philadelphia: L.H. Everts & Co., 1884), vol. I, 755.

Tyler was not the only man to leave Pennsylvania for the South. George McHenry, a native of the state and a former director of the Philadelphia Board of Trade, had been one of the delegates at the Charleston Convention. An avowed opponent of Douglas and "squatter sovereignty," he joined the Southern delegates who bolted and helped select John Breckinridge as the "state rights" candidate of the party. Tirelessly he campaigned for the Kentuckian, but Pennsylvania voted for Lincoln. As the secession crisis became increasingly acute, McHenry found his political beliefs coincided with those of the Confederates and on March 30, 1861, he left his home for Europe. During the war he lived in London and served as one of the South's chief propagandists, authoring books and pamphlets critical of the North, explaining why Pennsylvania should join the Confederacy and why England should recognize the independence of the South. In none of his efforts did he succeed.[6]

In 1860, John Hughes, the nephew of Francis W. Hughes, had been the unsuccessful Democratic congressional candidate for the Schuylkill-Northumberland district. His father and brother lived in New Bern, North Carolina, and in June 1861, without telling anyone but his uncle, he left Pottsville and went to his father's home. Once in Dixie, he joined a Confederate company and rose to the rank of captain.[7]

Harry Ingersoll, a second unsuccessful congressional candidate in 1860 and a son of Charles Jared Ingersoll, was as vocal a critic of the Union goverment as he "was violent for the South & secession." In 1864, rather than live in "Lincoln's despotism," he and his South Carolina–born wife moved to London. John Ingersoll, another of Charles Jared Ingersoll's sons, had taken up residence in Mississippi before the war started and his son, Charles, donned the gray. Edward and Charles Ingersoll, two of John's brothers, remained in Philadelphia during the war, but both believed that the South had a constitutional right to secede from the Union.[8]

Admittedly the Ingersoll family was unrepresentative of Pennsylvanians, but nearly everyone in the state knew of families with relatives in the slave states.[9] Some natives of the Keystone State

WHY

PENNSYLVANIA

SHOULD BECOME

ONE OF THE

CONFEDERATE STATES

OF

AMERICA:

BY A NATIVE OF

PENNSYLVANIA.

LONDON:

J. WILSON, 93, GREAT RUSSELL STREET,

BLOOMSBURY.

M.DCCC.LXII.

Cover of George McHenry's pamphlet proposing that Pennsylvania join the Confederacy.

served in the Confederate army,[10] and at least one Pennsylvania soldier traded the blue for the gray rather than suffer the rigors of being a prisoner of war.[11] Prominent Confederates with ties in Pennsylvania included General John Pemberton and Josiah Gorgas, both natives of the commonwealth; General John Winder, whose brother, William, lived in Philadelphia, and Alexander Stephens, whose father was a native of Perry County and who had cousins living there.

Yet, despite these ties, Pennsylvanians tolerated little disloyalty in 1861. Naturally the exodus of Confederate sympathizers in April 1861 removed some of the most vocal defenders of the South, and others who might have spoken up feared that mobs would damage their property. Mindful of the rioting in their city, Philadelphians critical of the war were careful not to express their views in public. When a war meeting was held in Kittanning in April, James Alexander Fulton refused to attend but would do nothing further to make known his true feelings about the conflict. Workers found it prudent not to voice criticism of the war. In Warsaw Township, sixty businessmen announced that they would refuse to hire men who had proclaimed "secessionist sympathies." Therefore it was not surprising that Sidney George Fisher wrote in his diary that it was "at the risk of any man's life that he utters publicly a sentiment in favor of secession or of the South." Added Sarah Wister in her diary on April 18, 1861, "There is a Treason law out which will keep people very straight."[12]

Naturally patriotism was important in creating this intolerance of pro-Southern opinions, but other factors were also significant. One such factor was that businessmen did not suffer the depression they had feared. For several months after the fall of Fort Sumter many thousands of men and women were out of work and stores were empty, but instead of calling for an end to the conflict, the unemployed pledged themselves to support the war. Food was relatively inexpensive, and few were starving. Had orders for war materiel not flooded Philadelphia and Pittsburgh in the summer of 1861, it is possible that the jobless would have rioted. Government contracts removed this threat. As the army expanded at an unprecedented rate, orders for wagons, ammunition, swords, uniforms, canteens, canned meat, blankets, and ships poured into Pennsylvania. Thus, most workers were only temporary economic casualties of the war.[13] Employed laborers had few reasons to criticize the fighting in 1861.

Prowar feeling was further strengthened when newspapers began to print stories about treason. It was falsely alleged that the Knights of the Golden Circle intended to set simultaneous fires in Boston, New York, and Philadelphia. During the first months of the war an old woman sold pies to the soldiers at Camp Curtin, outside Harrisburg. One day she poisoned her wares, and seven of her customers died. Later that year two soldiers died after drinking tainted whisky. At Carlisle Barracks authorities discovered that a lieutenant was sending out messages to the rebels, giving them information about troop movements. The soldier fled from his post but was caught in York County. Another man was arrested at Camp Curtin after he was seen taking mysterious notes in a small black book.[14]

With frightening frequency newspapers reported that contraband goods including bullets were being sent to the South. Besides seizing ammunition and lead, Philadelphia and Pittsburgh police uncovered large quantitites of uniforms, bandages, and other war materiel bound for Dixie. Several men were arrested for helping the South. Orders were issued to seize a resident of Reading, who was accused of preparing to ship quantitites of iron to South Carolina. The man's son was a Confederate soldier, and he himself had lived in the Palmetto State before the war. Diligent authorities seized him and found in his possession several bank notes from Charleston and large amounts of gold.[15]

In October another suspected spy was captured. J. Wallace Packard had gone to the South with his employer, a Philadelphia sewing-machine manufacturer and an outspoken defender of Southern rights. His boss opened a firearms factory in Dixie, and Packard was supposedly sent to the North to purchase supplies for the factory. If he was a spy, he was anything but a clever one, for upon arriving in Philadelphia, he registered at a hotel as a resident of Richmond. The keeper summoned authorities, who searched the guest's valises and discovered a secessionist letter and $600 in gold. Packard was sent to Fort Lafayette, where, after taking a loyalty oath, he was released.[16]

Two spies were caught in Harrisburg in August. Thomas Carson, a resident of Baltimore and a landowner in Virginia, carried letters from Southerners to Yankees. Walter Kelley, a British subject, was arrested by suspicious agents, who discovered a large amount of money and letters from the South hidden in his clothing.[17]

Three men were arrested in Philadelphia after they tried to sell a government detective, whom they thought a Confederate agent, overcoats, surgical equipment, and weapons for the Confederate army. One of the men was released from Fort Warren after he became insane, but his two co-conspirators were not allowed to leave the federal fortress until the United States district court in Philadelphia had prepared indictments against them.[18]

If arrests were effective in preventing the sale of goods to the Confederacy, they were equally successful in lessening loyal opposition to the government. Enough arbitrary arrests were made to convince critics of the Lincoln administration to keep their views to themselves. Ellis B. Schnable of Philadelphia was imprisoned in Connecticut for making allegedly treasonable speeches, but his case was far less spectacular than that of Pierce Butler. The former husband of actress Fannie Kemble had visited his family in the South before the war began. When he returned to Pennsylvania he strongly defended slavery and secession but told his family "that Southern as his sympathies are, & right as he believes them in their cause, he a born & bred Pennsylvanian would never take up arms against his own country." Nonetheless his enemies circulated a false story that he had accepted a Confederate commission and was in the North solely to purchase arms for the rebels. On August 19, 1861, his room was searched and he was arrested and sent to Fort Lafayette. Orders for his seizure had come from the War Department, but Secretary of War Cameron had no personal knowledge of the affair. No really damaging evidence about Butler had been found among his personal papers, but he spent a month in jail. He was released from Fort Lafayette in New York after he took an oath of allegiance and promised not to visit the South without a government passport. Federal authorities considered the case closed.

Butler, however, did not. Irritated and humiliated, he sought vindication in the courts. In April 1862, the Pennsylvania Supreme Court issued a writ which was served on Cameron, ordering him to answer charges for false arrest. Preparations were made to defend the former secretary of war, but after Lincoln assumed the blame for having ordered the arrest, Butler, satisfied that his honor had been avenged, let the matter drop.[19]

Scores of others were arrested for various offenses, but few incarcerations were as bizarre as that of William Winder of Philadelphia, who was arrested on September 11, 1861, for allegedly carrying on unpatriotic correspondence with Secretary of State Seward. Winder, who owned property in North Carolina, was the brother of a Confederate general and of Charles Winder of Washington, D.C., who was also jailed for disloyalty on September 11. The real reason for William Winder's imprisonment was that he had made a nuisance of himself after the conflict began by giving unsolicited advice to members of Lincoln's cabinet.

Among Winder's personal papers was correspondence with Confederate leaders and with such Northern "peace" men as Clement Vallandigham. Especially noteworthy were letters from his brother, Charles. These suggested that Charles sought a position in the Confederate government as minister to Mexico and that both men's sympathies lay with the South. In one note, dated February 2, 1861, Charles predicted that before August 1, 1861, Jefferson Davis would occupy the White House in Washington; in another, sent sometime in April, he wrote, "I know we [Confederates] are better organized, that we have a better cause & that in the coming contest, if it must come, we are *more* than a match for them." Other messages indicated that the two deluded themselves into believing that they could bring about a peace between the North and the South.[20]

Imprisonment did not silence William Winder's pen, for he deluged government officials with pleas demanding to know the nature of his offense. Seward eventually decided that Winder was harmless and ordered his release if he would take a loyalty oath. To everyone's surprise Winder refused to take an oath of allegiance. A month later Seward submitted a milder oath, but he again refused on the grounds that he was guilty of no crime and therefore the taking of an oath should not be a condition for his release. Not until November 26, 1862, was he released on parole.[21]

Arbitrary arrests were one way to help silence critics of the government; suppression of anti-administration newspapers was another. In April, anonymous critics had threatened the editor of the Uniontown *Genius of Liberty,* and mobs had closed the *Palmetto Flag;* in May, they invaded the office of the Beaver *Western Star;* and in August, they destroyed the offices of Easton's Democratic journals. On August 19, a Democratic political rally had been held in Easton, and speeches had been made that were critical of the war. After the gathering had dispersed, rowdies burned in effigy one of the speakers, Congressman Philip Johnson, and then they visited the offices of the Easton *Sentinel* and the Easton *Argus,* where they destroyed furniture and wrecked the press rooms.[22]

That same day another mob partially destroyed the West Chester *Jeffersonian* building. That paper had long antagonized Unionists, since it had defended secession and had claimed that the war would benefit only the "niggers." To many it was surprising that rioters had not attacked it until August. Two days after the riot federal deputies seized the type, the presses, and financial account books of the *Jeffersonian.* Editor John Hodgson vowed that the government would pay for suppressing his paper.

Hodgson had become notorious in his community for urging Democrats not to volunteer for the army and for calling Lincoln's election the great mistake "of the age." He refused to sign a loyalty statement although authorities told him that it was necessary for him to do so to get his property back. His response was defiant, insisting that he would rather "die" than to make such an

Fort Warren 15 March 1862

Hon. Simon Cameron

Sir

I was by order from you through a telegraphic despatch, Rat [...] to [...]

I was taken from Philadelphia [...] placed in confinement being [...] from whence I was transferred to this Fort, in which I am confined, still ignorant of the Cause which induced you to issue that order. The object of my writing this letter is to obtain from you information at who[se] instance & upon what representations you were influenced to the issue of the order for my Confinement in [...]

I believe I do not err in supposing the order could not have been of your own motion, but was upon Statement of party, or parties who might not [...] them [...]

I am [...] would not witting[ly] mislead you. And I trust that my volume [...] or your coolness to afford me the information desired, will not [...]

I [...] myself entitled to this consideration at your hands, & I am unwilling to doubt your inclination to accord it to me.

I am, Sir, very truly,
Your Obt. Servt.
W. H. Winder

affirmation. Like Winder he hoped to embarrass the government in the courts, and after three trials he was awarded $504.33 to compensate him for damages caused by federal agents.[23]

Surprisingly enough, not until August 22, 1861, did government officials suppress the publication of the *Christian Observer*. That the journal was published simultaneously in Richmond and Philadelphia was reason enought for Republicans to suspect that it was disloyal. Though editor Amasa Converse agreed that secession had been premature, he never endorsed the war and he called for an honorable and a "Christian" peace with or without reunion. Moreover, he frequently printed Northern "peace" resolutions and articles more critical of the abolitionists than of the secessionists. For example, one letter published in the August 22 issue stated that antislavery leaders were "more dangerous" than rebels. Another letter, supposedly from a Virginian, referred to alleged atrocities of Yankee soldiers in his state and concluded that "reunion is an utter impossibility."[24]

On August 22, 1861, Converse was arrested. The editor protested that he had not encouraged disloyalty, but before long he fled to Richmond, where he continued to publish his paper.

Even clergymen found it necessary to avoid criticizing the war. When the Reverend Henry A. Wise, Jr., an Episcopal minister in West Philadelphia and a son of the former governor of Virginia, omitted the prayer for the president at Sunday morning worship services, one prominent parishioner rose and requested Wise to add the prayer. The rector refused and was forced to leave the pulpit before he could finish the service or preach his sermon. Shortly thereafter he was threatened by angry townsmen and he moved to Richmond. Another Philadelphia minister, the Reverend W. T. Brantley, decided that he could no longer live safely in the North, and he and his family went to Georgia, the home of his wife's relatives.[25]

Despite this climate of fear, a few Democratic newspapers refused to support the war wholeheartedly. Some, such as the *Democratic Watchman*, which was published in Bellefonte, favored an immediate end to the fighting. On July 18, 1861, the paper boldly declared, "We are ready for peace now, we long for peace, we pray for peace, but the northern people—[and] the Southern people—it appears, are not ready for it." The Bedford *Gazette* shared these sentiments, though it was more moderate in its opposition to the war. Proposing an convention of the loyal states to devise a compromise to end the fighting, its editor warned of dire consequences to Pennsylvania laborers and capitalists if the conflict continued. Journalists in Carlisle, Montrose, Selinsgrove, and Smethport insisted that the "imbecile who occupies and disgraces the Presidential chair" would not terminate the war until the federal government was a military despotism and the slaves were free. Though these journals were lonely voices "crying in the wilderness," they were convinced that the masses would eventually hail their bravery and willingness to defy public opinion to speak the truth.[26]

Admittedly support for the war was widespread in 1861, but discontent was not limited to a few journalists. The conflict was less than three months old before a group of Venango County Democrats assembled to make known their feelings about the strife. Resolutions were passed recommending that a national convention be summoned to end the conflict and declaring that the sacrificing of human lives for "the frivolous pretext of war" without congressional authorization was "unjustifiable."[27] This was too much for the July 24, 1861, Franklin *Venango Spectator,* which lamented that such gatherings would cut the throat of the Democracy with "a very dull razor."

The Venango meeting was not the first such gathering held in the state. That honor belonged to a "peace" assembly which had convened in Cross Creek, Washington County, on June 8. Participants at this gathering had denounced all efforts to subjugate the South, stating, "Coercion can never carry with it the least weight in favor of reconciliation and peace." To preserve "our beloved Union by fighting under present circumstances," according to one resolution, "is simply preposterous."[28]

News of these two meetings encouraged other malcontents to assemble and voice their displeasure of the efforts to coerce the

South. In August, peace gatherings of varying hostility to the government were held in all corners of the commonwealth. In Lennox Township in strongly Republican Montrose County, antiwar Democrats met secretly on several occasions. Participants at these assemblies called the war a mockery and argued that the Union could be maintained "only on grounds of friendship, love and good will." Similar gatherings met in Chester, Wayne, and Elk Counties.[29]

More typical were meetings of McKean County Democrats, which condemned secessionists and those Northern politicians who fanned the flames of sectional agitation. For in 1861, Pennsylvania's Democracy was stumbling about, unsure of how to function as a loyal opposition party during wartime. On the subject of war, Democrats could agree on only one point: the conflict should not become an abolitionist crusade. Some thought that the government should be supported in all its activities; others insisted that they were only obligated to endorse Lincoln's constitutional actions. Many wanted peace as soon as possible and favored a political rather than a military solution to the crisis; and a small but vocal minority wanted peace at any price. As the pro-peace factions gained power in the Democracy, many war Democrats joined the Republicans, for they were persuaded that they could demonstrate their loyalty only by merging with Republicans and forming a Union party pledged to support Lincoln's war aims. Not only did this enhance the chance for victory of pro-administration candidates—for war Democrats-turned-Unionists were nominated for office almost exclusively in non-Republican districts—but it also forced Democratic politicians to be on the defensive; that is, they had to explain why, if loyal, they did not join the Union party.[30]

The election of 1861 was the least important of those held during the war years, for no national or major state offices were on the ballot. Nonetheless, voters had to select men to fill all of the positions in the Pennsylvania House of Representatives and one-third of those in the state senate. The issue about which Pennsylvanians were most concerned was the repeal of the tonnage tax levied on the Pennsylvania Railroad, and this was unrelated to the war. Unionists—this was the new name that Republicans took for themselves during the war—were most willing to exploit the disloyalty issue, warning that one could tell a traitor when he heard "a doughface talking about conforming to the Constitution in our efforts to punish traitors. . . . None are loyal but those who pledge life, fortune, and sacred honor in the common cause of our country," announced the Harrisburg *Telegraph* of August 15, 1861.

On the whole, the campaign did not stress the issue of loyalty to the government. According to the Philadelphia *Public Ledger* of October 8, 1861, "All the candidates profess to entertain Union sentiments, and this profession is doubtless sincere." Even the increasingly Unionist Philadelphia *Evening Bulletin* noted on September 6, 1861, that the Democrats were not running any "Secession, White Feather, or Peace Movement" candidates in the state. Furthermore, it added,

> the few men who advocate submission to the South, destruction of the Union and exaltation of slavery as the supreme power of the land—all which is done under the craven and treacherous cry of Peace are so few in number and so despicable in character, that they are totally insignificant. They do not dare show themselves in any political movement here.

On election day it was apparent that the only issue of interest to the voters was the repeal of the tonnage tax. Political observers noted that it was no coincidence that, except for the Philadelphia delegation, every member of the House but one who voted to rescind the tonnage tax and who ran for reelection was defeated. In the Senate only two of the eleven whose terms expired were returned to office, and both had oposed repeal. The question had not been decided on party lines, but the Democrats were the beneficiaries of the protest.[31]

On the local level the war issue had occasionally been important. Efforts were made in Philadelphia to defeat Robert Ewing, the Democratic candidate for sheriff and a former slaveowner, because he had been a vice-president of the Democratic peace meeting of January 16. Ewing protested that he had not attended the gathering or even read the resolutions, and he noted that twenty years before, he had freed all of his slaves. Moreover, as a further proof of his loyalty, he reminded voters that his son was a Union soldier. Nonetheless, some supporters of the war urged the electorate to vote for his opponent. Republicans won most of the city contests, and at first it appeared as though Ewing had lost by a mere 150 votes. Soldier ballots reversed the election result, however, and angry Republicans took the case to court.[32]

During the last weeks of October, Philadelphia newspapers repeatedly listed voting irregularities: non-Pennsylvania soldiers voting, polls not opening on election day, votes not being counted, and voters being denied ballots. Many called for the repeal of the law, and on October 20, 1861, the Philadelphia *Sunday Dispatch* declared that soldier voting was "as fatal a foe to good discipline as could be devised," for it promoted political quarrels in the army.

In Luzerne County Democrats lost several offices after the soldier vote had been tabulated, and they began to investigate stories of fraud. It was decided that Ezra Chase, the party candidate for district attorney, would test the constitutionality of the law in the courts. According to the 1838 Pennsylvania Constitution, voters had to cast ballots within their home election districts, and the state supreme court ruled that soldiers could not vote outside the boundaries of the commonwealth. Justices Walter Lowrie and George Woodward wrote the opinion of the court, which the May 22, 1862, Philadelphia *Evening Bulletin* praised as being based on common sense and the law. Republicans were not unduly upset with the verdict, for their candidate became sheriff of Philadelphia—though not until he could expel Ewing from the office. Chase received his position in Luzerne County, and so both parties were able to point to victories won because of the decision.

By the end of 1861 antiwar sentiment was weak but growing. Fear of arrests or of mobs forced most pro-peace Pennsylvanians to be silent, but this would soon change. Political and military events in 1862 would create a war-weary public, and many would be willing to criticize the efforts to triumph over the Confederacy.

NOTES

1. Washington *Reporter and Tribune,* January 10, 1861; Columbus (Ga.) *Sun,* March 5, 1861.

2. Some even suspected that James E. Harvey was guilty of treason, but there is no evidence of this. Harrisburg *Telegraph,* April 26, 1861; Uniontown *Genius of Liberty,* April 25, 1861; Ebensburg *Alleghanian,* May 2, 16, 1861; "Wister's Dairy," pp. 278–80; Crofts, "James E. Harvey," *passim.*

3. Philadelphia *Public Ledger,* April 17, 1861; "Wister's Dairy," p. 275; William C. Wright, *The Secession of the Middle Atlantic States* (Rutherford, N.J., 1973), p. 161.

4. Reed to Buchanan, April 29, 1861, Buchanan MSS; "Wister's Dairy," pp. 278–80.

5. Philadelphia *Inquirer,* April 16, 19, 1861; "Wister's Diary," p. 275.

6. George McHenry, *The Position and Duty of Pennsylvania* (London, 1863), *passim;* George McHenry, *The Cotton Trade* (London, 1863), *passim;* George McHenry, *The African Race in America,* pp. 13–14; George McHenry, *Why Pennsylvania Should Become One of the Confederate States of America* (London, 1862), *passim.*

7. Arnold Shankman, "Francis W. Hughes and the 1862 Pennsylvania Election," *Pennsylvania Magazine of History and Biography* 95 (1971): 387.

8. *Fisher Diary,* pp. 379, 437, 499; Irwin Greenberg, "Charles Ingersoll: The Aristocrat as Copperhead," *Pennsylvania Magazine of History and Biography* 93 (1969): 192–94; R. Sturgis Ingersoll, *Sketch of the Ingersoll Family of Philadelphia* (Philadelphia, 1966), pp. 12–14.

9. Perry County offers examples of the links between the state and the South. One native of the county raised a regiment for the Confederates, and several others fought for the rebels or had children who joined the confederate army. H. H. Hain, *History of Perry County, Pennsylvania* (Harrisburg, Pa., 1922), p. 554. The story of Dr. Stephen Duncan, on the other hand, shows that not all native Pennsylvanians living in the South were secessionists. Duncan, the largest resident slaveowner in Mississippi in the 1850s, strongly opposed secession and fled Natchez in 1863. See William K. Scarborough, "Slavery—The White Man's Burden," in Harry Owens, ed., *Perspectives and Irony in American Slavery* (Jackson, Miss., 1976), pp. 103–35.

10. Hundreds of graduates of the University of Pennsylvania, Dickinson College, and Jefferson Medical School donned the gray. Most, of course, were natives of the South.

11. Luther Dickey, *History of the 103d Regiment, Pennsylvania Veteran Volunteer Infantry* (Chicago, 1910), p. 77.

12. Fulton, "Western Pennsylvania," p. 88; Easton *Express,* August 9, 1861; *Fisher Diary,* p. 385; "Wister's Diary," p. 278.

13. Philadelphia *Public Ledger,* April 16, July 9, 10, 1861; Wilkes-Barre *Luzerne Union,* Nobember 6, 1861.

14. Philadelphia *Sunday Dispatch,* May 5, 1861; Stroudsburg *Jeffersonian,* December 5, 1861; Janet Book, *Northern Rendezvous* (Harrisburg, Pa., 1951), p. 54.

15. Pittsburgh *Gazette,* April 22, 1861; Harrisburg *Telegraph,* August 22, 1861.

16. U. S. War Department, *The War of the Rebellion: A Compilation of the Official Records of the Union and Confederate Armies* (Washington, 1880–1901), series 2, 2: 295, 308, hereafter cited as *O.R.*

17. Philadelphia *Evening Bulletin,* August 23, 1861; Altoona *Tribune,* August 29, 1861.

18. *O.R.,* ser. 2, 2: 829–55.

19. Ibid., pp. 507–508; "Wister's Diary," pp. 274, 281, 304, 322–27.

20. Ibid., pp. 155, 721–31, 739–46; William Winder, *Secrets of the American Bastile* (Philadelphia, 1863), *passim;* "Proceedings Relating to State Prisoners, 1862," pp. 1–27, Record Group 59 (RG 59), National Archives (NA).

21. Elizabeth McCall to George McCall, October 27, 1862, McCall Family Papers, HSP; New York *World,* November 6, 1861.

22. Uniontown *Genius of Liberty,* April 25, 1861; Beaver *Argus,* June 5, 1861; Easton *Express,* August 20, 21, 1861.

23. Ray Abrams, "The *Jeffersonian:* Copperhead Newspaper," *Pennsylvania Magazine of History and Biography,* 57 (1933): 268–77.

24. Christian *Observer,* June 27, July 4, 11, August 22, 1861; New York *Day Book,* August 26, 1861; Shankman, "Converse," *passim.*

25. Wellsboro *Tioga Agitator,* June 5, 1861; Chester Dunham, *The Attitude of the Northern Clergy Towards the South* (Toledo, Ohio, 1942), pp. 144–46.

26. Bellefonte *Democratic Watchman,* July 11, August 22, 1861; Bedford *Gazette,* April 12, 26, October 25, 1861; Montrose *Democrat,* August 15, 1861; Smethport *McKean County Democrat,* April 18, 1861; William Russ, Jr., "Franklin Weirick: 'Copperhead' of Central Pennsylvania," *Pennsylvania History* 5 (1938): 245–56, hereafted cited as "Weirick."

27. Franklin *Venango Spectator,* July 17, 1861.

28. Washington *Reporter and Tribune,* August 29, 1861; Harrisburg *Telegraph,* July 3, 1861.

29. Bedford *Gazette,* August 9, 1861; New York *Day Book,* August 20, 1861; Clearfield *Raftman's Journal,* September 4, 1861; Shippen *Cameron Citizen,* September 18, 1861.

30. Shippensburg *News,* August 24, 1861; Stanton Davis, *Pennsylvania Politics 1860–63* (Cleveland, 1935), p. 202.

31. Christopher Dell, *Lincoln and the War Democrats* (Rutherford, N.J., 1975), pp. 112–13.

32. Philadelphia *Evening Bulletin,* October 5–9, 1861.

4

"John Brown's Soul Has Stopped Marching On"

"[I wish] horice Greely may axidently B Shot."*

"There is no need for a people opposed to each other being bound together. We may still be a great people, though a smaller country."**

Antiwar sentiment had hibernated in 1861; in 1862, it finally awoke from its slumber. Even Democrats in favor of the war—and in a few cases Unionists—became disenchanted with the progress of the Union Army and with the ever-increasing centralization of power in Washington. No longer were there surplus volunteers for the army, and as many Pennsylvanians were as interested in evading military service as in donning the blue. Despite the activities of Thaddeus Stevens, only a minority of the commonwealth's citizens wanted to free the blacks, and even if a majority of the residents of the Keystone State personally despised slavery, a substantial number wished to have no social or political contact with Negroes. After Lincoln announced that he would issue the Emancipation Proclamation, Democrats ex-

*Samuel Houston to Sister, Margaret, September 1, 1862, Houston MSS, microfilm copy at Pennsylvania Historical and Museum Commission.
**Peter Walker, *Some Thoughts on the Pacification of the Country for the Consideration of the North and the South* (Philadelphia, 1862), p. 3.

ploited prevalent racial antipathies, and this was a key factor in their impressive electoral victories in 1862. Less than a year after war critic William B. Reed had confided to a friend that he dared not make his true beliefs known, he was sending fellow Democrats copies of his political tracts in which he called for a cessation of hostilities. Truly 1862 was a year of change.

In 1861, Pennsylvania congressmen docilely supported the war; one year later a few openly broke with the Lincoln administration, stating that they could no longer endorse its policies. Typical of the new, militant anti-Lincoln congressmen was Colonel Charles John Biddle, a former Whig and the son of famed banker Nicholas Biddle, who was elected in the summer of 1861 to fill a vacancy created when Edward Joy Morris resigned his seat. Biddle had distinguished himself in the Mexican War and had opposed secession in 1861. At the start of the war he had been elected a lieutenant colonel of the 13th Pennsylvania Reserves, and though he weighed barely one hundred pounds and was a rigid disciplinarian, he quickly won the respect of his men. None dared call him a Southern sympathizer, but he was unwilling to become an uncritical defender of Lincoln. Shortly before he left for Washington, several of his Philadelphia friends held a public dinner in his honor. Because of prior commitments, he could not be present, but he sent his hosts a letter in which he called for a vigorous suppression of the rebellion and in which he insisted that nothing be done to curtail civil liberties.[1]

In Congress Biddle frequently castigated his colleagues for tolerating executive usurpations of power. "A party that can silence opposition and muzzle the press," he warned, "is the worst kind of tyrant." As time passed he feared that abolitionists were trying to promote a "black millennium" by turning "the fertile regions of the South into a howling wilderness of revolted negroes." Biddle told his friend Lewis Coryell that this was hypocritical since the most vocal critics of slavery often lived in states discriminating against free blacks.[2] Before long Unionists were denouncing Biddle as an enemy of the people.

Other Pennsylvania congressmen also made known their dissatisfaction with the government. Philip Johnson and Sydenham Ancona joined Ohio antiwar leader Clement Vallandigham and eleven other Democrats in composing an address calling for the restoration of the old Union and the preservation of civil liberties. In addition, Ancona, who had voted for Vallandigham for speaker in 1861, opposed the confiscation acts and legal tender bills, and he proposed that the secretary of state free all Confederate prisoners who took a loyalty oath. William Lehman rebuked abolitionists for suggesting that, once conquered, the South would forfeit its former status in the Union and become a federal territory. Such talk, he thought, would strengthen Confederate morale and pro-long the war.[3]

Even Hendrick B. Wright, a Union Democrat from Wilkes-Barre, began to criticize the administration. Fearing that Lincoln was making the war a struggle in behalf of an "inferior caste" of black men, he warned that such a policy would alienate the border states, Pennsylvania, and Ohio more than "the plagues of Egypt." On several occasions he denounced the Unionists for passing legal tender bills, which he believed were unconstitutional. According to Wright, if Congress needed money, it could levy direct taxes and raise all the funds it needed.[4] Men of both parties listened to him since his views were those of war Democrats, men whose votes would be crucial in any close election.

Most surprising of all was Republican Senator Edgar Cowan's criticism of the government. In 1861, when he was elected to succeed William Bigler, Democrats had nothing good to say about him. Soon they had reason to change their minds, for he opposed the confiscation acts, disliked the conscription bills, and disapproved of the legal tender acts. Furthermore, ignoring the advice of the Pennsylvania Senate to vote for the expulsion of Senator Jesse Bright of Indiana, he was one of only two Unionists to defend the Hoosier from charges of disloyalty. The Harrisburg *Patriot and Union* of July 19, 1862, praised him for acting more like "a patriot than a partisan" and for doing "his own thinking and voting." Unionists, however, considered him to be a renegade who had forgotten to whom he owed his election.[5]

It is difficult to determine who led the antiwar forces in the state legislature. In the Pennsylvania house the most persistent critics of the war were Levi Tate and Charles Lamberton, and in the state senate Hiester Clymer headed the pro-peace forces. These three strongly opposed efforts to abolish slavery in the District of Columbia and hoped to bar blacks from entering Pennsylvania. In 1862 most of their colleagues ignored them.[6]

Just as some Democratic politicians became more bold in opposing the war, so did some party newspapers more openly manifest their displeasure with the conflict. Nothing that the government did pleased John Hodgson of the West Chester *Jeffersonian.* When Lincoln called for new taxes, the *Jeffersonian* claimed that no funds would be needed if the president would get rid of the corruption in Washington. Hodgson also opposed the issuance of paper money, the emancipation of the slaves, and the conscription of soldiers. He insisted that Lincoln was unfit to be president since he believed the chief executive to be a "jester and buffoon" and a "smutty joker."[7]

On July 10, 1862, Hodgson published the following doggerel, which he claimed was the work of a schoolboy:

> God made man,
> And man made money.
> God made bees,
> And bees made honey.
> God made the *Union*
> Nice and slick.
> In came old Lincoln
> And spoiled it quick!

Readers of the *Jeffersonian* were treated to excerpts from the speeches of Jefferson Davis, Clement Vallandigham, and Charles J. Biddle, and they were assured that England, France, and even Spain would soon recognize Confederate independence. Hodgson was as unwilling to report Union victories as he was to acknowledge that Southerners occasionally destroyed Yankee property.

On the other hand, he frequently printed lurid accounts of Northern soldiers pillaging Dixie and of black rapists and criminals promoting miscegenation and disorder in both the North and the South.[8] Peace Democrats considered the paper to be "one of the best in the State," and they agreed with the Montrose *Democrat* of January 3, 1862, that it should continue its personal war against the antislavery faction of the North.

It was no surprise therefore that Unionists disliked the *Jeffersonian*. Dr. Franklin Taylor warned his sister's suitor, Eber, "You must stop taking the *Jeffersonian*, it won't do." When Eber refused to take this advice, their friendship terminated.[9]

Another paper hostile to the war was the Selinsgrove *Times* of Snyder County, a Unionist stronghold. Ignoring the political opinions of the county, editor Franklin Weirick urged young men not to enlist in the army. Union soldiers disliked him so much that a group of them once tried to lynch him; he was saved only when he reluctantly muttered, "Three cheers for the Union." Mobs threatened to destroy his printing office, and many called for his arrest. For a while his press was suppressed, but soon he was back at work. Enjoying his infamy and probably seeking martyrdom, he claimed not to fear insolent rowdies or "Presidential dungeons, the fortresses of the modern Caligula."[10]

Among the other journals sharply critical of Lincoln were the Chambersburg *Valley Spirit* and the Ebensburg *Democrat and Sentinel*. The first of these alleged that the war was being waged for emancipation and spoils. "Under the banner of plunder and the black flag of fanaticism and negroism," it stated, the Unionists were "trampling the Constitution under foot and marching on to destroy the Union they profess to uphold." Scandals were so prevalent, it added, that "smelling committees" had to be assigned to every department of the government in Washington "to drive away the thieves." The Ebensburg paper also argued that it was the so-called Unionists who favored perpetual dismemberment of the nation.[11]

Supporters of the war rarely discriminated between "peace" editors and those who were only mildly opposed to the Lincoln administration. In 1862, the owners of two journals of the second category were forced to "pay" for their alleged treason. Though John Bratton of the Carlisle *American Volunteer* was urging men to join the army to defeat the rebels, soldiers at nearby Carlisle Barracks came to regard his paper as a disloyal sheet, and on October 24, 1862, members of the Anderson Guards sacked his office. When the local sheriff and Bratton went to the army post to complain, they were given an unfriendly reception. For several days Democrats patrolled the town and threatened to arrest any soldier walking about Carlisle after 10:00 P.M.[12]

Two months before, the editors of the influential Harrisburg *Patriot and Union,* which epitomized loyal opposition, were arrested. Like the *American Volunteer,* the *Patriot and Union* encouraged men to enlist in the army, but periodically it printed the peace sentiments of some of its readers, clearly stating its disagreement with these views. The paper was a racist journal, and it strongly opposed any efforts to change the status of the slaves. Until Lincoln became the emancipator, the *Patriot and Union* was content to dismiss him as a well-meaning man under the influence of malicious advisers. There would be no reason to expect that the editors of this paper would be arrested.

On August 4, 1862, as a joke, two printer's helpers prepared and circulated a bogus handbill alleging that General James Lane was in town to recruit blacks for two colored regiments. This conceivably could have promoted opposition to the government, and George Bergner, postmaster of Harrisburg and editor of the rival Union newspaper, *The Telegraph,* was probably the man who sent a copy of the circular to Washington. General Henry Halleck and the chief of the Secret Service, Lafayette Baker, ordered the arrest of the management of the *Patriot and Union.* On the night of August 6, editors Ormond Barrett and Thomas McDowell and two of their employees were sent to the Old Capitol Prison. No charges were ever preferred against them.

The incident gave the Democracy an opportunity to denounce the government for muzzling the press, and on August 23, officials sheepishly released the prisoners. A crowd of 1,000 greeted the "martyrs" when their train arrived in Harrisburg.[13] Many wondered why such cases were not tried in local courts, and some questioned the propriety of jailing men for the misdeeds of their employees.

Philadelphia had no peace journal until 1863, but its antiwar leaders began to make their views known in 1862. When the English author Anthony Trollope visited the city in February 1862, he wrote, "In Philadelphia I for the first time came across live secessionists,—secessionists who pronounced themselves to be such."[14]

On April 27, 1861, Lincoln issued a proclamation which suspended the writ of habeas corpus covering the line from Philadelphia to Washington. Within a matter of weeks scores of individuals were arrested and transported to military prisons. Many prominent lawyers doubted the constitutionality of such acts, and after the decision of Chief Justice Roger Taney in the Merryman case, criticism of political arrests mounted in Philadelphia. Unionists, desirous of clothing their acts with at least a semblance of legality, prevailed upon the distinguished Philadelphia lawyer Horace Binney to write a pamphlet giving his views on the subject. Binney obliged them, and in a well-reasoned booklet he argued that the power to suspend the writ belonged to the chief executive.[15]

Several prominent Philadelphians disagreed and composed replies to dispute Binney's work. George Wharton, Tatlow Jackson, Edward Ingersoll, Jonathan Montgomery, J. C. Bullitt, and several anonymous authors agreed that only Congress could suspend the writ; for the president to assume this power would be tyrannical and destructive of constitutional liberties. All chided Binney for refusing to accept Taney's decision in the Merryman case.[16]

The rapidity with which these replies appeared in print amused the Philadelphia *Evening Bulletin.* On May 7, 1862, it reported that the city's "secessionists" ate together and spent their time together writing pamphlet responses to Binney. "In one single family," it sarcastically noted, "there have been two pamphlets issued on the subject, and it is supposed all the other members of the family are busy with new ones." Binney was astounded by the "galaxy of pamphlets" written in response to his tract. After having read as many as he could to "find if there is any political or constitutional law in them," he revised his work but only mildly modified his arguments.[17]

By July, the Democrats apparently saw no further need to write legal tracts. Noted the July 24, 1862, *Evening Bulletin:*

> They have even ceased writing pamphlets to Mr. Binney about the suspension of the writ of habeas corpus; but this, it is suspected, is because Jeff. Davis has suspended the writ, and they cannot reply to Mr. Binney or attack Mr. Lincoln for a measure which has been adopted by their dear friend Jeff.

If Democrats tired of writing polemics on the writ of habeas corpus, they had energy enough to author pamphlets advocating the restoration of the Union by compromise. Charles Ingersoll wrote a lengthy tract entitled *A Letter to a Friend in a Slave State.* In this he called the war a mistake on the part of both the North and the South: "Had the South known that war was to follow, secession would not have been resorted to. Had the North known secession was to be the consequence, they would not have tolerated the slavery agitation." Ingersoll denounced the abolitionists and suggested that peace could be had only if Democrats controlled the government.[18]

Unionists, of course, disagreed with this evaluation, but they realized that Ingersoll's pamphlet was persuasive. Sidney George Fisher deplored his brother-in-law's lack of criticism of the South, but he was forced to admit that the *Letter* was a "strange mixture of extravagant ideas and good sense." In May, Judge Martin Russell Thayer wrote a response to the tract in which he criticized Ingersoll's willingness to appease Southern "traitors" and his lack of sympathy with the Lincoln government.[19]

William B. Reed also wrote pamphlets critical of the government, but he did not always sign his name to them. Before the war he had offered to serve as an intermediary between the North and the South, and he claimed that Seward had assured him that Fort Sumter would be evacuated. He communicated this information to the Confederates, and therefore, when he learned that the fort would not be surrendered, he concluded that Seward had deliberately made a fool of him. On two occasions he composed pamphlets critical of Seward's diplomacy, suggesting that the secretary of state really did not want to end the war. Moreover, he blamed Seward for tolerating corruption in the government and for ordering the arbitrary arrests of his opponents. "The Ship of State is among the reefs and breakers," he wrote, "with gloom and danger threatening outside. The pilot to weather the storm is not among those on deck. The hands that steered it into peril cannot be trusted for rescue—the chief mate least of all."

Reed's most famous work was his *Vindication* of his political beliefs. This tract was circulated privately until some enemies published it in an imperfect edition. The author then added an appendix and printed a corrected version. The *Vindication* painted a dismal picture of Union efforts to suppress the rebellion, emphasizing the number of soldiers who had been killed or wounded, and the huge sum of money needed to finance the bloodshed. "Every day dissipates some theory of conquest or submission," he argued, "and renders more probable the stupendous shame of European intervention—not merely recognition but active military interposition, which at once settles the contest to our ignominy." Reed feared it was necessary to recognize the independence of the Confederacy, blaming the "abolition party . . . for this dread necessity. The blood of the Union is on them." The *Vindication* was quite popular, and demand outran supply.[20]

Former Senator William Bigler was another who was disillusioned with the war. He proposed that Lincoln call for a convention of the loyal states to devise a peaceful solution to the conflict and that both the North and the South hold referendums to decide whether to continue the war. The probable results of such ballotings, he predicted, was that both sides would agree to reunion. If the Confederates refused to hold such an election after the North had done so, he argued, they would be completely discredited and all Northerners would enthusiastically support the war.[21]

William B. Reed was one of the ablest of the antiwar men in the North. In 1862 he published a pamphlet, *A Paper Containing a Statement and Vindication of Certain Political Opinions,* in which he called for recognition of the Confederacy. *(Courtesy Historical Society of Pennsylvania.)*

As was to be expected, Unionists strongly denounced Charles Ingersoll, Reed, and Bigler as traitors and suggested that they be arrested. This was no idle threat, as Ingersoll was to find out; in fact, in 1862, more Pennsylvanians were arrested for disloyalty than in 1861. By 1862, most cases involving alleged treason were under the supervision of the War Department rather than the State Department. Since Seward had been prone to arrest all whom he suspected of unpatriotic activities, Pennsylvania's Democracy was initially pleased that the change had been made. Peace Democrats expected Stanton to end arbitrary arrests, but they were to be disappointed, for he was even more eager to imprison war critics than Seward.[22]

Overzealous officials sometimes arrested citizens for refusing to inform on their neighbors, for unknowingly purchasing stolen horses, or for using treasonable language in public. One man was jailed for stating, "I will not go to war, and they cannot make me. I would rather serve in the rebel army for five cents a day than accept the bounty." In April 1862, at the suggestion of a Unionist that a group of secessionists was overrunning Fayette County, a squad of soldiers went there to rout the "rebels." This caused great excitement, but the "seccessionists" had already fled.[23]

Many of those arrested were told that their offense was discouraging enlistments. Often the accused were released without trial because of lack of evidence against them. On the other hand, when John Apple of Philadelphia protested that he had not discouraged men from joining the army, he was told that "we will find a[nother] charge against you."[24]

In Luzerne County three prominent Democrats, County Register George Kulp, District Attorney Ezra Chase, and Ira Davenport, were seized. At first they were not told the reason for their imprisonment, but it was suggested that they had discouraged men from joining the army. Chase promptly obtained and published a number of affidavits from soldiers and local citizens stating that he was a member of a volunteer militia unit, that he had urged men to join the Union forces, and that he had contributed funds for recruiting soldiers. Government agents quickly arranged for the release of the three Democrats after they posted a $500 bond; they were never brought to trial.[25]

Undoubtedly the most celebrated arrest was that of Charles Ingersoll for making an allegedly disloyal speech in Independence Square on August 23, 1862. In his address he had argued that the "despotism of the Old World can furnish no parallel to the corruption of the Administration." Mocking political arrests, he had noted, "If they arrest you, they must feed and clothe you and lodge you, and, in these hard times, there is something in that." On August 25, indignant federal officers arrested Ingersoll and prepared to send him to a federal fort. Judge John Cadwalader, however, forced them to cancel their plans when he issued a writ of habeas corpus for the prisoner, and Secretary of War Stanton ordered Ingersoll's release.[26]

Once freed, Ingersoll became increasingly defiant, and he claimed to "doubt whether we have either [a] constitution or country left us." On one occasion he challenged Congressman William D. Kelley to a duel for having called him and William B. Reed "traitors." Sidney George Fisher mused that if his brother-in-law challenged "everyone who calls him a traitor, he will have fighting enough. His passions are as extravagant as his opinions." Later that year the diarist reported that Ingersoll celebrated the Union defeat at Fredericksburg in December 1862, and called the Legal Tender Act unconstitutional.[27]

Perhaps the most ludicrous arrest was one which took place a few weeks after the 1862 election when the Reverend Charles Hay of Harrisburg, an avid supporter of the war, was seized and sent under guard to Baltimore. His offense was insisting that Unionists be allowed to care for wounded Yankee soldiers! An angry delegation confronted Stanton, and the clergyman was quickly released.[28] Many citizens began to wonder about the purpose of the arrests, and Unionists were forced to admit that sometimes the wrong people were imprisoned. On December 19, 1862, the Harrisburg *Telegraph* lamely explained that war justified such extreme action and that no man-made law was perfect.

Although it was true that arbitrary arrests often imprisoned the

the wrong people, still it would be erroneous to assume that no disloyalty was planned or committed in the commonwealth in 1862. Some unpatriotic Philadelphia merchants sent goods to Maryland, knowing that they would later be shipped to the Confederacy. In January 1862, the Reverend J. B. Wilmer, formerly rector of Philadelphia's St. Mark's Church, secured permission to return to the South, where he owned much property. A search of the twenty trunks he was taking with him uncovered maps, documents, letters, information about troop movements, and enough pairs of shoes, boots, and rolls of gray cloth to equip several Confederate soldiers. Officials let him continue his journey, but his baggage remained behind.[29]

Federal officials were also on the lookout for people whose pro-Southern sentiments might lead them to commit disloyal acts at some future date. Government records therefore included such things as a sworn statement from a resident of Philadelphia that one of his neighbors anticipated a Confederate invasion. When the Southerners arrived, the statement alleged, this neighbor promised to furnish them with coffee and other supplies.[30]

Some Pennsylvanians were also worried about potential traitors. Unionists mistakenly believed that the Knights of the Golden Circle (KGC) had a lodge in Franklin County, and a man in Lancaster offered a $100 reward for information that would enable authorities to arrest members of the KGC and bring them to trial. Others thought that persons belonging to a similar group, the Sons of Liberty, flourished in Philadelphia. A resident of Mercersburg wrote Thaddeus Stevens to suggest that the government require every citizen to take an oath that no promise "past or future to any Society, *secret* or open, shall be as obligatory as that to support the State & National Laws' Government."[31] Democrats insisted that there were no treasonable organizations in the state, commenting sarcastically that the only members of the KGC of which they had knowledge were the contractors and political leaders who were engaged in robbing the U.S. Treasury of sixty million dollars each year.[32]

Secret societies were but one of the problems facing the

Unionists. As the tables below show, prices were rising rapidly, and many disgruntled citizens blamed the government for this inflation. The rapid increase in the cost of living in 1862 contributed to the growing opposition to the war.

Table 2
Inflation in Philadelphia, November, 1861–November, 1862

Item	*Cost*		
	November 1861	*March 1862*	*November 1862*
			all prices are given in cents
1 lb. sugar	75-78	72-74	91-96
1 gal. molasses	45-50	50	60
1 lb. currants	12	12	15
1 gal. kerosene	60	34	100
1 lb. roasted coffee	20-28	25-30	34-40
1 quart beans	8-10	9-10	12
1 lb. black tea	50-80	75-100	75-100
1 lb. cheese	10	10	12
1 lb. ham	10-12	12	12

Source: Philadelphia *Public Ledger,* November 26, 1862.

Table 3
General Rises in the Price of Goods in Philadelphia
March 1861–November 1862

X represents the average price of an item in March, 1861

Item	*price March 1861*	*November 1862*
Clothing	X	110-125 X
Fuel	X	200 X
Shirts	X	150 X
Jewelry	X	110 X
Boots	X	110-120 X
Hardware	X	125-135 X
Paper	X	200 X
Gold	X	130 X
Medicine	X	150-200 X
Twelve Spools of Cotton	X	200 X

Source: Ibid.

Table 4
**Wages and Prices of Goods in Schuylkill County
November 1862–November 1863**

	November 1862	*November 1863*
	all prices are given in dollars	
Wages		
Laborer per week	6.00	12.00
Miners per week	7.50	18.00
Miners per day (contract)	2.00	5.00
Powder per keg	4.00	4.75
Whale Oil per gallon	.90	1.25
Iron Rails per ton	45.00	90.00
Lumber per thousand feet	12.00	28.00
One mule	150.00	240.00
Corn per bushel	.60	.90
Oats per bushel	.45	.90
Hay per ton	12.00	30.00

Source: Paul Hartranft, *History of Schuylkill County, Pennsylvania* (New York, 1881), p. 64.

Table 5
Prices of Goods in Lancaster County, 1862–65

	January 1862	*January 1863*	*January 1864*	*January 1865*
			all prices are given in dollars	
Wheat per bushel	1.30	1.60	1.65	2.50
Corn per bushel	.50	.70	1.00	1.60
Oats per 32 lb.	.33	.50	.80	.80
Rye per bushel	.62	.85	1.25	1.50
Butter per pound	.22	.25	.30	.50

Source: Klein, *Lancaster County Since 1841,* p. 50.

Nowhere was there more dissatisfaction than in the mining regions of the state, where less coal was produced in either 1861 or 1862 than in 1860. Speculators had so inflated prices in 1861 that merchants and homeowners turned to other sources of fuel, and this eventually forced hoarders to unload their supplies. Shortages suddenly became surplus, and the market was glutted. Excessive competition of mineowners resulted in a profit squeeze and in the spring of 1862, the Pennsylvania Coal Company reduced the price it charged for coal by fifty cents per ton.[33]

Meanwhile the miners were finding it increasingly difficult to make ends meet. In May, they struck for higher wages, and the mines were forced to close. Coal was essential for running the trains which transported the troops, and Governor Curtin sent 200 infantrymen to Pottsville to quell the disturbance. Less than one month after the strike was ended, Mauch Chunk, Glendon, Bethlehem, and several other mining towns experienced the worst flooding to hit the region since 1850. Hundreds of homes, scores of bridges, and millions of dollars' worth of personal property were destroyed, and an undetermined number of residents were killed. For months some mines could not be worked and again there was a coal shortage. This calamity was especially serious in these hamlets since community ties in many Pennsylvania towns were almost nonexistent.[34]

Frustrated miners were bewildered by natural disaster, increasing inflation, fluctuating coal prices, and the start of a state military draft, and they were afraid of Negro strikebreakers. Therefore it was not surprising that they were critical of the government and sympathetic to advocates of peace. They had no way of knowing that their wages would rise dramatically in 1863, and in 1862, their votes helped provide the margin of victory for the Democrats in the October elections.

Unlike 1861, 1862 was a major election year, and Democrats intended to exploit antiwar sentiment to their advantage. On July 4, they met at Harrisburg to select their state ticket. Presiding at the convention was Francis W. Hughes, who was chosen to manage the campaign and to help compose the party platform. Though critical of the administration, the resolutions were mild in regard to the war. The Democrats pledged to support the government in its constitutional efforts to restore "the Union as it was" and to preserve "the Constitution as it is." Unionists were denounced for belonging to "the party of fanaticism," and racism was omnipresent in the party resolutions. "The negro race are not entitled to and ought not to be admitted to political or social equality" with whites, the Democrats declared, for blacks were "an inferior but dependent race." Hughes insisted that his was the loyal party and that there were but two groups of men in the North; one was "the friends of the Constitution and the other its enemies."[35]

Public reaction to the convention was predictable. Virtually all Democrats agreed with the Reading *Gazette and Democrat* of July 12, 1862, that the resolutions were "eminently national, conservative, and patriotic." One exception was the editor of the Huntingdon *Globe,* who thought they suggested disloyalty and therefore his paper would not support them; local peace Democrats retaliated by establishing a new party organ, the *Monitor,* which enthusiastically endorsed the state ticket.[36]

As was to be expected, Unionists denounced James Barr, the editor of the Pittsburgh *Post* and the Democratic candidate for surveyor general, and Isaac Slenker, the Democracy's nominee for auditor general. Barr was called corrupt and imbecilic, and Slenker was dismissed as a sympathizer with treason.[37] Neither allegation was true.

Compared with the canvass of the previous year, the 1862 campaign was quite spirited. On the county level scores of conventions and hundreds of rallies were held. Since it was not yet fashionable to condemn the war openly in most parts of the state, local resolutions tended to denounce both secessionists and abolitionists, to condemn arbitrary arrests, and to pledge loyalty to the Constitution. Ridgway Democrats, for example, promised to denounce violations of civil liberties with "a courage defying chains—imprisonment—fortresses—Bastiles—aye—even the powers of Earth and Hell."[38]

A massive campaign rally was held in Independence Square on August 23. Francis Hughes told the large crowd that the administration was waging a war against the Constitution and that the soldiers were being forced to fight for the emancipation of the blacks. He publicly pledged his support for the restoration of the Union, but he argued that the subjugation of the South could only lead to eternal disunion, anarchy, and despotism. The Democrats, some of whom carried signs proclaiming "no nigger equality," enthusiastically endorsed Hughes's views. The rally was relatively tame, although the speech of Charles Ingersoll was so intemperate that it led to his arrest.

Unionists called the Democratic assemblies "political Gull Traps" full of "sugar coated treason" and alleged that at several meetings participants had cheered for Jefferson Davis. Most commonwealth voters, however, were too disillusioned with the war to believe these stories.[39]

Democrats did more than hold rallies; they also published pamphlets and wrote scores of newspaper articles and editorials critical of the administration and the war. The most radical of these called for a national convention of the people to restore the Union and to show "that no mad advocate of a 'higher law'—the dictum of those whose perverted minds cannot read the language of the HIGHEST . . . [would] be permitted longer to misrepresent the people."[40] They printed letters from disillusioned soldiers who had "given up all hopes of a restoration [of the nation] and who look forward to cessation of hostilities and a compromise," editorials purporting to show that the national debt was so high that it could *"never,* NEVER be paid," and a letter from former Senator Bigler stating that the war could have been averted if only the Crittenden Compromise had been adopted.[41]

Probably the most important campaign issue concerned the status of blacks. Workers feared black competition and miscegenation. They sincerely believed "the white man is superior to the negro" and they maintained "this is a government of and for white men." A letter sent to Unionist Eli Slifer reflected the widespread concern with the "black menace":

There are 45 Negroes at the Union Water Works and 50 are here at the big dam in Elwood and they said that they would wait till the white men would all go to war. [Then] they would have their fun with the white women. Now I want you to write as soon as you get this if we shall leave them go or if we may shoot them.[42]

Democrats exploited the Negrophobia and denounced Lincoln's proposed emancipation proclamation, arguing that the abolition of slavery was unnecessary to the preservation of the Union. Moreover, they alleged, such a proclamation would destroy the last vestiges of Southern unionism and would promote the exodus of blacks to the North, where they already filled the jails and poorhouses. On October 9, 1862, the Easton *Argus* presented the question: "How would you like to have a gang of forty or fifty niggers coming to your house, demanding food, or

Table 6
Composition of the Pennsylvania Legislature, 1860–1865

Senate

Year	Republicans (Unionists)	Democrats	Union Republicans
1860	21	12	
1861	27	6	
1862	22	10	1
1863	21	12	
1864	17	16	
1865	20	13	

House of Representatives

Year	Republicans (Unionists)	Democrats	Union Republicans	Union Democrats
1860	67	33		
1861	71	29		
1862	32	51	13	4
1863	45	55		
1864	52	48		
1865	64	36		

Source: Tribune Almanacs for 1860–65. All figures are for January 1 of the year indicated. Thus, for example, 1864 figures reflect the results of the 1863 election. The entire membership of the House of Representatives was elected each year; only one-third of the state senate seats expired each year. For figures on the Pennsylvania Democracy and electoral competitiveness, 1861–64, see Joel Silbey, *A Respectable Minority: The Democratic Party in the Civil War Era* (New York, 1977), p. 151. Sibley considers state and congressional contests.

threatening to burn down your barns and houses?" Democrats also condemned the abolitionist talk of recruiting black soldiers as "barbarious, unchristian, and unnecessary" and an insult to white volunteers. Many Pennsylvania soldiers did in fact despise their black brethren and considered them to be a curse to the nation.[43]

Privately a few Democrats made known their peace sympathies. William Garvin hoped for the election of "a democratic House that would boldly refuse to sustain the war—that would refuse a drafting law—and that would declare itself for compromise." Congressman William Stiles prayed that the voters would finally realize that the war would bring "onerous taxation upon us" and would call for an end to the bloodshed.[44]

Unionists feared that a Democratic success would result in an ignominious end to the war, but not until the end of September were they able to find a satisfactory campaign issue, the alleged treason of Francis W. Hughes. Affidavits professing to prove that the Pottsville lawyer was a traitor filled prowar newspapers. To be sure, Hughes had made a number of foolish statements in 1860 and 1861 and before the outbreak of the war had composed a resolution suggesting that Pennsylvania join the Confederacy, but this was not treason as defined by the Constitution. Whatever voters thought about his loyalty, they continued to support Democratic candidates. One Unionist lady was not upset about the prospects of a Democratic victory, for she believed that "if they do make it clean as a hurricane does the shore, I'll be glad; there is room for improvement at Harrisburg."[45]

The election was not a clear-cut victory for either party, but the Democrats were the main beneficiaries. In the legislature they gained four seats in the House and two in the Senate. (See Table 6.) More important was that their congressional representation jumped from seven to eleven. Unionists correctly pointed out that their vote would have been higher if soldiers had been able to cast ballots. Moreover, they stated, many potential voters had been occupied in repelling the Confederate forces who had invaded the state in October and were therefore unable to go to the polls on election day. Democrats, on the other hand, insisted that their

Pottsville, Schuylkill County,
January 9. 1863.

Hon. Simon Cameron,
Harrisburg,
Dear Sir,

In the month of February, 1861, in the Supreme Court Room, in Philadelphia, Francis W. Hughes told David B. Green Esq. now Adjutant of the 129th Regiment of Penna. Vols; that, in the event of the secession of the South, he considered it was both "the duty as well as the interest" of Pennsylvania to unite with the South and cut herself loose from the other States of the Union, and that he was willing to be nominated as a candidate for Governor of the State on such a platform, and would stump the State on the question, and believed he could be elected on such a platform. This fact is stated in writing by Mr. Green himself.

In the fall of 1860, John Hughes, the law partner and the nephew of Francis W. Hughes, was, through the instrumentality of Francis W. Hughes, made the Democratic nominee for Congress in the District composed of Schuylkill and Northumberland counties. Francis W. Hughes advocated his election with all the energy and eloquence he was capable of, but he was fortunately defeated. In the

First page of a letter from Charlemagne Tower to Simon Cameron alleging that Francis W. Hughes stated in February 1861 that "he considered it was both 'the duty as well as the interest' of Pennsylvania to unite with the South." *(Courtesy Library of Congress.)*

vote total would have been greater if deputy marshals had not been stationed at the polls to register men for the draft. This irregularity, they declared, was responsible for the defeat of several of their candidates.[46]

Nonetheless, Democrats were jubilant, and, for his successful management of the campaign, a delegation of the party faithful presented Hughes with a handsome silver set. For many the election marked a turning point. Some, such as the Carlisle *American Volunteer,* no longer felt any reason to continue to support a government that it thought was engaged in an unholy war. On October 23, 1862, editor Bratton warned: "More than one tyrant has lost his head for crimes against his country not half so aggravated as those committed by this miserable man Lincoln. Let him resign and go home and thank his God that a worse fate did not overtake him." A few boldly dared to declare that the South was invincible, and at a massive rally in Philadelphia on October 31 the mood of the crowd was expressed by a sign reading "John Brown's Soul has stopped marching on." Fireworks were displayed, and Charles Ingersoll proclaimed the election results to be "a victory for the Constitution and the Union."[47]

Unionists were glum. One soldier sadly commented that there was "more disunion at home than ever," and he feared that the war would never end until there was a "very different feeling at home." A group of Philadelphia Unionists thought it necessary to form a club for "loyal men" to promote patriotism and established what came to be known as the Union League. Within a few months similar organizations were founded throughout the North, and these were to become a major source of pro-government propaganda in 1863 and 1864.[48]

For Democrats not all was joy and happiness. The war continued, the national debt rose, arbitrary arrests went on, and the slaves were declared free. Furthermore, Democrats realized that mobs might persecute them if they were too open in expressing their peace views. Some paid a price for voting Democratic in 1862; their Unionist employers fired them. One boss, a young lady in Chester County, told a discharged Irish worker, "We can never have the same feeling towards you again; it would be disagreeable for you to remain and even more so for us. There is no law of God or man that gives a man the privilege to do that which he knows to be wrong."[49]

John Bell Robinson sadly noted that members of his church and Unionists who had been his friends before the war now called him a traitor and said they wished to hang him. His only offense, he said, was to defend the institution of slavery and to condemn the war.[50]

By the end of 1862, the antiwar movement was growing in size and strength. An increasing number of Pennsylvanians were concluding that continuation of the conflict was useless, and in 1863, peace men would have a prominent role in state politics.

NOTES

1. Edwin Glover, *Bucktailed Wildcats* (New York, 1960), pp. 30, 36–37, 58; Ebensburg *Democrat and Sentinel,* December 4, 1861.

2. Biddle to Coryell, April 21, 1862, Lewis Coryell MSS, HSP, hereafter cited as Coryell MSS; *Congressional Globe,* Thirty-seventh Congress, 2nd session, March 6, June 2, July 8, 1862, pp. 1111–12, 2504–2505, 3183–84; see also Charles John Biddle, *Address of the Democratic State Central Committee* (Philadelphia, 1863), p. 7.

3. Clearfield *Raftman's Journal,* May 21, 1862; Reading *Gazette and Democrat,* August 16, 1862; *Congressional Globe,* Thirty-seventh Congress, 2nd session, April 23, June 9, 1862, pp. 1795, 2622.

4. Ibid., January 20, 1862, p. 405; Hendrick B. Wright, *Objects of the War* (Washington, 1862), *passim.*

5. *Congressional Globe,* Thirty-seventh Congress, 2nd session, December 18, 1861, January 24, February 5, May 6, June 27, 28, 1862, pp. 130, 471, 654–55, 1965, 2960–62, 2993–94.

6. *L.R.,* March 11, 13, 1862, pp. 504–506, 512, 614; Pittsburgh *Post,* April 28, 29, 1862; Harrisburg *Patriot and Union,* March 21, May 10, 1862.

7. West Chester *Jeffersonian,* January 18, February 1, April 19, May 10, 24, 1862.

8. Ibid., January 4, May 24, June 2, 1862; Ray Abrams, "*The Jeffersonian:* Copperhead Newspaper," *Pennsylvania Magazine of History* 48 (1933): *passim.*

9. Annie Taylor to brother, Charles, February 23, 1862, Charles Taylor MSS, in possession of Professor Charles Hobson, editor, The Papers of John Marshall, hereafter cited as Taylor MSS.

10. Muncy *Luminary,* September 30, 1862; Tunkhannock *North Branch Democrat,* October 1, 1862; Pottsville *Miners' Journal,* October 4, 1862; William Russ, "Franklin

Weirick: 'Copperhead' of Central Pennsylvania," *Pennsylvania History* 5 (1938): pp. 246–52.

11. Chambersburg *Valley Spirit*, February 19, May 21, 1862; Ebensburg *Democrat and Sentinel*, July 2, 1862.

12. Carlisle *American Volunteer*, August 14, 1862; Jessie Sellers Colton, ed., *The Civil War Journals and Correspondence of Matthias Baldwin Colton* (Philadelphia, 1931), pp. 17, 84–85.

13. Harrisburg *Patriot and Union*, August 7–25, 1862.

14. Anthony Trollope, *North America* (New York, 1863), p. 289.

15. Horace Binney, *The Privilege of the Writ of Habeas Corpus*, 2nd ed. (Philadelphia, 1862), *passim.*

16. See, for example, George Wharton, *Remarks on Mr. Binney's Treatise on the Writ of Habeas Corpus* (Philadelphia, 1862), pp. 13–20; Edward Ingersoll, *Personal Liberty and Martial Law* (Philadelphia, 1862), p. 19; Tatlow Jackson, *Authorities Cited Antagonistic to Horace Binney's Conclusions* (Philadelphia, 1862), p. 8, and his *Martial Law: What Is It and Who Can Declare It?* (Philadelphia, 1862), pp. 18–19; J. C. Bullitt, *A Review of Mr. Binney's Pamphlet* (Philadelphia, 1862), *passim;* Jonathan Montgomery, *The Writ of Habeas Corpus and Mr. Binney* (Philadelphia, 1862), *passim;* [Anonymous], *A Reply to Horace Binney's Pamphlet* (Philadelphia, 1862), *passim.*

17. Charles Binney, *The Life of Horace Binney* (Philadelphia, 1902), pp. 334–63.

18. This was published in Philadelphia in 1862.

19. *Fisher Diary*, p. 424; Martin Russell Thayer, *Reply to Ingersoll* (Philadelphia, 1862), *passim.*

20. Shankman, "Reed," *passim;* see also William K. Scarborough, ed., *The Diary of Edmund Ruffin, II: The Years of Hope* (Baton Rouge, La., 1976), p. 521.

21. John Bell Robinson, *Pictures of Slavery and Anti-Slavery* (Philadelphia, 1863), pp. 374–88.

22. Ellis Lewis to Stanton, January 14, 1862; George W. Woodward to Stanton, January 14, 1862, Stanton MSS, LC.

23. J. Burchinal to Slifer, April 2, 14, 1862, Slifer-Dill MSS; Pittsburgh *Gazette*, August 29, 1862; John Marshall, *American Bastile* (Philadelphia, 1869), pp. 180–83.

24. Montrose *Democrat*, November 25, 1862; Marshall, *American Bastile*, p. 402.

25. Wilkes-Barre *Luzerne Union*, September 10, 1862; Tunkhannock *North Branch Democrat*, September 24, 1862.

26. Philadelphia *Public Ledger*, August 26–September 2, 1862.

27. Tunkhannock *North Branch Democrat*, October 8, 1862; *Fisher Diary*, pp. 431, 439–40, 444.

28. Philadelphia *Evening Bulletin*, October 29, 30, 1862.

29. Ibid., January 8, October 2, 1862; Harrisburg *Telegraph*, January 9, 1862.

30. Sworn statement of George Wood, September 24, 1862, Case Files of Investigation by Levi Turner and Lafayette Baker, 1861–66, Microfilm Reel 14, NA.

31. John Agnew to Stevens, March 20, 1862, Stevens MSS; Frederick Shiver Klein, *Lancaster County Since 1841* (Lancaster, 1955), pp. 48–49; Philadelphia *Constitutional Union*, n.d., quoted in Uniontown *Genius of Liberty*, July 31, 1862.

32. Harrisburg *Patriot and Union*, April 29, 1862.

33. Ibid., December 12, 20, 1861, May 9, 1862; Philadelphia *North American*, May 8, 1862; Pottsville *Miners' Journal*, June 7, 14, 1862; Hartranft, *History of Schuylkill County*, p. 63.

34. Rowland Berthoff, "The Social Order of the Anthracite Region, 1825–1902," *Pennsylvania Magazine of History and Biography* 89 (1965): 262–63; Harold Aurand, *From the Molly Maguires to the United Mine Workers* (Philadelphia, 1971), p. 27.

35. *Appleton's Annual Cyclopaedia for 1862* (New York, 1870), pp. 703–704.

36. Samuel Barton to James Simpson Africa, July 24, 1862; Oliver Barrett to Africa, October 28, 1862, Africa MSS, Pennsylvania Historical and Museum Commission.

37. *Union County Star and Lewisburg Chronicle,* July 8, 1862; Clearfield *Raftman's Journal,* July 16, 1862; Pittsburgh *Gazette,* July 17, 1862.

38. Harrisburg *Patriot and Union,* August 14, 1862; Tunkhannock *North Branch Democrat,* September 17, 1862; Lock Haven *Clinton Democrat,* October 16, 1862.

39. George Manley to Slifer, July 12, 1862, Slifer-Dill MSS; Pittsburgh *Gazette,* September 23, 1862; Shippensburg *News,* July 26, 1862.

40. Jacob Dewees, *To the People of Pennsylvania* (Pottsville, 1862), *passim.*

41. Bellefonte *Democratic Watchman,* September 26, 1862; Meadville *Crawford Democrat,* October 14, 1862.

42. J. Weaver to Slifer; September 8, 1862, Slifer-Dill MSS; Uniontown *Genius of Liberty,* July 10, 1862.

43. West Chester *Jeffersonian,* May 24, 1862; Tunkhannock *North Branch Democrat,* September 24, October 29, 1862.

44. William Garvin to William Bigler, July 12, 1862, Bigler MSS; Stiles to Coryell, July 1, 22, 1862, Coryell MSS.

45. Arnold Shankman, "Francis W. Hughes and the 1862 Pennsylvania Election," *Pennsylvania Magazine of History* and Biography 95 (1971): *passim;* Colton, *The Civil War Journals* p. 59.

46. George Wolff Fahenstock Diary, October 11, 15, 1862, HSP: *Congressional Globe,* Thirty-seventh Congress, 3rd session, February 23, 1863, pp. 1216–17; see also Silbey, *A Respectable Minority,* pp. 145–51.

47. Philadelphia *Inquirer,* November 1, 1862.

48. Zeriah Monks to Hannah Rohrer, October 27, 1862, Monks MSS (microfilm in Emory University Special Collections), hereafter cited as Monks MSS; George Lathrop, *History of the Union League of Philadelphia* (Philadelphia, 1884), *passim.*

49. Annie to Charles Taylor, October 22, 1862, Taylor MSS.

50. Robinson to Samuel Cox, December 26, 1862, Cox MSS, Brown University.

5

"We Are in Favor of an Immediate Armistice"

"Peace, peace, *on any terms,* at any price: anything to end this fratricidal war."*

"The brutal and bloody tyranny of Robespierre, of Danton and Marat may yet find their parallel in the acts of the present despotism."**

With the passage of time antiwar sentiment grew in Pennsylvania. In January 1862, General George McCall's wife, Elizabeth, had been one of the most loyal defenders of the government; ten months later she confessed that she was "the worst disunionist in the world," having reluctantly concluded that separation was preferable to continuation of the conflict. What had changed her mind? In large part, the answer lay in the fact that, when her husband had run for political office in October 1862, Unionist newspapers had called him a traitor, and she was convinced that these false allegations had caused his defeat. Furthermore, she tired of church sermons on the "burning wrong" of slavery, of newspaper articles defending violations of "our once boasted and loved Constitution," and of government proclamations hostile to a compromise solution to the war.[1]

*Alexander Fullerton, Jr., *Coercion a Failure, Necessarily and Actually* (Philadelphia, 1863), p. 16.
**C. Butler to Lewis Coryell, February 17, 1863, Coryell MSS.

In 1863, Mrs. McCall, one of the leaders of Philadelphia society, did little to make public her disillusionment with the war, but many previously silent members of the city's social elite openly denounced the conflict. To be sure, Charles Ingersoll and William B. Reed were known to favor peace, but not until 1863 would George Biddle, Edward Ingersoll, or George Wharton echo their sentiments and lend their prestige to the antiwar movement. Whereas in 1862 open criticism of the war was rare, by the end of 1863 few Democrats would continue to defend the conflict.

During the winter of 1862–63 war weariness was so strong that scores of peace meetings were held in Pennsylvania, mainly in Armstrong, Washington, Venango, Westmoreland, Crawford, Northampton, Pike, and Fayette counties.[2] Never before in the Keystone State were so many willing to oppose the war.

Typical of these gatherings was one held on February 13 in Menallen Township and reported in the February 19, 1863, issue of the Uniontown *Genius of Liberty*. Those assembled at this meeting denounced the Republican party as "fiends in human shape" and Lincoln as "alien in heart to our Constitution." Clement L. Vallandigham, the Ohio Copperhead leader, on the other hand, was praised for his patriotism and statesmanship. As for the war, delegates resolved

> That inasmuch as two years of sanguinary and expensive war have failed to show the efficacy of coercive measures in restoring the Union, we think that experience alone ... should dictate a resort to some other measure of "calming the troubled waters" and to that end we are in favor of an immediate armistice and cessation of hostilities and an honest and earnest effort to settle the difficulties of the Union by peaceful remedies.

For the most part peace arguments advanced at the Menallen gathering and at other rallies were already known to the public; these included statements that ninety percent of the people were sick of the war, that the Union was one of consent and could not be restored by force, and that abolitionists were opposed to peace. In

1863 as in 1861 and 1862, peace men questioned the patriotism of the president and blamed the war more on puritanical New Englanders who had provoked the slaveholders beyond human endurance than on the Southerners who had struck the first blow.

A more vigorous opposition to the administration was also evident in Democratic newspapers. As was to be expected, the Bellefonte *Democratic Watchman,* Mauch Chunk *Carbon Democrat,* Meadville *Crawford Democrat,* Selinsgrove *Times* and Tunkhannock *North Branch Democrat* continued to denounce the government, but no longer were they lone voices in the wilderness. Joining the peace chorus were the Easton *Argus* and Lewistown *True Democrat,* two widely respected Democratic journals. Peace sentiment had become so respectable that the *Argus* dared print a poem entitled "Abe's Visitor" in its August 13, 1863, issue. The tone of the poem can readily be seen in the following excerpt, in which the Devil speaks to President Lincoln:

> "How are you my Abe? Is the list nearly filled
> Of sick men and dying of wounded and killed,
> Of widows and tears, or orphans unfed
> Of poor honest white men struggling for bread?"
>
> "Dear devil," quoth Abe, "I'm doing my best
> To promote the interest of you and the rest.
> But then you remember, I'm only the tool
> Of Seward and Chase, and that other old fool
> Who the Navy controls, and who always condemns
> Any modern plan of capturing Semmes."

That the *Argus* dared to print such literature emboldened others, and before long more and more editorials and articles in the York *Gazette,* Erie *Observer,* and Wilkes-Barre *Luzerne Union* were pro-peace in their sympathies. Most gratifying of all to war critics was the establishment of new journals in Kittanning, Johnstown, and Philadelphia strongly opposed to the conflict.

In December 1862, James Alexander Fulton founded the Kittanning *Mentor* because the local party organ, the Kittanning

Armstrong Democrat, was prowar, "and hence obnoxious to more than half of the Democrats in the county." Local Unionists were infuriated by the appearance of such a sheet, and they deluged authorities with requests for Fulton's arrest. One Sunday, while the editor was teaching at a Sabbath school, vandals cut down 300 apple and peach trees in his orchard, and on April 30, 1863, rowdies destroyed part of his printing office. Neither incident silenced him, for the *Mentor* was a financial success, and Fulton's friends warned that, if Unionists again dared to harm his property, they would pay a surprise visit to the Kittanning *Free Press.*[3]

The contents of the *Mentor* fully justified the allegation that it was among the most outspoken of all peace journals. Fulton continually called for a national convention and denounced the abolitionists. To him the best solution to the antislavery agitation was the colonization in Latin America or Africa of Horace Greeley and William Lloyd Garrison, "who could never be missed except for the peace that would reign in their absence."[4] Fulton solicited correspondence from disenchanted soldiers, and on August 26, 1863, he gladly printed a letter of Private Edward Plyer, who had voted for Lincoln in 1860. The Yank wrote a friend, "I wish to God this war was ended or if I was safe at home, the negro worshippers might fight it out themselves."

Three months after the *Mentor* started publication, another antiwar journal, the Johnstown *Democrat,* appeared. Editor James F. Campbell spared no invective in discussing the antislavery crusade, since he believed that "amalgamation, abolitionism, and Republicanism are simply the three stages of the same disgusting disease." Like Fulton, he blamed the "pious descendants of the Pilgrim fathers" for all of the nation's miseries, and he printed soldier letters calling for an end to the fighting.[5] On occasion readers were treated to his compositions, one of which was published on August 19, 1863:

> We're going to fight for darkies now, Glory hallelujah.
> At Lincoln's negro altars bow, Glory hallelujah.
> Come, jolly white men, come along, Glory hallelujah.

Fall in, and sing this merry song, Glory hallelujah.
O, when we get the negroes free, Glory hallelujah.
As good as niggers we shall be, Glory hallelujah.

More important than the establishment of Fulton's or Campbell's paper was the appearance on March 25, 1863, of the
Philadelphia *Age*. Not since the demise of the *Pennsylvanian* two
years before had there been a Democratic daily in Philadelphia,
the second largest city in the nation. To be sure, the *Evening
Journal* sometimes published antiwar editorials, but Democrats
did not consider it to be a party organ. Party regulars were
determined to have their own journal, and finally Adam
Glossbrenner, formerly a secretary to Buchanan, William Welsh,
editor of the York *Gazette,* and Felix Grund[6] obtained the capital
needed to publish a four-page daily. The *Age* called for a national
convention of the states to end the war, criticized the abolitionists,
and reported the sufferings of Confederate prisoners in Yankee
jails; it also printed articles on a variety of subjects including
history, literature, music, art, and science as well as poetry.

Unionists agreed with the Harrisburg *Telegraph* of March 27,
1863, that the new paper was a "pestilential publication," and they
were displeased by the rapid increase of its circulation. On the
afternoon of May 8, 1863, a member of the paper's staff put a sign
on the *Age* bulletin board protesting the arrest of Clement
Vallandigham. This incensed a crippled veteran, who tore it
down. A mob quickly gathered and smashed some windows, but
police persuaded the crowd to disperse.[7] Despite this incident, the
Age refused to modify its antiwar views.

The *Age* and the *Mentor* were not the only papers to face mob
violence in 1863. Two editors, Henry Smith of the *Fulton County
Democrat* and H. J. Stahle of the Gettysburg *Compiler,* were jailed
for alleged disloyalty; angry bands of Unionists visited the offices
of the Butler *Democratic Herald,* Ebensburg *Democrat and
Sentinel,* and Huntingdon *Monitor.* Though the first of these
suffered no vandalism, the other two sustained thousands of
dollars' worth of damages.[8]

These incidents so disturbed Democrats that they called on members of the party to retaliate in kind. The Carlisle *American Volunteer* of May 28, 1863, urged its readers to seek "an eye for an eye," and it proposed that thereafter two abolitionist journals be gutted for each Democratic paper destroyed. Representatives from many Pennsylvania Democratic organs met on June 17 and passed resolutions in defense of a free press; a similar meeting was held in Philadelphia on August 11.[9]

Just as the Democratic editors had become more vigorous in opposing the war in 1863, so did party members in the legislature and in Congress become more aggressive in denouncing the conflict. The first question before the legislature was the selection of a successor for Senator David Wilmot. Since the Democrats had a majority of one on a joint ballot in the legislature, it was reasonable to expect that one of their leaders would be elected. Simon Cameron, however, was eager to regain his old senate seat, and friends assured him that, if he were a known candidate for the office, he could control that vote. Cameron declared his candidacy and met with Thomas Jefferson Boyer, a Democratic legislator, who offered to sell his vote. Boyer had previously informed Democrats that "he intended to lead Cameron to a distinct offer .. and then reject the bribe, expose him and vote against him." The ruse worked, and Cameron offered Boyer $25,000 and a position as paymaster in the army.[10]

On January 13, the Democratic caucus decided to support Charles R. Buckalew, a moderate war critic, for senator. They also spread the word that a number of men were outside the legislative chambers ready to assault any apostate Democrat who voted for a Unionist. Buckalew was elected to the United States Senate, and Democrats exulted that for once Cameron's money could not buy him power. To Unionists the election was an outrage, and Buckalew was denounced as a disciple of Calhoun.[11]

If Unionists were distressed when Cameron was defeated in his bid to replace Wilmot, they were even more upset when the Democratic legislators championed the case of Albert D. Boileau, the editor of the Philadelphia *Evening Journal*. Boileau was arrested on January 28, 1863, because his paper had printed an article unfavorably comparing Abraham Lincoln's intellectual capacities with those of Jefferson Davis. Two days later the Democratically controlled house adopted a resolution protesting the jailing and calling upon Governor Curtin to go to Washington to demand Boileau's release. Furthermore, they passed a bill making it a crime to send any man to a prison outside of the state before he had been charged with a crime. Unionists were unhappy, for they feared that any law curtailing arbitrary arrests would promote treason. Fortunately for them the Senate was persuaded not to approve of this measure.

Finally the governor felt it necessary to take notice of the situation. By expressing his own moderate criticism of the jailing, he would deprive his political rivals of an issue that could be important in the upcoming gubernatorial contest. Therefore he proposed that Congress pass a law punishing treason and providing a speedy and impartial trial "so that the guilty may justly suffer and the innocent be relieved."[12]

Democratic legislators did more than champion Boileau, who was released after formally apologizing for having published the offensive editorial. They also introduced a resolution to prohibit the immigration of free blacks to the state, prevented Andrew Johnson from speaking in the hall of the Pennsylvania House of Representatives, and passed resolutions on April 13, 1863, which called the Emancipation Proclamation "unwise, unconstitutional and void" and demanded the convening of a convention of the states to end the war. Naturally the senate refused to endorse these resolutions, but that the house called for an end to the conflict showed how powerful antiwar sentiment had become in 1863.[13]

In comparison with the legislature, Pennsylvania's congressional delegation was more restrained. Biddle and Cowan still criticized the government, and they were joined by Jesse Lazear and John Stiles, who opposed all efforts to "exterminate" the South. Stiles was especially critical of Lincoln, who, he thought, was a despot more devoted to the Negro than to the Union.[14]

Since public officials were willing to criticize the war, it was not surprising that private individuals were also displaying great dissatisfaction with the conflict. In a widely circulated book John Bell Robinson attempted to prove that slavery was a moral good and that continuation of the hostilities could never restore the nation, for "the only bond of this Union was love." Alexander Fullerton, another writer, agreed that cannon and bayonets could never restore a Union based on friendship and patriotism. In his opinion peace at any price was better than war.[15]

Had the Democrats limited their denunciations to personal letters, books, or obscure tracts, the Unionists might have dismissed antiwar activities as the vagaries of a few fanatics. However, they could not view lightly the formation of the Central Democratic Club in Philadelphia on January 8, 1863, which made available a public forum for peace advocates. The club constitution asserted that all power in Pennsylvania belonged to its white residents and that the people need not support any government officials or politicians who willfully disregarded the Constitution. Annual dues of $10 made the group too expensive for workers to join, but many meetings were open to the public.[16]

At the inaugural meeting the club's president, Charles Ingersoll, spoke, along with James Van Dyke and George Wharton. Ingersoll declared to an applauding audience that, if he were a member of Congress or of the Pennsylvania legislature, he would vote against appropriating any more money for military purposes. Van Dyke contented himself with calling the Lincoln administration "corrupt, imbecile, and profligate," and Biddle was an even more moderate critic of the war. Unionists were displeased with the gathering, and the Philadelphia *Evening Bulletin* of January 9, 1863, insisted that it was fortunate that Ingersoll was not a legislator, adding, "but if he were, it would be hard to find his match in . . . political folly and partisan malice." At the second meeting, which was held on January 29, just after the arrest of Albert Boileau, Peter McCall warned that the administration was encouraging the people to seek redress of their grievances outside the law.

Since neither gathering led to the arrest of any of the speakers, weekly meetings were scheduled and a number of visiting Democrats, including Senator James Wall and the Reverend Chauncey Burr of New Jersey, Mayor George Sanderson of Lancaster, and Richard O'Gorman of New York addressed the Central Democratic Club. At times it seemed as though there was a contest to determine who could most severely criticize the government and escape imprisonment in a federal fortress. Burr called Lincoln a greater traitor than Jefferson Davis at one session. At another William B. Reed called for an armistice and, if necessary, recognition of Confederate independence. In his first speech since the start of the war Edward Ingersoll urged the Democrats to protect themselves from the revolutionary activities of the abolitionists. He stated:

> Whether the appeal be to the ballot-box or the hideous but not less popular appeal to the cartridge box be forced upon the people, I have not a particle of doubt of the result. . . . Maintain your laws peacably if you can, forcibly if you must.[17]

When compared to these harangues, the speeches of O'Gorman, Wharton, Biddle, Wall, and Sanderson were moderate in tone.

At one meeting members of the audience hissed a prowar speaker, who had been invited by mistake. On other occasions listeners cheered for Jefferson Davis and the Confederacy. It was to be expected that some citizens would desire to close the Central Democratic Club—forcibly if necessary. On May 9, when Wall spoke police guarded the building lest there be a riot. During another gathering, held in August, a dozen soldiers armed with bayonets and muskets invaded the premises and routed the audience.[18] Despite these two attempts to suppress its activities, the organization continued to sponsor antiwar activities.

Although nearly all soldiers condemned the antiwar Democrats as disloyal, a few admired their courage, and a small number joined them in denouncing the administration. Jacob Weidensall knew few members of his regiment who were not Democrats or supporters of General "McLelan." Despite his desire to "stick to the Government to the last," he believed that there was "a screw loose some place or this war would be over ere this." Another military man, Adam Bright, was critical of abolitionist journals, which he believed did "more harm than good." A number of his comrades back home accused him of being disloyal, but he replied, "If some of my patriotic friends had soldiered as long as I have, they would not be half so patriotic as I am." A third soldier wrote, "Loyal as I am, I would not serve my country with niggers for my companions. I do not like the animals and can scarcly [sic] believe them fully human."[19]

Unionists realized that not all of the men in blue supported their program and that some were disloyal. For example, a Pittsburgh officer, Lieutenant Frank Robinson of the 56th Pennsylvania Volunteers, was arrested and threatened with a court martial for bragging that "Jeff. Davis ought and would be our next President."[20] It was the rare veteran who would speak out against the war in 1863, but the number would slowly but steadily increase as the war lingered on.

To those who believed that the South had to be suppressed by force of arms the actions of the peace Democrats were treasonable. These men reasoned that the nation was fighting for its very existence and that preserving the Union was far more important than safeguarding civil liberties. Therefore they excused arbitrary arrests, newspaper suppressions, the suspension of the writ of habeas corpus, and the increasing centralization of power in Washington. They welcomed the formation of the Union Leagues as a means of sustaining the Lincoln administration in its efforts to defeat the Confederacy. Convinced that the overthrow of the rebellion was the work of the Lord, they could not admit that antiwar Democrats were sincere in their beliefs.

Defenders of the war demeaned their critics by giving them such names as "Copperhead" and "Butternut." The first of these two terms was used in Indianapolis, Indiana, shortly after the secession of South Carolina. A Hoosier noted that the emblem of South Carolina was the rattlesnake and claimed that it would be more appropriate to have the copperhead snake as the symbol of the Palmetto State since it struck without warning. Several months later an Ohioan suggested that traitorous Confederate sympathizers in the North were like copperheads since they also gave no notice before attacking. Though copperhead snakes frequented the Alleghany Valley, not until 1863 was the term widely used in Pennsylvania's prowar journals to designate Southern sympathizers. To their chagrin, Unionists discovered that some Democrats were proud to be called Copperheads. In fact, peace men cut out the head of the goddess of liberty from copper pennies to make "Copperhead" badges. Their rivals denounced them for mutilating coins and sarcastically commented that a Copperhead was a man who outraged the "good sense" of the nation. "Butternut" gained considerably less acceptance in Pennsylvania as a term of opprobrium. It referred to the "dirty brown" colored cloth worn by many poor families in Ohio, Indiana, Illinois, and Kentucky who opposed the war and since this cloth was not commonly used in the mid-Atlantic states, the term was not germane to Pennsylvania.[21]

As already noted, peace Democrats openly espoused their beliefs in 1863, and this frequently alienated their neighbors. Unionists urged their friends to boycott Copperhead merchants, to fire their "secessionist" employees, and to shun their antiwar acquaintances. Delia Colton reported that a lady neighbor greeted a visiting male acquaintance by saying, "Sir, I understand you are a seceshionist [sic], is it so?" When the man responded affirmatively, she replied, "Very well, I cannot receive you then." The surprised visitor grabbed his hat and departed. When a soldier received a letter from a man who wrote that Lincoln would rather free the slaves than end the war, the Yank warned his correspondent, whom he called a "child of the devil," to be "careful what you do when, if ever, the soldiers come home."[22]

A few supporters of the war went beyond ostracizing antiwar Democrats and helped to destroy offices of newspapers whose loyalty they questioned. Sometimes they forcibly ejected Copperheads from railroad cars, and in one case they chased a man whose face was covered with lather from a barber shop after he dared to criticize the government. When some congregants in the Lutheran church in Middletown suspected that their minister had "secession" sympathies, they made it known that, if this were true, he would have to leave town "even if his preaching equal[led] that of Martin Luther." On occasion the property of Copperhead leaders was destroyed; besides cutting down trees in the orchard of James Alexander Fulton, prowar rowdies desecrated a tombstone of one of Francis W. Hughes's relatives in Pottsville's Mt. Laurel Cemetery.[23] In a number of instances Unionists arrested Democrats for such allegedly disloyal offenses as refusing to pray for the success of Lincoln and for arguing that the administration was corrupt.[24]

Though few opponents of the war hoped for Confederate victory, a small number of Pennsylvanians did give aid and comfort to the enemy. Despite the blockade, several merchants and farmers continued to send goods to the South, and government agents spent a considerable amount of time trying to identify unpatriotic businessmen. In April 1863, they seized a Confederate agent who had purchased $4,000 worth of clothing and miscellaneous supplies which he was hoping to send to the South via Baltimore. On his person were Confederate bonds and banknotes and letters from Philadelphians to residents of Dixie. Less than two weeks later government detectives sent Benjamin Jackson and Louis Solomon to Fort Delaware for trying to ship goods to the Confederacy. Jackson, a merchant with stores in New York and Georgia, had purchased $600 worth of morphine, iodine, chloroform, and quinine; Solomon had bought fourteen boxes of needles, hats, and shoes for Southerners. In June, Dr. John W. Ramsay, a Confederate spy, was caught in Uniontown; his mission was unknown. One month later, in July, officials jailed three men for piracy. The accused were allegedly "fitting out" a schooner with which they planned to attack Northern ships and destroy a lighthouse in Delaware.[25]

Perhaps the best evidence that only a few in the Keystone State were disloyal came during the Confederate invasion in June and

July 1863. To be sure, a number of citizens did help the rebels but many did so out of fear. To Confederates these Copperheads who displayed signs of friendship were cowards; Colonel Thomas Jenkins supposedly told one peace man that, if he really believed the South was right, he would don the gray. The man refused, and Jenkins later declared that such men would be hanged in the Confederacy. Although Southerners gathered information from peace men, they treated them no differently from other Pennsylvanians and stole their horses, food, and money.[26]

Some Copperheads were so distressed at this, one lady declared, that they marched into Carlisle with tickets which were to have protected them from the rebels. They visited the men who had sold these to them and demanded their money back, claiming that they had "made the signs, but it did no good."[27]

After Gettysburg, Unionists would no longer associate with those who had befriended the Southerners. No "respectable" lady would converse with these men and women, and Cassandra Blair observed that "they must form a party among themselves." Even close friends were snubbed, she reported, and one neighboring family whom everyone had liked before the invasion now found itself ostracized.[28]

Despite Unionist allegations that many Democrats welcomed the Southerners, such was not the case. Colonel Charles J. Biddle helped organize militia forces to repel the invaders, and many Democrats joined such companies. The Philadelphia *Age* gladly reported Lee's defeat and welcomed the routing of the enemy. Decimus and Ultimus Barzizi, a Confederate prisoner of war, met many Pennsylvanians sympathetic to the South, but he reported that Copperheads wanted peace only because "they regarded it as the shortest and surest way to the reconstruction of the Union, not that they thought we were right, and they were wrong." This was an accurate observation; to the Copperheads the old Union of their fathers could be restored only if the war ended in a stalemate; a Confederate victory in Pennsylvania would have been as upsetting to them as the issuance of the Emancipation Proclamation.[29]

NOTES

1. Elizabeth to George McCall, October 21, November 17, 1862, McCall Family Papers, HSP. For more on the hostility of Philadelphians to abolition see Russell Weigley, "A Peaceful City: Public Order in Philadelphia from Consolidation Through the Civil War," in Allen F. Davis, ed., *The Peoples of Philadelphia* (Philadelphia, 1973), p. 165.

2. Meadville *Crawford Democrat*, February 3–March 24, 1863; Easton *Argus*, February 26, March 19, 1863; Indiana *Democrat*, April 16, 1863; Washington *Reporter and Examiner*, May 20, 1863; Uniontown *Genius of Liberty*, February 19, 26, March 5, April 23, 1863.

3. James A. Fulton, "It Happened in Western Pennsylvania, 1862-65" ed. Cecil Fulton (Dover, Del., 1962), pp. 78–91.

4. Kittanning *Mentor*, December 16, 1862.

5. Johnstown *Democrat*, July 15, 1863.

6. In August 1863, Grund disassociated fhimself from the paper because he could not agree with its antiwar editorial policy.

7. New York *Tribune*, May 9, 1863; York *Gazette*, May 12, 1863.

8. Ebensburg *Democrat and Sentinel*, February 4, June 3, 1863; Pittsburg[h] *Dispatch*, April 22, 1863; Johnstown *Democrat*, May 20, 1863; Gettysburg *Compiler*, July 13, 27, 1863; Coudersport *Potter County Journal*, July 29, 1863.

9. Carlisle *American Volunteer*, May 28, 1863; Philadelphia *Inquirer*, June 19, 1863.

10. Christopher L. Ward Diary, January 11, 13, 1863, HSP; *Report of the Select Committee of the House of Representatives on the Subject of the Alleged Frauds in the Election of United States Senator* (Harrisburg, 1863), *passim;* Christopher Dell, *Lincoln and the War Democrats* (Rutherford, N.J., 1975), p. 175.

11. Wellsboro *Tioga Agitator*, January 21, 1863.

12. Arnold Shankman, "Freedom of the Press During the Civil War: The Case of Albert Boileau," *Pennsylvania History* 42 (1975): 305-15.

13. *L.R.*, January 15, February 16, March 5, 26, 1863, pp. 34, 195, 330–31, 365, 377, 386, 565–67; Jacob Dewees to Crittenden, February 4, 1863, Crittenden MSS; William K. Scarborough, ed., *The Diary of Edmund Ruffin*, (Baton Rouge, La., 1976) 2:567.

14. *Congressional Globe*, Thirty-seventh Congress, 3rd session, January 27, February 4, 18, 23, March 2, June 2, 1863, pp. 538, 541, 554, 714–15, 1087–88, 1214–17, 1446, 2505; *Appendix*, February 28, 1863, pp. 159–61.

15. John Bell Robinson, *Pictures of Slavery* (Philadelphia, 1863), pp. 70, 130, 267; Fullerton, *Coercion a Failure, passim*.

16. *Constitution and By-Laws of the Central Democratic Club, Organized January 1863* (Philadelphia, 1863), pp. 5–6, 9.

17. Philadelphia *Sunday Mercury*, March 22, 1863; Philadelphia *Age*, March 30, April 13, 20, June 15, 1863; Uniontown *Genius of Liberty*, April 2, 1863.

18. Philadelphia *Evening Bulletin*, February 4, May 12, June 12, September 14, 1863; Harrisburg *Patriot and Union*, August 20, 1863.

19. Jacob Weidensall to Brother, April 14, 1863, Weidensall MSS, George Williams College, hereafter cited as Weidensall MSS; Aida Craig Truxall, ed., *Respects to All* (Pittsburgh, 1962), pp. 41-42; Samuel Croft to Sister, February 12, 1863, Croft MSS, Washington and Jefferson College.

20. Clearfield *Raftman's Journal*, February 11, 1863.

21. Indianapolis (Ind.) *Journal,* December 25, 1860; Clearfield *Raftman's Journal,* April 29, 1863; Philadelphia *Evening Bulletin,* March 20, 1863.

22. Jessie Sellers Colton, ed., *The Civil War Journals of Matthias Colton,* (Philadelphia, 1931) p. 140; Harrisburgh *Telegraph,* February 25, 1863.

23. Robert Weidensall to Father, April 18, 1863, Weidensall MSS; Harrisburg *Telegraph,* April 4, 6, 1863; Philadelphia *Age,* August 17, 1863.

24. Carlisle *American Volunteer,* March 12, 1863; William Itter, "Conscription in Pennsylvania During the Civil War" (Ph.d. diss., University of Southern California, 1941), pp. 160–61, hereafter cited as "Conscription."

25. Philadelphia *Public Ledger,* April 2, 1863; Philadelphia *Evening Bulletin,* April 14–22, July 11–16, 1863; Ludwell Johnson, "Commerce Between Northeastern Ports and the Confederacy," *Journal of American History* 54 (1967): 37; Uniontown *Genius of Liberty,* June 4, 1863.

26. Harrisburg *Telegraph,* July 18, 1863; W. H. Logan to William Cairnes, July 17, 1863, Cairnes MSS, in possession of Mrs. Roy Keene, Christiana, Pennsylvania, hereafter cited as Cairnes MSS; see also Edwin B. Coddington, "Pennsylvania Prepares for Invasion, 1863," *Pennsylvania History* 31 (1964): 157–75.

27. Cassandra Morris Blair, *Letters of '63, Written in York, Pennsylvania, During the Occupation of that Town by the Confederate Troops in the Summer of 1863* (Detroit, 1928), pp. 27–28; see also Coddington, "Pennsylvania Prepares for Invasion," pp. 162–63.

28. Blair, *Letters of '63,* pp. 44–45.

29. R. Henderson Shuffler, ed., *The Adventures of a Prisoner of War, Decimus et Ultimus Barzizi* (Austin, 1964), p. 71.

6

"Judge Woodward Is Every Inch a Copperhead"

"Oh, that we had a Vallandigham in the old Keystone for the present crisis."*

"We regard the [gubernatorial] election in your state [Pennsylvania] as more important than in N. York. We are working earnestly for it."**

Unlike Ohio, Pennsylvania had no peace Democrat with the leadership qualities of a Clement Vallandigham. The Keystone State's antiwar congressmen and legislators were content to be followers rather than innovators, and of the leaders of Philadelphia's peace faction, who were also members of the city's aristocracy, a few were suspicious of the masses and democracy.[1] Although Vallandigham's pro-peace views were extreme, by 1863 many Pennsylvania Democrats shared his disgust with the war. When he addressed the Central Democratic Club in Philadelphia in March 1863, a sizable crowd attended the meeting and gave him a warm reception. So great was his popularity that he also received invitations to speak at Lancaster and Pittsburgh, and the Democracy of Allen and Buffalo Townships in Washington County held

*Wilkes-Barre *Luzerne Union,* March 11, 1863.
**Charles Mason to Peter McCall, August 31, 1863, McCall MSS, Cadwalader Collection, HSP.

122

meetings at which they proposed that he be the party's next presidential candidate. Even the Pittsburgh *Post,* which had few kind words for him in 1861, began to argue that the rebels hated him more than any other Northern "statesman" because his speeches encouraged the development of Union sentiment in the South.[2]

Thus it was to be expected that news of his arrest, trial, and banishment would disturb his Pennsylvania friends, but few would have predicted the magnitude of the protest in his behalf. Newspapers called his forced exile a "climax" to the wickedness of the Lincoln administration and suggested that unless arbitrary arrests were discontinued, the people would find it difficult to obey the law. Angry editorials had followed the incarceration of Charles Ingersoll one year before, but Democrats had staged no protest rallies for him. Such demonstrations, however, were held for Vallandigham, who more than any other man personified the peace Democracy. Meetings were held in Philadelphia, Union, Pike, Cambria, Fayette, Erie, Venango, Dauphin, Carbon, Lancaster, and Schuylkill counties.[3]

Shortly after soldiers led Vallandigham to the Confederate border, Ohio Democrats nominated him for governor. Pennsylvania also had a gubernatorial election that year, and her Democracy also selected a peace man, George W. Woodward, as its candidate. In many ways the election campaign in the Keystone State was equal to Ohio's in excitement and importance. Woodward made few public statements on the war after the start of hostilities and left no collection of personal papers after his death, but from the contents of the few letters he wrote just before and during the conflict and from the speech he made in Philadelphia on December 13, 1860, he appears to have been as strong an opponent of the war as Vallandigham. Perhaps the greatest difference between the two was that Vallandigham's opinions were widely known; Woodward was able to campaign while still serving as a judge, and therefore he excused himself from expressing his views on political matters until after the election.

George Woodward, a justice of the Pennsylvania supreme court, was one of the ablest legal minds of his generation. A strong opponent of the abolitionist movement, he did not believe that the South could be defeated militarily. In 1863 he ran for governor of the state on the Democratic ticket and lost to the incumbent, Governor Andrew G. Curtin. *(Courtesy Historical Society of Pennsylvania.)*

Both Unionists and Democrats agreed that Woodward was a man of ability and that his personal characteristics were exemplary. Even the most severe critics of the Democrats expressed surprise that their rivals should nominate as capable a man as the scholarly Wilkes-Barre judge. Apparently few people knew his true views on the war, for at the very time that the Philadelphia *Evening Bulletin,* the Philadelphia *Press,* and the *Union County Star and Lewisburg Chronicle* were calling him a Southern sympathizer and apostle of Calhoun, the equally prowar Philadelphia *Inquirer* of June 19, 1863, was insisting that he was "a citizen of unimpeachable character, an able jurist, and a patriotic gentleman." Another Union journal, the Pittsburgh *Dispatch,* announced on July 28, 1863, that he was a "jurist of acknowledged ability, widely-known throughout the state as but little committed to the extreme doctrines of the [peace] party." Apparently Southerners were also ignorant of his views, for the Turnwold (Ga.) *Countryman* of July 14, 1863, denounced the Democratic platform and urged Pennsylvanians to "change their position and travel *Wood* ward—that is, to Fernando."

The Democratic candidate, the son of a judge and the father and uncle of several more jurists, had been born six weeks after Abraham Lincoln. After graduating from what later became Hobart College, he studied law and at the age of twenty-one was admitted to the bar. He quickly established the reputation of possessing one of the finest legal minds in the state and he distinguished himself as a delegate to the 1837–38 Pennsylvania Constitutional Convention. In 1841, he was appointed a judge for the Fourth Judicial District of Pennsylvania and he served in this position until 1851; one year later he was elected to a fifteen-year term on the state supreme court. Yet his life was not free from disappointment. Because of opposition from Simon Cameron he had been denied a seat in the United States Senate in 1845. Later that year Cameron's lobbying against him and lack of support from James Buchanan cost him a seat on the United States Supreme Court. But the tall, lanky Democrat bore his defeats with unusual grace. Rarely did he seek office; in fact, at the very time he was nominated for governor, he was on a fishing trip, and friends had to notify him of his selection.[4]

Many agreed with James Buchanan that the nomination of Woodward was the best that could have been made "under all of the circumstances" then affecting the Democracy. Nonetheless the nominee had one unfortunate trait: to outsiders he appeared to be self-poised, coldhearted, and calculating. Therefore, to avoid making many public appearances and speeches, he decided not to resign from the bench. This action also helped him to keep from the public his true feelings about the war. Like Calhoun, he believed that the Union could be preserved only by maintaining state rights and that the Negro race was inferior and incapable of exercising the franchise intelligently. Shortly before his nomination he wrote a friend of his unhappiness with political affairs. He was most upset at the lack of "constitution loving citizens whose hearts were large enough to embrace the whole country and whose heads were clear enough to see that a centralized despotism would be the death of popular liberty."[5] Since many peace men knew him to be one of their own, there was no real need for him to oppose the war; to war Democrats questioning his patriotism he merely noted that his two sons were Union soldiers.

Woodward's Unionist opponent was incumbent Governor Andrew G. Curtin. The governor, who was in poor health, had only reluctantly accepted the Unionist nomination. Democrats had denounced his administration as corrupt, imbecilic, and inefficient, and this made him think that only by defeating Woodward at the polls could he vindicate himself. At first the Democracy welcomed Curtin's renomination, convinced that he would be easy to defeat, and on August 6, 1863, the Philadelphia *Age* thanked the "Abolition Convention for giving us such a candidate."

Though the election was not held until October, Democrats were actively wooing voters as early as June. When he learned of the Confederate invasion of the state, Charles J. Biddle publicly resigned from his position as chairman of the Democratic State Central Committee so that he could help protect the commonwealth from the enemy. Woodward accepted the resignation and called upon all able-bodied Pennsylvanians to heed the governor's call for volunteers and "expel the invaders from our borders." Democratic newspapers printed the exchange of letters between the two men to prove their loyalty and to prevent Unionists from ignoring the role of the Democracy in defeating the Southerners. The plan worked, and on June 30, 1863, both the Philadelphia *Evening Bulletin* and the Philadelphia *Inquirer* praised Biddle as "a brave soldier" for his patriotism. A few Unionists tried to minimize this contribution and claimed that, while the Confederates were pillaging the commonwealth, "Charles the Valiant" was busy drilling in Philadelphia by himself. Democrats countered by passing resolutions blaming Lee's invasion on the "inefficiency of Gov. Curtin."[6]

Unionists hoped to convince the voters of Woodward's disloyalty by printing extracts from his speech of December 1860, in which he had called slavery an "incalculable blessing." Next to these excerpts they listed cases of cruelty to slaves which disproved his claims. The Harrisburg *Telegraph* of August 7, 1863, asked whether he counted among the "incalculable blessings" the "ruined homes, desolated states, widowed women, orphaned children, money expended, life sacrificed, and the perpetuity of our Union endangered. These are thy blessings, O Woodward."

Democrats, however, saw nothing wrong with the speech, and hoping to win support from the electorate, they too circulated pamphlet copies of the address and printed sections of it in their newspapers. Admittedly Woodward had ignored the many evils of human bondage, but it was easy to persuade voters already convinced of the inferiority of the blacks that slavery was the natural condition of Negroes. Furthermore, Philadelphia Democrats including George Wharton, Peter McCall, and Charles J. Biddle asked Bishop John Henry Hopkins, the Episcopal Bishop of Vermont and a former resident of Pennsylvania, to write a pamphlet explaining the Biblical position on slavery. Hopkins' *Bible View of Slavery* skillfully argued that human bondage was sanctioned both in the Old and New Testaments.[7] Peace Democrats sent thousands of copies of the sixteen-page tract to potential voters, and party organs printed selections from it on their editorial pages. Before long it was one of the most widely read pieces of pro-Woodward literature.

Bishop Alonzo Potter of Philadelphia and nearly one hundred Pennsylvania Episcopal clergymen who were Unionists wrote Hopkins that it was unworthy of a servant of Jesus to advocate the continuation of slavery and claimed that he had distorted the Bible. Therefore they publicly disassociated themselves from his text, and their protest became a Unionist campaign tract. The Vermont preacher refused to modify his position, dismissing their arguments as "a protest against the Almighty." Since the question of the Bible's position on slavery divided the voters, it was not very useful to Unionists.[8]

In 1862, the Unionists had tried to prove that Francis W. Hughes was disloyal; in 1863, they questioned the patriotism of George W. Woodward. Newspapers argued that his election would be equal to Pennsylvania's being admitted to the Confederacy. Because the judge's views on the war were unknown, administration spokesmen warned, he was potentially more dangerous than Vallandigham. The Lancaster *Express* of September 17, 1863, posed the question: "If Jefferson Davis had the power to elect the Governor of Pennsylvania . . . whom would he choose? George W. Woodward, who with brazen effrontery from the very steps of Independence Hall, upheld the right of secession and the blessings of slavery, or Andrew G. Curtin, who with untiring energy has urged forward troops and supplies to the national armies?" If Pennsylvanians elected "the Jesuitical Judge Woodward," insisted the Bellefonte *Central Press* of August 14, 1863, "we might as well have Jeff. Davis as President to complete the infamy." Woodward, said his opponents, was the candidate of the KGC.

At a Union meeting held in Philadelphia on August 26, Nathaniel B. Browne, who had been postmaster of the city during the Buchanan administration, declared that the election of Woodward would be a calamity; once in office the judge would try to carry out the principles of Calhoun. Since Woodward dismissed the charges of Browne as those of a renegade slanderer, Charles J. Biddle wrote and published a letter to Browne asking for verification of the allegations. Browne, now an officer of the Union League, confessed that he did not know Woodward personally and was unfamiliar with the judge's current sentiments on the war. He also stated that he had based his remarks on the speech Woodward had delivered on December 13, 1860. Because Woodward had then defended slavery and had encouraged secession, he said, he was obviously a disciple of Calhoun. Unionists circulated Browne's response, but they realized that his arguments were weak. Democrats sarcastically wondered why Browne, who had praised the speech in 1860, later found it objectionable.[9]

Curtin's backers knew that they needed more substantial evidence of Woodward's disloyalty to sway the voters, and by the end of September they were spreading stories purporting to give concrete examples of his traitorous sentiments. Lemuel Todd told Unionist audiences that Woodward had stated to a friend of his, a Judge Hale, that he favored the doctrine of secession and called for recognition of Southern independence. Rufus Shapley, a Democrat, wrote Woodward to find out whether he had made such a statement to Judge *Hall*. Naturally the Democratic candidate, who knew no Justice Hall, denied the allegation and stated that "so far from ever avowing belief in secession or favoring recognition of the Southern Confederacy, I am, and always have been opposed to both and am in favor of suppressing the rebellion by which both are supported. . . . Neither secession nor the malignant fanaticism that caused it will ever find an advocate in me." Unionists pointed out that Woodward had not refuted their allegation since he had not spoken about Judge Hale, but he would say nothing more on the subject.[10]

Another Curtin supporter, Congressman John M. Broomall, traveled about the commonwealth, telling of a conversation he claimed to have had with Woodward shortly before the war broke out. At that time, he stated, the judge had told him that, if disunion did occur, he hoped that Pennsylvania would join the Confederacy. Democrats denied the veracity of the story, but the judge said nothing and, considering the content of his letters to Jeremiah Black in 1860, it is probable that Broomall was telling the truth. At any rate, he was willing to repeat his story in Congress in 1864.[11]

The electorate showed interest in Broomall's allegation, but they still lacked evidence of disloyalty on the part of Woodward after the start of hostilities. Unionists made a special effort to provide this evidence. Judge Thomas Cunningham of Beaver County, who had been a vice-president of the Charleston Convention in 1860, declared at a Curtin rally in Washington, Pennsylvania, that in the fall of 1862, when he and Woodward were having a friendly talk about the war and politics, Woodward had told him that the best solution to the nation's difficulties would be for the Union Army to withdraw all of its forces south of the Mason-Dixon Line and offer terms of compromise or peace to the rebels.[12]

Another supporter of Curtin, George Hart of Philadelphia, claimed that when he and Woodward were fellow passengers on a stage coach near Gettysburg on July 7, 1863, he had heard the judge vehemently denounce the Lincoln administration, saying that the "abolition" war was unconstitutional, that he had no interest in its result, and that the North by continuing the struggle could get neither honor nor credit.[13] Whether Hart—or, for that matter, Cunningham—was telling the truth or making up fabrications, Woodward never said. Since he thought that the North was becoming a despotism, he might well have made the statements attributed to him.

Most spectacular were the allegations Unionists made about his son, George A. Woodward. According to Woodward's opponents, when the boy was severely wounded at Gettysburg, his father had told him that he should have been shot in the heart for fighting with the Union Army. Naturally this created quite a sensation, and in a letter written from his hospital bed in Washington, D.C., Major Woodward refuted these statements about his father. First, he declared that, while he and his father did not always agree about the war, the judge was not disloyal and in his presence had never uttered a word of sympathy for the secessionists. Next, he noted that his father had contributed a substantial sum of money to help outfit a company of the 2nd Pennsylvania Volunteer Regiment. Finally, he stated that he had received only a minor bullet wound at Gettysburg but had been more severely hurt while fighting in Virginia in 1862. After this first misfortune his father had cared for him for four months and never once did he rebuke him for fighting against the South.[14] Unionists made no efforts to challenge the veracity of this letter.

The only other Democrat running for a major state office was Walter Lowrie, who sought reelection as chief justice of the state supreme court. Efforts were made to convince voters that he too was disloyal. First, the Unionists printed stories in their newspapers accusing him of endorsing the activities of Confederate privateers, but his friends insisted that his court decisions were deliberately being misrepresented. At a Union meeting held in Alleghany County on September 14, Thomas Bingham claimed that two months before, two hungry Yanks who had come to Lowrie's house seeking food were refused by him with the statement "that he would prefer giving bread to Rebels rather than [to] Union Soldiers." The Chambersburg *Franklin Repository* of September 30, 1863, asked its readers if they could "vote for such a man as that." It is not known if Lowrie responded to Bingham's allegations.

Although the results of the smear campaign were uneven, a number of voters apparently were convinced that, if not all Democrats were traitors, all traitors were Democrats. Unionists, however, did not overemphasize the issue of loyalty for fear of alienating Democrats, who were proud of their party affiliation but who disliked Woodward. To woo these voters they emphasized the importance of keeping an experienced executive such as Curtin in office during the crisis. They declared that the governor had not been inefficient during the Confederate invasion; he had consulted with the War Department only because he needed federal funds to equip and feed the volunteers. State money had not been available then because the state legislature was not in session.

Unionists took great care to deemphasize the race issue. They argued that the Emancipation Proclamation was an act of humanity and not an effort to make the Negro a citizen. General Lovell Rousseau told a Philadelphia crowd that blacks were inferior to whites but insisted that the government's freeing of the slaves was justified because rebels had "no rights to slave property nor any other kind of property"; no right "to anything else than to be hanged."[15]

It is likely that Curtin's margin of victory came from the votes of soldiers and their families. The governor had won the respect of the Yanks by promptly answering all of their letters, doing what he could to arrange for the transportation of the bodies of dead volunteers to their families, and calling for the establishment of a national cemetery at Gettysburg. On August 28, 1862, he further enhanced his popularity with the men in blue by presenting a sword to General George Meade in appreciation of his services to the nation. Since even Democratic soldiers were unwilling to forgive Woodward for his role in depriving them of the right to vote outside of the commonwealth, the judge had almost no friends among the Yanks. Nearly every soldier deluged his family and friends with letters warning that Woodward's election would be a dire calamity. Few in the army said anything good about Copperheads. Scores of these soldier letters were reprinted in the Unionist press.[16]

One notable feature which distinguished this campaign from those of 1861 and 1862 was passionate insistence of Democrats that election of their candidate was essential to persuading Lincoln to get rid of his radical friends. Unlike Thaddeus Stevens, whose motto "the Union as it was, God forbid," Woodward called for a *status quo ante bellum*. Hiester Clymer told rallies in Somerset and Canonsburg that, if Vallandigham and Woodward were elected, they would unite with the governors of New York and New Jersey "in calling from the army the troops from their respective states." These soldiers would not go back to the field unless Lincoln summoned a convention of the states to solve the national difficulties.[17] Many really believed that somehow Woodward would be able to end the war; they were convinced that he could stop the draft in the Keystone State.

On June 30, 1863, the Meadville *Crawford Democrat* assured its readers that "Judge Woodward is every inch a Copperhead and will receive the full vote of his party." This, in fact, was the judge's problem. He was assured the vote of the peace men; to defeat Curtin he needed some support from war Democrats. Upset at charges that he was disloyal, he denied that he was a traitor. When James Buchanan considered it necessary to urge him not to rule that the conscription law was unconstitutional, he became angry, assuming that Buchanan was questioning his patriotism. In his curt reply to the former president, he stated that the matter was currently before the state supreme court and he thought it best to keep his views private until he had heard all the legal arguments on the question. Yet, he was obviously worried about what the voters were thinking about this matter, and he hastily composed letters encouraging soldiers to suppress the rebellion.[18]

On October 13, the day of the election, the Philadelphia *Age* and other Democratic journals printed a letter from General George B. McClellan in which he denied supporting Curtin and said that, if it were in his power, he would "give to Judge Woodward my voice and my vote." Unionists urged the electorate to ignore this last-minute appeal and printed a letter the general had written one year before which praised Governor Curtin for his efforts to repel the Confederate invaders from Pennsylvania. The Lancaster *Express* of October 16, 1863, warned that McClellan's letter meant that he had "voluntarily cast his political fortunes with Woodward and Vallandigham. He must share their fate." The paper concluded, "It requires no prophet to foretell that a man who says his views 'agree' with those [of Woodward] . . . can never be President of the United States." Others echoed these sentiments, and in 1864, the general, who had been reluctant to write the letter,[19] probably regretted having composed it.

Unionists would take no chance of losing the election to a Copperhead, and they busily insured that many soldiers and government employees woul be able to vote at home. Dozens of letters were sent to Secretary of the Commonwealth Eli Slifer and to Unionist campaign chairman Wayne McVeagh urging that Union soldiers be allowed to return to Pennsylvania to cast ballots for Curtin. A typical note read: "You will please recommend the following [men] to the chairman of the State Central Committee for a furlough; all [are] right for Andrew G." Thaddeus Stevens asked Secretary of the Treasury Salmon P. Chase to mobilize Treasury clerks from Pennsylvania and make sure that they participated in the election. In fact, so many government employees in Washington were returning home to vote that a group of them chartered a steamboat to Philadelphia. Secretary of War Stanton also sent potential voters home, and he claimed that his action was responsible for Curtin's reelection.[20]

On October 13, 1863, Pennsylvanians reelected Curtin governor. Less than 16,000 votes out of over 500,000 cast separated the two men, and Woodward ran considerably better than Vallandigham did in Ohio.[21] (See Table 7.)

Table 7

1863 Vote for Governor

County	Curtin	Woodward
Adams	2,689	2,917
Allegheny	17,708	10,053
Armstrong	3,146	2,977
Beaver	3,037	2,056
Bedford	2,430	2,704
Berks	6,005	12,627
Blair	3,283	2,386
Bradford	6,722	2,954
Bucks	6,266	6,836
Butler	3,328	3,054
Cambria	2,164	3,000
Cameron	318	216
Carbon	1,542	2,119
Centre	2,714	3,058
Chester	7,988	5,498
Clarion	1,618	2,598
Clearfield	1,531	2,483
Clinton	1,607	1,911

Table 7 (cont.)

1863 Vote for Governor

County	Curtin	Woodward
Columbia	1,801	3,342
Crawford	6,141	4,236
Cumberland	3,431	4,075
Dauphin	5,065	3,875
Delaware	3,462	1,789
Elk	336	722
Erie	6,259	3,260
Fayette	3,091	3,791
Forest	91	58
Franklin	3,876	3,710
Fulton	761	1,022
Greene	1,484	2,960
Huntingdon	3,260	2,167
Indiana	3,961	1,955
Jefferson	1,754	1,698
Juniata	1,456	1,737
Lancaster	13,341	7,650
Lawrence	3,063	1,251
Lebanon	3,658	2,653
Lehigh	3,696	5,526
Luzerne	7,022	9,808
Lycoming	3,414	3,865
McKean	727	622
Mercer	3,907	3,408
Mifflin	1,709	1,626
Monroe	684	2,712
Montgomery	6,238	7,489
Montour	1,119	1,447
Northampton	3,465	6,538
Northumberland	2,469	3,356
Perry	2,328	2,296
Philadelphia	44,274	37,193
Pike	270	1,184
Potter	1,470	619
Schuylkill	6,506	8,547
Somerset	3,064	1,738
Snyder	1,758	1,231
Sullivan	359	713
Susquehanna	4,134	2,932
Tioga	4,504	1,617
Union	2,024	1,250
Venango	3,295	2,979

Table 7 (cont.)

1863 Vote for Governor

County	Curtin	Woodward
Warren	2,274	1,386
Washington	4,627	4,371
Wayne	2,211	3,152
Westmoreland	4,404	5,581
Wyoming	1,379	1,418
York	5,512	8,069
Total	269,496	254,171

Source: Tribune Almanac for 1864, p. 58.

Democrats lost six seats in the Pennsylvania House, giving Unionists a majority of four, but they won several senate races and were but one vote short of being able to control that body. Unionists did elect Daniel Agnew to the state supreme court, but they knew that the election was not much of a triumph. Had there been a major Southern victory just before October 13, Woodward might well have been chosen and Lowrie been reelected chief justice of the supreme court.

Unionists celebrated, and Democrats were glum. One Pennsylvanian, a student at Princeton University, sadly noted that "the Elections are over at last & I very much fear the Union [is] too." The Easton *Argus* warned that its readers would have to endure at least another year and a half of "needless" bloodshed and fruitless battles because of the "imbecility and fanaticism of the Administration."[22]

Democrats quickly convinced themselves that had a fair election been held, Woodward would have won. Fraudulent votes, they said, constituted Curtin's margin of victory and they purported to show mathematically that more votes were cast than there were eligible voters. Furthermore, they noted that several employers had warned their workers that they would lose their jobs if they voted Democratic. Thus, the people had not been free to express their true will on election day.[23]

In truth there had been numerous frauds in several counties.

THE 1863 PENNSYLVANIA GUBERNATORIAL ELECTION

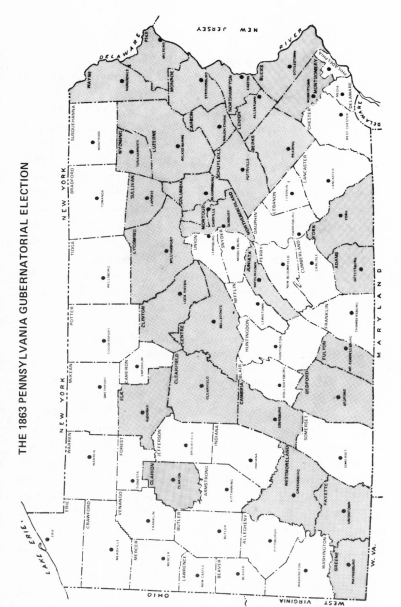

[░] Shaded Counties Voted for Woodward

[ ] Counties that voted for Curtin

Contrary to law, soldiers had been stationed at the polls in Snyder and Crawford counties. In one township in Washington County a mob had stood in front of the polls, stuffed ballot boxes, and harassed Democratic voters. In other villages Unionists had voted several times, nonresidents and minors had cast ballots, and Democratic votes had been lost or stolen. Charles J. Biddle asked Democratic leaders to document incidents of fraud for possible litigation, but he later abandoned plans for court action.[24]

Unionists probably committed a majority of the electoral outrages, but Democrats were not themselves completely blameless. They also bribed voters, imported out-of-state residents to cast ballots, denied qualified Unionists the right to participate in the election, and in a variety of other ways violated the law.[25]

Unionists dismissed the complaints of the Democrats as being the wails of poor losers. The Conneautville *Courier* of October 28, 1863, sarcastically noted:

> Just think of it, a *soldier* going down South and fighting beside a nigger, and then coming home a poor cripple to vote for a black abolitionist for governor, and there is no clause to be found in the Constitution even by Judge Woodward to prevent it. What a horrid outrage!

Curtin's victory temporarily dampened the spirits of the Copperheads.[26] Convinced that Woodward, Pennsylvania's counterpart to Vallandigham, had been cheated in the election, they bided their time, waiting for an opportunity to turn out of office those in control of the government in Washington. They knew that by himself Woodward could do little to end the war by compromise; only a change of presidents, they believed, could achieve the desirable end of saving the country.

NOTES

1. Joshua Francis Fisher, *The Degradation of Our Representative System and Its Reform* (Philadelphia, 1863), *passim;* Sophia Cadwalader, comp., *Recollections of Joshua Francis Fisher* (n.p., 1929), p. 241.

2. Pittsburgh *Post,* February 17, April 14, 1863; Philadelphia *Inquirer,* March 7, 1863; Washington *Reporter and Tribune,* May 20, 28, 1863; Uniontown *Genius of Liberty,* February 19, 1863.

3. Easton *Argus,* May 28, 1863; Philadelphia *Age,* June 2, 3, 1863; Erie *Observer,* June 13, 1863.

4. See the writer's sketch of Woodward in James Robertson and Richard McMurry, *Rank and File: Civil War Essays in Honor of Bell Irvin Wiley* (San Rafael, Calif., 1976), pp. 93–111.

5. Buchanan to Nephew, James, July 10, 1863, Buchanan MSS; Woodward to Lewis Coryell, June 1, 1863, Coryell MSS.

6. Chambersburg *Franklin Repository,* August 19, 1863; Meadville *Crawford Democrat,* September 22, 1863.

7. In 1864, Hopkins expanded his argument and published his tract in book form. See his *A Scriptural, Ecclesiastical and Historical View of Slavery, Addressed to the Right Rev. Alonzo Potter* (New York, 1864).

8. Ibid., pp. 44–49; Philadelphia *Evening Bulletin,* September 26, October 8–12, 1863.

9. Woodward to Black, September 10, 1863, Black MSS, LC; Philadelphia *Age,* August 12, 1863; see also N. B. Browne, *An Address Delivered Before the Union League in the 24th Ward of the City of Philadelphia and Its Opening Celebration, May 9, 1863* (Philadelphia, 1863), p. 7; Christopher Dell, *Lincoln and the War Democrats* (Rutherford, N.J., 1975), pp. 246–47.

10. Montrose *Democrat,* October 1, 1863; Harrisburg *Telegraph,* October 5, 1863.

11. Lancaster *Express,* September 26, 1863; *Congressional Globe,* Thirty-eighth Congress, 1st session, March 24, 1864, pp. 1221–22.

12. Lancaster *Examiner and Herald,* September 30, 1863; Philadelphia *Public Ledger,* October 10, 1863.

13. Philadelphia *Evening Bulletin,* October 3, 1863.

14. *Address of the Democratic Central Committee of September 19, 1863, Letter of Major George A. Woodward, and Letter of Judge Woodward* (Philadelphia, 1863), *passim.*

15. Philadelphia *Evening Bulletin,* August 2, October 12, 1863; Muncy *Luminary,* September 29, 1863.

16. William Hamilton to Boyd?, August 25, 1863, Hamilton MSS, LC; Captain T. G. Orwig to Slifer, September 3, 1863, Slifer-Dill MSS; Coudersport *Potter County Journal,* September 23, 1863.

17. York *Gazette,* August 25, 1863; Montrose *Democrat,* October 8, 1863; *Address of Hon. William Bigler, Delivered at New Hope, Bucks County, September 17, 1863* (Harrisburg, 1863), pp. 4–11.

18. Philadelphia *Evening Bulletin,* September 18, 28, October 5, 1863. Interestingly enough, this cost Woodward some peace votes. Alexander Harris, *A Review of the Political Conflict in America* (New York, 1876), p. 350.

19. According to Alexander McClure, early in the campaign McClellan had offered to endorse Curtin, but the governor did not accept the offer. Meanwhile Pennsylvania Democrats courted the general and told him that Woodward would win with or without his support; only then would McClellan write the desired letter commending the judge. Chambersburg *Franklin Repository,* n.d., quoted in Harrisburg *Telegraph,* October 31, 1863; George McClellan to Charles Biddle, October 12, 1863 (rough draft of letter), McClellan MSS, Illinois State Historical Library.

20. William Griffith to Alexander Frey, October 6, 1863, Slifer-Dill MSS. Soldiers known to favor Woodward were not allowed to go home. Uniontown *Genius of Liberty,* October 29, 1863. On the fears of Unionists that they might lose the election, see Joel Silbey, *A Respectable Minority* (New York, 1977), p. 146.

21. Joel Silbey perceptively notes that 89,000 more Pennsylvanians voted in 1863 than did in 1862. Democrats did reasonably well, and their share of the vote declined by just under 2 percent. Silbey, *A Respectable Minority,* p. 147.

22. W. H. Logan to William Cairnes, November 6, 1863, Cairnes MSS; Easton *Argus,* n.d., quoted in Harrisburg *Patriot and Union,* October 23, 1863.

23. Easton *Sentinel,* October 9, 1863; York *Gazette,* November 10, 1863.

24. Biddle to James Simpson Africa, October 30, 1863, Africa MSS, Pennsylvania Historical and Museum Commission.

25. Clearfield *Raftman's Journal,* October 21, 1863.

26. Particularly upsetting to Copperheads were the lavish Republican celebrations in honor of Curtin's victory. The Union men of Lewisburg in Union County, for example, staged a giant ox roast, still believed to have been the largest gathering in the town's history. Signs in evidence at the affair included "Jeff. Davis, You Shan't Come Here" and "Copperheads Beg for Peace—We Fight for It." Charles M. Snyder, *Union County, Pennsylvania, a Bicentennial History* (Lewisburg, Pa., 1976), p. 67.

7

"All Seem Bent on Avoiding the Draft"

"For God's sake, resist the draft!"*

Q: Why does Abe with his Conscription Act differ from the butchers that drive bullocks to the slaughter house?
A: Because butchers drive the fat of the land to the slaughter pen, but Abe drives none but the poor.**

Pennsylvanians have justly been proud of their state's record during the Civil War. By April 1865, perhaps as many as 320,000 residents of the Keystone State had donned the blue, a figure exceeded only by the more populous Empire State. As late as the summer of 1862, Pennsylvania, with a population of less than three million, had more men in uniform than New York, with a population of nearly four million. But as the war became more onerous, political opposition to it was so widespread that provost marshals barely had time to solve problems in one township before difficulties arose in two others. Most frightening of all there were stories of alleged conspiracies in Berks, Columbia, and Clearfield counties to resist the draft and to aid the Confederacy. Though tales about these disloyal groups were often exaggerated, it was true that several enrollers were murdered while carrying

*Johnstown *Democrat*, April 18, 1863.
**Ibid., October 14, 1863.

out their official duties and that desertions were common in Pennsylvania. Moreover, some Pennsylvania families helped Keystone Yanks desert by sending them civilian clothes in packages marked "food" or "medicine."[1]

In 1861, after it had become apparent that the war would last years rather than weeks or months, many ninety-day volunteers lost their enthusiasm for soldiering, and officers found it difficult—if not impossible—to persuade their men to reenlist for three years. Some Yanks bitterly declared, "Should we decline [to reenlist] . . . we are told that we will be discharged in such a way as not to leave the service with honor."[2]

By 1862, volunteers were so scarce that congressional legislation was needed to provide men for the army. However, the Militia Act of July 17, 1862, which authorized state drafts to supply the military with needed manpower, was so inadequate that a comprehensive conscription law had to be enacted on March 3, 1863. This second law, like that of 1862, exempted those men who were physically or mentally unfit or who were the sole support of aged or infirm parents. To help avoid the problems of 1862, an elaborate system of conducting the draft was set up involving a provost marshal and enrollment officers for each congressional district. These men were placed under the direction of federal draft officials for each state and the provost marshal general in Washington. A draftee was to be given ten days' notification, and, if he wished to escape military service, he could furnish a substitute or pay a $300 commutation fee. Draft resisters and those who obstructed the orderly prosecution of the law were subject to two years' imprisonment and a $500 fine.[3]

The law had been passed despite the opposition of several of Pennsylvania's Democratic congressmen. Sydenham Ancona, who had failed in his efforts to reduce the commutation fee to $200, warned in February 1863 that, unless the government ceased its infringement of civil liberties, he would find it impossible to continue his support of the war. Later that year he said that the Conscription Act of March 3, 1863, was "oppressive, unjust, and unconstitutional" because it was calculated to create a "military despotism," to give the federal government powers belonging to the states, and to deprive alleged deserters of trial by a jury of their peers.[4]

Lame-duck Congressman Charles J. Biddle alleged that provost marshals provided by the law would promote anarchy and tyranny since they could summarily arrest anyone obnoxious to them or to their superiors. He told his colleagues that the principles behind the Conscription Act differed little from those that motivated the despotic governments of France or Russia. Myer Strouse and John Stiles echoed these sentiments when they too voiced criticism of the draft law.[5]

A few days after the enactment of the Conscription Act of March 3, 1863, the Democrats of Crawford County assembled and passed several resolutions about the draft. One of these declared that it was unworthy for any American to "accept the office of enrolling marshal" under the federal law. At another meeting in the county provost marshals were likened to pimps, spies, and political informers. The judgement was harsh, for most of Pennsylvania's provost marshals were solid citizens. There were, of course, exceptions; one was a drunk who embezzled several thousand dollars from the government and at least two others had drinking problems.[6]

Whatever the characteristics of the provost marshals, the draft itself was quite unpopular. The Easton *Argus* of June 18, 1863, stated that military conscription was as unpopular as an epidemic of smallpox and that enrollment officers in most towns were as welcome as "a pack of mad dogs." It was not uncommon for enrollers to report that uncooperative citizens pelted them with rotten eggs and vegetables or that women chased them out of their houses.

Since most of those who were willing to support the draft law were Democrats, Unionists called their rivals unpatriotic cowards. Naturally the Democracy denied the allegation. The Meadville *Crawford Democrat* insisted on June 16, 1863, that "the butternuts are willing to fight for Uncle Sam, but they are not inclined to fight for Uncle Sambo." One editor printed a letter from an angry soldier who declared that he was disillusioned after discovering that the war was being waged to promote emancipation rather than to save the Union. He had hoped that Northerners would have enough courage to stand [up] for their rights and not suffer another draft to be made in such a war as this." Franklin Weirick of Selinsgrove urged his friends to resist the draft until its constitutionality was affirmed in the courts. Until then, he said, "none but abject slaves will cheerfully or without earnest protest submit to it."[7]

Particularly galling to Democrats was the $300 commutation, which they interpreted as being an effort to make the conflict a rich man's war but a poor man's fight. Whereas the wealthy could buy their way out of the service, the impoverished farmer would be "ruthlessly swept into the ranks to waste his blood and sacrifice his life." Moreover, some stated, a number of provost marshals withdrew the names of Unionists from a draft wheel and thus "the lottery of death" was more likely to select the name of a Democrat than that of a supporter of the war. When the only "free American of African descent" in Ebensburg was drafted, he tried to raise enough money to hire a substitute and asked for donations. Local Democrats, who were poor, contributed a total of five dollars, but the president of the local Union League, who was a wealthy man, pledged only to "give a *dollar and take it out in shaving.* "Here then," wrote a resident of that city to a friend in Johnstown, "is the boasted philanthropy of the Union League."[8]

Though Democrats disliked the conscription act, most submitted peacefully. When W. H. Logan, who denounced the Lincoln Administration as a "fanatical abolition party" was drafted, he "patriotically bought a ticket of Exemption." Peter Gray Meek, the Copperhead editor of the Bellefonte *Democratic Watchman,* was also drafted, and, like Logan, he paid the commutation fee rather than resist the draft.[9] Even the Johnstown *Democrat,* which called for opposition to the law, explained on July 8, 1863, that it did not advocate "armed resistance. The ballot box is our remedy," editor James Campbell told his subscribers, "and by yielding obedience to the law, distasteful though it may be, we may consistently require like obedience from our enemies when the law is on the side of the Constitution."

Scarcely a county in Pennsylvania was free of draft problems in 1862 or 1863. The most serious difficulties arose in the coal-mining regions and counties in the central, southeastern, and southern parts of the state. Yet even in western Pennsylvania, where Unionist sentiment was stronger than in any other region of the commonwealth, a number of men made known their dissatisfaction with the draft. In 1862, men opposed to conscription in Fayette County allegedly constructed a fortified log cabin and announced that they would resist the law. The army sent troops to two rebellious townships to restore order, and it was later discovered that the men were angry because they believed their county had not been given proper credit for volunteers already furnished for the service. Francis W. Hughes and Charles R. Buckalew urged the protesters to refrain from illegal acts and to seek redress of all wrongs in the courts.[10]

Draft officials reported a number of problems in the western part of the state in 1863. General William Brooks decided to remove Negro recruits from Pittsburgh lest there be a riot. In Washington County members of antiwar organizations were supposedly active in six townships, and the provost marshal called for troops after someone shot at enrollers serving notices on draftees. One enroller in Greene County reported that a group of men threatened to hang him. When he returned from Pittsburgh, accompanied by twenty-three soldiers, the ringleaders fled to Virginia. After he arrested five deserters, he encountered no more trouble. Many of Mercer County's 900 draftees spoke about resisting the conscription law, but most later changed their minds and found a substitute or paid the $300 commutation fee.[11]

George Eyster, the provost marshall for Fulton and Bedford counties, which were located in the south central section of the state, wrote of similar troubles. His enrollers complained that they could not complete their work because women were harassing them; such disruptions in Fulton County declined markedly after Eyster was instructed to arrest the unruly ladies. Unidentified persons burned the sawmill of one Bedford County enroller and the barn of another. The two men resigned, and after a third enroller in the county was shot, morale plummeted. Federal officials authorized the use of troops stationed at Carlisle for trouble spots, and the draft was then completed without further problems.[12]

In nearby southeastern counties draft officials met much opposition. In Lancaster, on July 15, 1863, as the names of draftees were being drawn, a mob of German-speaking residents gathered about the county courthouse to prevent the provost marshal from carrying out his work. The mayor asked the malcontents to disperse, but they ignored his pleas. Only when a posse of soldiers arrived would thy return to their homes. Abraham Bertolet, an enrolling officer, was murdered in Montgomery County while trying to arrest William Howe, a deserter. Howe was later apprehended and hanged. Mahlon Yardley, the provost marshal for Pennsylvania's 5th district, reported that one of his men was forced to flee a tailor shop in Bucks County when the proprietor menacingly raised a club at him. Another was trying to enroll employees at a tannery, but he gave up because he feared being attacked by a large dog. As he left, the men who had been uncooperative, called him a "d——n dirty rascal" and threw stones and fired shots at his wagon. Yardley also noted that some unpatriotic men were observing the movements of his agents and were warning deserters whenever enrollers approached their homes.[13]

In Philadelphia threats of draft riots in 1863 caused some residents to suggest that the enrollment be postponed. Fearing that any delay would only encourage similar agitation elsewhere in the state, the army sent General George Cadwalader to the city to suppress any outbreaks of violence. The general, who had helped quell Philadelphia's nativist riots in 1844, made it known that he would tolerate no nonsense, and city officials reported no major draft problems that year.[14]

Agents in the central counties of the commonwealth were not so fortunate as those in Philadelphia. In 1863, twenty of the twenty-eight enrollers for Clearfield County resigned; seventeen of the twenty-five in Jefferson County and eight of thirteen in McKean County quit their jobs. Enrollers reported obstruction in Centre and Northumberland counties, where secret societies supposedly flourished, and in Cambria County, where one government agent was told to quit his work or to "make peace with his God." Morale, already low, tumbled even further after a man arrested for assaulting an officer was freed on a writ of habeas corpus. Reuben Keller, former postmaster of Williamsport in Lycoming County, allegedly urged local Democrats to resist the draft and said that, if the government dared to arrest any of them, they should retaliate by burning the property of Unionists. Though these words frightened the local provost marshal, there were fewer difficulties than he expected. Similarly, bands of Democrats in Union County spoke about causing trouble, but their actions did not measure up to their words. However, there was a disturbance when Union officers tried to arrest James Hummel, a deserter, at the funeral of his sister. Hummel wounded one soldier in the melee before he was fatally shot in the lungs. Women mourners attacked the injured Yank, and he was forced to flee the church.[15]

Such incidents spread to other parts of the commonwealth. Provost marshals in Pike, Monroe, Lehigh, and Northampton counties deluged their superiors with accounts of the many difficulties that they were facing in their efforts to carry out the law.[16]

The most serious problems of all occurred in the coal-mining regions of the state. The miners, many of whom were Irish, had no desire to fight for the Negro, and peace men easily convinced them that emancipation was the sole aim of the war. Uneducated, overworked, underpaid, and exploited, they saw no reason to leave their families and risk their lives to take up arms against Southerners, who had never bothered them. Despite efforts of enrollers to avoid trouble with the miners, serious affrays marred the drafts of 1862 and 1863.

During the state draft of 1862 enrollers reported that women and boys threw hot water, stones, sticks, and other missiles at them. Some miners refused to be enrolled, and others ignored their draft notices. On October 16, a riot broke out in Tremont, Schuylkill County, when a train transporting draftees to Harrisburg was stopped by a crowd of 1,000 miners, who were determined to prevent the induction of their friends. Order was restored only after Bishop James Wood, the spiritual leader of Pennsylvania's Catholics, toured the area and ordered local priests to deliver sermons calling for obedience to the law.[17]

In 1863, there was even more resistance to the draft in this area. In Carbon County an official of a coal-mining company was murdered in his home because he had allegedly supplied draft officials with information about his employees. Charlemagne Tower, the provost marshal for Schuylkill County, reported that local citizens fired shots at a number of his enrollers and threatened others. He declared that his agents could not enroll the eligible males in some townships unless they were accompanied by troops; sometimes he was forced to seize the payroll books of mining companies to help him compile the draft lists. Many claimed that the Molly Maguires were responsible for resistance to the laws, but there is no real evidence that this group flourished during the war.[18]

Others blamed the Knights of the Golden Circle (KGC) for the widespread hostility to the draft, but it is not likely that there were any KGC lodges in the Keystone State. With good reason Democrats declared that the only knights in the state were in the imaginations of panicky Unionists. One man, however, accused the supporters of the war of organizing peace lodges for political purposes. Samuel Bigler insisted that Frank McReynolds, an employee of the governor, traveled about the state to establish branches of the "Nights [sic] of the Golden Circle" so that he could later expose its members and denounce Democrats for having joined a disloyal organization.[19]

But if Democrats did not form KGC lodges, some did join mutual protection societies which were critical of the war and the conscription laws. Government detective William Lyon was sent to Reading in 1863 to investigate reports that meetings were being held in Berks County to promote discontent with the conscription law.[20] On April 8, Lyon, who had once been police chief of Reading, ordered the arrest of four men for organizing antiwar meetings, and believing that the farmers and industrial workers of the county were so opposed to the government that they would never convict any one of discouraging enlistments, he sent the captives to Philadelphia for trial.

His fears were well founded, for on April 9, 300 angry farmers marched into Reading to protest the arrests. Only with great difficulty were they persuaded to return to their farms. Later that month, on April 21, peace Democrats staged a meeting in the city at which Congressman Sydenham Ancona, Jehu Glancy Jones, and Hiester Clymer enumerated the Lincoln administration's violations of civil liberties. The speakers castigated the government for arresting peaceable citizens "on charges and pretenses founded on mere rumor and without the slightest foundation in fact" and for carrying them outside the jurisdiction of the local courts. One resolution adopted at the gathering stated that, if there were any secret groups in the county, it should "be presumed they are for no other purpose[s] than the protection of their rights . . . [and against] the execution of unconstitutional laws." Arbitrary arrests must cease, the protesters warned, or "resistance by force to an invasion of [their] personal freedom [would be] a virtue."[21]

Meanwhile, the attention of both Democrats and Unionists focused on the hearing in Philadelphia at which Philip Huber, Dr. Augustus Illig, Gabriel Filbert, and Harrison Oxenrider were charged with conspiring to resist the government. Detective Lyon testified that on March 21, 1863, he had concealed himself in a pile of straw in the barn of Jacob Zeller. There Huber, a resident of Lancaster County, had addressed a rally of nearly a hundred men who gathered inside of the barn and who had paid an initiation fee of one dollar. According to Lyon, Huber had called the war an unholy crusade and had warned his listeners that someday they might have to kidnap President Lincoln. At one point during Lyon's testimony Huber became excited and stated in a loud voice, "It is a lie, I swear it openly."

In his cross examination of the witness, J. Glancy Jones, Huber's attorney and a former Democratic congressman, forced Lyon to admit that he had no evidence that Illig, Filbert, or Oxenrider had attended the gathering and that, although he had heard Huber's speech, he had not been present at another meeting which had been held a few hours later at Zeller's house.

Other witnesses testified that Huber had offered a biblical defense of slavery at this second meeting, had said that he would desert to the forces of Jefferson Davis if drafted, and that he claimed that two million men belonged to his organization. Jones argued that the money raised from initiation fees was to be used to hire lawyers to test the constitutionality of the conscription law, but the judge refused to dismiss the charges against the four Democrats. He allowed the accused to be released on bail and scheduled another hearing for May 5.[22]

At this second hearing the prosecution announced the arrest of a fifth man, Henry Seidel, and produced new witnesses who testified that Huber had conducted several peace meetings in the state in February and March. At one such gathering Huber had allegedly called the conflict a "nigger" war, stating, "God has put a curse on negroes and Abe Lincoln had put himself above God by trying to remove that curse." At another assembly he had reportedly shown his audience the secret grip of his order. According to one prosecution witness, Huber had told the members that, if they met a Confederate soldier, they should raise their hats three times and say "HO-RD," a secret word that would protect them from harm." The "RD" supposedly stood for Richmond; no one was able to explain the meaning of "HO." Testimony was also given that Huber had urged Democrats to fill their guns with salt or buckshot and shoot at the legs of enrollers seeking to draft them.

Jones was baffled by these accusations, but he nonetheless produced a number of witnesses who testified that nothing illegal had taken place at the meetings and who emphasized that Huber merely wanted to scare—but not to kill—enrollers.[23]

The case was continued to June 2, but no new testimony of any importance was given at that time. Jones produced witnesses who alleged that Huber was collecting money to purchase flags and that his meetings were nothing more than political rallies to elect a Democratic successor to Governor Curtin. The government realized that its case was increasingly getting weaker, and it decided that no good would come from continuing the hearing. Seidel was discharged, and the four remaining "conspirators" were released on bail. There was talk of holding a trial, but none was ever held.[24]

One of Huber's contentions was that the conscription act was unconstitutional; many others in the commonwealth also questioned its validity; and some brought the issue before the courts. Judges could not agree on the matter, for at the very time that Judge John Cadwalader affirmed its constitutionality in Philadelphia, Justice Walter Lowrie rendered a verdict in Pittsburgh which strongly suggested that the national government lacked the authority to enact a draft law. That the Supreme Court of Pennsylvania would have to rule on the question was obvious to many lawyers, but even though the court had heard arguments against the law in September, Judge Woodward was in no hurry to render a verdict until after the October elections. At that time government attorneys, believing the question to be no concern of a state court, deliberately refused to participate in the trial.[25]

On November 9, in the case of *Kneedler* v. *Lane,* the court ruled that the conscription law of March 3, 1863, was unconstitutional. Delivering the opinion of the court was Chief Justice Walter Lowrie, who declared that Congress had no power to draft the state militia, that a citizen of Pennsylvania could not be subjected to the rules of war until he was a member of the army, and that the law seriously threatened the rights of the states. He strongly denounced the government's contention that the writ of habeas corpus could be denied to men between the time they received their draft notices and actually joined the army. Justices James Thompson and George W. Woodward wrote concurring opinions, and the court issued an injunction forbidding the government from continuing the draft in the commonwealth.[26]

Just as the government had refused to present arguments

before the court, so did it refuse to consider the verdict binding. Authorities in Washington ordered that the draft be continued as usual, and provost marshals acted as though the court had issued no opinion on the case. To Unionists the episode was evidence that the Democrats—for a majority of the judges were Democrats—ought to bring about a collision between the state and national governments.

As might be expected, Democrats took a completely different view of the situation, calling the decision a courageous effort to uphold the law. The Philadelphia *Age* of November 12, 1863, for example, boldly proclaimed that the conscription law was no longer valid and therefore it was the "duty of every good citizen to resist its enforcement." In December, Congressman Philip Johnson introduced a resolution that would require Lincoln to agree with the verdict of the Pennsylvania Supreme Court or to submit the question to the United States Supreme Court; Congress rejected his proposal.[27]

If Unionists were not unduly worried about the case, it was because they correctly expected the verdict to be overturned once Daniel Agnew replaced Lowrie on the court. The case had been decided by a vote of three to two, and Agnew was known to be a strong supporter of the war. Shortly after the newly elected judge took the oath of office, Unionists asked the high court to dissolve its injunction, and despite Charles Ingersoll's persuasive arguments that the law was unconstitutional, by a vote of three to two the court reversed itself. The new chief justice, George W. Woodward, wrote a masterful minority opinion; but on January 16, 1864, the draft in Pennsylvania was again legal.[28]

The Democratic press, however, continued to denounce conscription. According to the Ebensburg *Democrat and Sentinel* the choices before the draftee were decidedly unappealing. He could submit to the law and end up in a hospital or get "cut into sausage meat under drunken, incompetent officers"; he could become a fugitive; he could mutilate himself to avoid the army; or he could sell all of his property to pay the exemption fee and discover that he would be liable for the draft a few months later. On August 6, 1864, the editor of this paper asked:

Does this Administration, after taking every available man we could spare, and leaving his bones to rot in some Southern soil, or else sending him home mutilated and crippled to us, expect us to give all our available means to support the Shoddy Government, and have our aged, and our young and our females to starve and perish for the want of the necessaries of life and make a charnel of our once beautiful country? The people are quietly but anxiously looking out for the last man and the last dollar. . . . Is it any wonder that the war is unpopular with the masses, indeed, with every one who is not making money out of it?

When the government exempted the insane from the draft laws, editor Franklin Weirick of the Selinsgrove *Times* wrote, "This is unquestionably for the benefit of the abolitionists, who are all crazy as march hares." The draft law so disturbed the editors of the Philadelphia *Age* that they wondered how much longer the nation could tolerate conscription and suggested that the people choose wiser rulers.[29] Perhaps the most vehement opponent of the draft was James F. Campbell, the editor of the Johnstown *Democrat,* who composed the following headline on September 28, 1864, when he listed the names of local draftees: "TO WHOM IT MAY CONCERN, MORE VICTIMS FOR THE SLAUGHTER PEN. ANOTHER WHIRL OF THE BLOODY WHEEL, THE LOTTERY OF DEATH. MOTHERS, SISTERS, AND WIVES, PREPARE YOUR MOURNING CLOTH."

Democrats also took great delight in pointing out the mistakes which enrollers sometimes made. They noted cases of elderly men being drafted and episodes in which innocent citizens were mistakenly shot by government agents who thought they were deserters. The writer of a story which appeared in the November 10, 1864, Montrose *Democrat* alleged that when soldiers came to the house of one deserter to arrest him, they insulted his wife, tore off her clothing, and injured her person. Other journals noted that men who openly announced their dislike of the draft were arrested and taken to federal bastiles and were deprived of jury trials near their homes. When a number of Democrats were arrested for draft evasion shortly before the 1864 presidential election and were released a few weeks later because there was no evidence against them, the Democracy protested that the government was deliberately using the draft laws to promote Lincoln's relection.[30]

Draft enrollers enountered about as much resistance in 1864 as they had in 1863. No fewer than five were killed while trying to arrest deserters, several were shot, and at least two others were warned that they would be killed if they carried out the law. One Unionist claimed that men eligible to be drafted were hiding in lumber shanties in the mountains of Clinton and Centre counties, where they eluded the enrollers and found employment at high wages. He suggested that the governor send bloodhounds to the local provost marshals to help them ferret out the potential draftees. Another supporter of the war alleged that weekly meetings of the KGC were being held in three townships of Bucks County. According to his letter, officers of the 174th Pennsylvania Volunteers were drilling the Knights, who marched about armed with guns.[31] Even in Unionist McKean County, lamented the *McKean County Miner* of January 26, 1864, desertion was common. Five deserters in one township were able to elude authorities because of the hostility of the local population toward the draft.

Undoubtedly the most incredible tale of draft resistance concerned the so-called Fishingcreek Confederacy of Columbia County. The rural county near the center of the state was a Democratic stronghold and the home of Seantor Buckalew. In July and August 1863, officials had to suspend the draft in one township after an unknown nocturnal visitor stole all of the record books, papers, and vouchers pertaining to the draft. A significant number of draftees failed to report in 1863 and 1864, and therefore it was not surprising that the local provost marshal and the farmers of the county eyed each other suspiciously. Tensions reached a new high on August 1, 1864, when Lieutenant J. Stewart Robinson, the assistant provost marshal for the district, was murdered while searching for draft dodgers.

Shortly after this incident Unionists began to fabricate stories that several hundred farmers and deserters had banded together and fled to a remote spot of the Fishingcreek Valley. There they had allegedly constructed a fort armed with four pieces of artillery smuggled from Canada. These men supposedly intended to violate the draft law and to help Southerners invade the state. Gullible draft officials believed that the story merited investigation, and they wired the War Department for help in suppressing the conspiracy.[32]

On Saturday, August 13, 1864, forty-eight soldiers armed with rifles and two cannon suddenly appeared in Bloomsburg and encamped in the agricultural fair grounds. Surprised and worried Democrats, fearful that the military planned mass arrests and the burning of their homes and barns, held a meeting on Sunday at the home of the Reverend John Rantz in nearby Benton Township. Although one or two speakers called for violent resistance, nearly all of those present opposed causing trouble unless the soldiers first committed acts of aggression against them.

During the next two weeks hundreds of army reenforcements led by Generals Darius N. Couch and George Cadwalader searched the countryside for the nonexistent arsenal. On the morning of August 31, nearly 100 residents of Columbia and neighboring Luzerne counties, all of whom were Democrats, were seized at their homes and marched to a church in Benton Township. Forty-four of the captives were designated as prisoners and sent to Fort Mifflin; the rest were allowed to return to their homes. Apparently Couch was afraid to admit that the expedition was a mistake—Cadwalader had already decided that there was no hidden arsenal in the county—and the arrests actually were nothing more than a way for the army to save face.

Naturally the episode outraged the Democrats in the area, and Senator Buckalew demanded to know the charges against the men. While the government was withdrawing most of its soldiers from Columbia County and trying to find an answer to Buckalew's query, the prisoners were suffering and starving in their damp and overcrowded cell. One man died, another became insane, and at least five contracted serious maladies. Embarrassed officials released twenty of the captives and the body of the deceased farmer and charged the rest with organizing to resist the draft.[33]

Trials for the twenty-three began in Harrisburg on October 17. The military tribunal hearing the case was inexperienced. Moreover, one of the three judges was replaced during the middle of the trial by a man who had heard none of the evidence previously presented; nonetheless, the new man helped judge the case. The evidence against the Columbia County farmers was reminiscent of that presented one year before at the Huber trial. Prosecution witnesses testified of having attended secret antiwar meetings which, they claimed, were supervised by the KGC. According to one witness, John Freeze, one of the defense lawyers at the trial, had addressed a gathering at which he had supposedly said that Illinois was about to secede from the Union and that Pennsylvania should follow suit. Others spoke about secret passwords and discussions of efforts to rescue drafted soldiers and to oppose the continuation of the "abolition war." When cross-examined, these witnesses had trouble remembering details about the secret ritual of the meetings. Moreover, they suddenly recalled that the children of several of the defendants were serving as soldiers and that many of the accused had generously contributed funds for soldier bounties. Defense witnesses admitted that meetings critical of the activities of the Union League had been held in Columbia County but denied that they had encouraged violence or were affiliated with the KGC.[34]

Two men "confessed" their crimes in return for a promise of immunity, but impartial observers reported no real evidence against the accused. Nonetheless only fifteen men were found innocent of all of the charges against them. Three received prison sentences and/or fines; others paid only fines. At no time did the judges indicate that they thought any of the farmers had belonged to the KGC; it was merely announced that the guilty had been members of a group opposed to the draft law. Predictably, Democrats, led by Senator Buckalew, and even Unionist Senator Cowan denounced the trial as a travesty, but they were powerless to overturn the verdict of the court. One man paid his fine, another was pardoned by President Lincoln, and the others were later pardoned by President Johnson. Aware that the trial had been a farce, some Unionist journals ignored the case, and on December 1, 1864, the War Department liquidated the Department of the Susquehanna, which had been involved in the matter, and replaced it with the Philadelphia-based Department of Pennsylvania.[35]

Although the Fishingcreek Confederacy had turned out to be a farce, local provost marshals continued to insist that illicit secret organizations were plotting treason in the state. Because government officials sincerely believed that there was a secret society promoting a Northwest Confederacy, they were reluctant to dismiss stories of disloyal activities in Pennsylvania.

During the summer of 1864, when Unionists were looking for campaign issues, Pennsylvania newspapers printed a letter in which William Riddles, a Phillipsburg Democrat, described the Democratic Castle, an organization he was forming to condemn the Lincoln administration for its war policy and for its frequent violations of civil liberties. The group was not disloyal, its founder wrote, for it called for a redress of all grievances at the ballot box. Unionists disagreed, noting that the Castle had a secret ritual and condemned all wars not fought in self-defense as being contrary to Christian principles. Therefore, prowar Pennsylvanians concluded, the Castle was actually a subversive organization that was promoting treason and encouraging its followers to violate the draft law.[36]

In December troops were sent to Knox Township in Clearfield County to arrest Thomas Adams, a deserter, and to investigate stories about the existence of a band of 1,000 men from Clearfield and neighboring Cambria County who sought to promote treason. At Adams's house an affray broke out, and one soldier and one townsman were killed. This incident came one month after Joseph Lounsberry, a deserter, had killed an army officer; furthermore, the local enroller had frequently complained to Provost Marshal H. S. Campbell about the difficulties he encountered when trying to serve draft notices in Clearfield County. All of these episodes convinced the government that it should take decisive action, and army officers arrested thirty-six men from the two counties. Many of the captives belonged to the Democratic Castle, but none was a deserter, a fact which the government preferred to forget. Incensed Democrats argued that none of the men had ever called for resistance to the laws; nonetheless, the army scheduled trials for the accused, and these began in February 1865.[37]

Events followed the familiar pattern of the Huber and Fishingcreek Conspiracy cases. Government witnesses testified to attending secret meetings at which there was talk of resisting the draft and of rescuing deserters. Two deserters had in fact been rescued a few months before, but the prosecution could not prove that the Castle had been responsible for the deed. Similarly, the government offered no evidence to back up its contention that money raised by the Castle was used to purchase guns; the defense insisted that these funds were being saved to help men too poor to hire substitutes. Lawyers for the accused further argued that nothing said at these meetings was more radical than what ex-Senator Bigler had publicly stated at a Democratic rally at Clearfield on August 13, 1864.

Three men were found guilty and were sent to jail and were fined for their alleged misdeeds; the rest were released and allowed to return to their homes.[38] The head of the Department of Pennsylvania was so disillusioned with these trials that he directed his subordinates to try their nonmilitary prisoners in civil courts.[39] Within a few weeks the war ended, and the army no longer worried about secret societies in Pennsylvania.

The draft laws were quite unpopular in the Keystone State, and many provost marshals found it difficult to enroll the men in their districts and spent much of their time trying to track down and arrest deserters. Occasionally they accidentally killed innocent men whom they mistook for fugitives from the army. Meanwhile, a number of men formed organizations unsympathetic to the draft laws but, since they preached that all wrongs could be corrected by electing Democrats to political office, they considered themselves to be no more disloyal than the Union Leaguers. That members of these secret groups made imprudent statements is quite likely, but Unionists unrealistically magnified their potential for danger. Because the nation was undergoing a bloody civil war, supporters of the government were hypersensitive to criticism of the war policy of Lincoln, and their fear helped promote the policy of arbitrary arrests.

As for the draft itself in Pennsylvania, it was at best only partially successful. About 8,500 draftees and 12,500 substitutes from the Keystone State were added to the army because of its provisions. Doubtless the conscription laws stimulated volunteering, but the state rarely met its quotas and on several occasions in 1862 Governor Curtin was forced to postpone the draft. Of the hundreds of men who were drafted in Venango County during the first months of 1864, between eighty and ninety paid the commutation fee, thirty furnished substitutes, twenty percent failed to report, and the remainder were exempted because of physical disabilities. "Not one of those originally drafted," noted the Franklin *Venango Spectator* of June 29, 1864, "has gone into Father Abraham's service." The same was undoubtedly true of many other counties.[40]

James G. Randall and David Herbert Donald, noting that the number of draftees and substitutes constituted a mere six percent of the total Union forces, have called Civil War conscription a failure.[41] The case of Pennsylvania provides much to substantiate this argument.

On February 10, 1864, the Johnstown *Democrat* well summed up the attitude of many people when it published the following doggerel:

> Fathers and sons, and old bachelors too
> Are sweating their brains to know what to do,
> But 'mid hope, fear, and a good deal of craft,
> They all seem bent on avoiding the draft.

NOTES

1. Sanford Higginbotham, William Hunter, and Donald Kent, *Pennsylvania and the*

Civil War, a Handbook (Harrisburg, 1961), pp. 2–3, 9; Robert Alotta, *Stop the Evil: A Civil War History of Desertion and Murder* (San Rafael, Calif., 1978), p. 82.

2. Alexander Harris, *A Review of the Political Conflict in America* (New York, 1876), p. 246.

3. Fred Shannon, *The Organization and Administration of the Union Army* (Cleveland, 1928), I: 305–307.

4. *Congressional Globe*, Thirty-seventh Congress, 3rd session, February 25, 1863, p. 1293; *Appendix*, February 28, 1863, pp. 162–63; Thirty-eighth Congress, 1st session, December 23, 1863, p. 95.

5. Ibid., Thirty-seventh Congress, 3rd session, February 23, 1863, p. 1215; Thirty-eighth Congress, 1st session, December 21, 1863, February 3, 1864, pp. 74, 374, 478; Harris, *Political Conflict*, p. 311.

6. Meadville *Crawford Democrat*, March 31, July 28, 1863; Euguene Murdock, *One Million Men: The Civil War Draft in the North* (Madison, Wisc., 1971), pp. 106, 116; hereafter cited as *Million*.

7. Tunkhannock *North Branch Democrat*, March 4, 1863; William Russ, "Franklin Weirick: Copperhead of Central Pennsylvania," *Pennsylvania History* 5 (1938): 250.

8. Johnstown *Democrat*, July 8, September 2, 1863; see also proceedings of meeting in Perry Township, Fayette County, April 10, 1863, cited in Uniontown *Genius of Liberty*, April 23, 1863.

9. Logan to William Cairnes, September 12, 1863, Cairnes MSS; Bellefonte *Democratic Watchman*, August 21, September 4, 1863.

10. Philadelphia *Public Ledger*, October 29, 1862; Tunkhannock *North Branch Democrat*, November 5, 1862.

11. Provost Marshal General's Bureau (PMGB), 24th district, Pennsylvania (Pa.), *Letters Sent* (L.S.), 4: 66, 69, RG 110, NA; Beaver *Argus*, August 12, 1863; *O.R.*, series 3, 3: 351–53, 543; Dennis Ziccardi, "Conscription, Draft Dodging and Desertion in Mercer County During the Civil War," *Mercer County History* 1 (1971): 59. For more detailed information on National Archives citations in this chapter, see Arnold Shankman, "Draft Resistance in Civil War Pennsylvania," *PMHB* 101 (1977): 190–204.

12. PMGB, 16th district, Pa., *Letters Sent*, 4: 38–39, 47, 51, 55, 59–60, RG 110, NA; *O.R.*, series 3, 3: 324–25, 341, 353, 550; Meadville *Crawford Democrat*, June 16, 1863; Bellefonte *Democratic Watchman*, July 31, 1863.

13. PMGB, 5th district, Pa., *Letters Sent*, 3: 11–12, 16, 79; 9th district, Pa., *Letters Sent*, 1: 143–44; *O.R.*, series 3, 3: 244–45, 357. On the Howe desertion and hanging, plainly a miscarriage of justice, see Alotta, *Stop the Evil*, pp. 89–91, 110–16.

14. Philadelphia *Evening Bulletin*, July 25, 1863; *O.R.*, series 3, 3: 543.

15. PMGB, 17th district, Pa., *Letters Sent* 2: 1; 18th district, *Letters Sent*, 2: *passim;* William Roshang to Eli Slifer, April 27, 1863; S. D. Munson to Slifer, November 24, 1863, Slifer-Dill MSS; York *Gazette*, May 13, 1863.

16. Philadelphia *Evening Bulletin*, June 12, 1863; *O.R.*, series 3, 3: 357; William Itter, "Conscription in Pennsylvania During the Civil War" (Ph.d. diss., University of Southern California, 1941), pp. 129–51.

17. Philadelphia *Public Ledger*, October 25–28, 1863; *O.R.*, series 1, 19 (pt. 2): 46, 468–69, 473–74.

18. Hal Bridges, *Iron Millionaire, The Life of Charlemagne Tower* (Philadelphia, 1952),

pp. 79–84; *O.R.,* series 3, 3: 330–33, 351, 372–73, 459, 543-54, 573, 590, 620, 629, 1004–1006.

19. Samuel Bigler to William Bigler, August 30, 1863, Bigler MSS. The writer has found no convincing evidence that the KGC existed in Pennsylvania.

20. *O.R.,* series 3, 3: 75, 187; Gettysburg *Compiler,* May 18, 1863.

21. Philadelphia *Evening Bulletin,* April 11, 23, 1863; York *Gazette,* April 28, 1863.

22. Philadelphia *Inquirer,* April 10, 1863; Philadelphia *Evening Bulletin,* April 10, 1863. Apparently Huber was sometimes also called William Hoover, see Alotta, *Stop the Evil,* p. 97.

23. Philadelphia *Public Ledger,* May 6, 1863; Philadelphia *Inquirer,* May 6, 1863.

24. Philadelphia *Public Ledger,* June 3, 1863, Philadelphia *Inquirer,* June 3, 1863.

25. Harrisburg *Patriot and Union,* September 1, 1863; Philadelphia *Evening Bulletin,* September 23-26, 1863; Charles Ingersoll, *Civil War Speeches* (Philadelphia?, 1865?), pp. 339–40.

26. Pittsburgh *Post,* November 10–16, 1863.

27. Philadelphia *Age,* November 12, 1863; Pittsburg[h] *Dispatch,* December 26, 1863; [anonymous], *The Votes of the Copperheads in the Congress of the United States* (n.p., 1864), p. 8.

28. Woodward became chief justice because of his seniority. Charles Ingersoll to Jeremiah Black, January 20, 1864, Black MSS; Ingersoll, *Civil War Speeches,* pp. 343-75; Philadelphia *Evening Bulletin,* January 16, 1864.

29. Philadelphia *Age,* February 1, 1864; Ebensburg *Democrat and Sentinel,* July 6, August 3, 1864; Russ, "Weirick," p. 247.

30. Franklin *Venango Spectator,* August 10–24, 1864; John Marshall, *American Bastile* (Philadelphia, 1873), pp. 629–31.

31. Murdock *Million,* p. 28; Joseph Quay to Governor Curtin, undated September 1864, letter, Slifer-Dill MSS; PMGB, 5th district, Pa., *Letters Sent,* 3: 244–45.

32. *O.R.,* series 1, 43 (pt. 1): 106, (pt. 2): ii, 354, series 3, 3: 550, 4: 607, 621; Philadelphia *Evening Bulletin,* August 23, 1864.

33. William Hummel, "The Military Occupation of Columbia County," *Pennsylvania Magazine of History and Biography* 80 (1956): 320–33; printed petition and documents relating to William Appleman (Bloomsburg, 1864), newspaper clipping folder, George Cadwalader MSS, HSP; May McHenry, "Military Invasion of Columbia County and Fishingcreek Confederacy" (Bloomsburg?, 1938), *passim.*

34. John Freeze, *A History of Columbia County Pennsylvania* (Bloomsburg, 1883), 395-525; Philadelphia *Inquirer,* October 26-November 3, 1864.

35. Hummel, "The Military Occupation of Columbia County," *passim;* William Schnure, "The Fishing Creek Conspiracy," *Northumberland County Historical Society Proceedings* 18 (1950): 95–115.

36. Clearfield *Raftman's Journal,* August 3, 1864.

37. Ibid., November 2, 1864, *O.R.,* series 1, 43 (pt. 2): 525-35; William Bigler to Edwin Stanton, February 27, 1864, Black MSS.

38. Clearfield *Raftman's Journal,* March 15–May 17, August 17, 24, 1865; Philadelphia *Evening Bulletin,* February 27, 1865.

39. Itter, "Conscription in Pennsylvania," p. 183.

40. See also Pittsburgh *Chronicle,* n.d., quoted in Uniontown *Genius of Liberty,* August 6, 1863.

41. James G. Randall and David Herbert Donald, *The Divided Union* (Boston, 1961), p. 315.

8

"My God! How Long Shall These Things Be?"

"Show us, [Oh, Lord,] a better mode of restoring the Union than by fire and bloodshed."*

"For over three years the people of the North have given men and money until the country is drained of both to assist in the prosecution of a war that has broken up the American Union forever—fastened upon the country a debt that can never be paid and is now conducted *solely* for the purpose of placing upon an equality with the white race, a parcel of ignorant, lazy Africans."**

If Unionists had hoped that the defeat of Woodward on October 13, 1863, would silence the Copperheads, they were to be sorely disappointed. In fact thereafter the peace men became even bolder in their denunciations of the Lincoln administration and in their calls for a peaceful resolution of the war. True, Democrats had agreed to abide by the decision of the voters in 1863, but after the ballots were counted, they insisted that Curtin had been fraudulently reelected. According to the Bellefonte *Democratic Watchman* of May 27, 1864, the crimes the Unionists had committed to deprive their candidate of the governorship were "unparalleled in

---

*Joshua Francis Fisher, *The Cruelties of War, by a Churchman* (Philadelphia, 1864), pp. 44–45, hereafter cited as *Cruelties.*
**Bellefonte *Democratic Watchman,* May 27, 1864.

modern history" and were "fouler" deeds than "had the word gone forth that no election was to be held at all and the right to vote [would be] denied them entirely."

To such opponents of the war, the future seemed quite gloomy. After Lincoln delivered his message to Congress of December 8, 1863, editor Peter Gray Meek of the *Democratic Watchman* became very despondent and concluded that the nation was in great trouble. In his "Carrier's Address" to his readers of January 8, 1864, he expressed some of his fears in the following verses:

> My God! how long shall these things be?
> How long shall right and liberty
> Be crushed beneath the iron heel
> Which despots make our necks to feel?
>
> Alas! the end seems distant yet.
> The sword, once more, for blood is whet.
> For Lincoln's message thunders war.
> And hell snuffs carnage from afar.
>
> They liberties are gone—and ye
> Once called the birthplace of the free
> Will soon become the tyrant's den
> Where despots bind the minds of men.

One of the reasons for the increase of opposition to the war in the months following Curtin's reelection was inflation and the speculation and corruption which it nurtured. Pittsburgh consumers in August 1864 had to pay twice as much as they had paid a year earlier for a pound of butter or a quart of milk. In June 1864, meat prices were so high in Pottsville that the local Unionist journal urged its readers not to buy any beef until the cattle monopolists and speculators became "honest." Coal prices then fluctuated from thirteen to fifty cents per bushel, and even supporters of the war predicted that costs would probably continue to rise. Businessmen too became worried, for pig-iron prices rose rapidly; the ton that had cost $30 in 1860 could not be bought for less than $80 in 1864.[1]

Democrats feared that continuation of the conflict would completely destroy the financial credit of the country. They distrusted a government that issued paper money without adequate financial backing and they feared that the national debt was rising so rapidly that it could never be paid off. "Love for the administration," quipped the Erie *Observer* on February 13, 1864, "flows from the fount of greenbacks and will go down with them below par." Another paper commented acidly that, if Lincoln was the government, he was a poor man indeed, for few governments had suffered as many financial reverses as his had in three years. This journal blamed greedy army contractors for much of the unnecessary cost of the war.[2]

Another factor contributing to the growing antiwar sentiment was the Lincoln administration's policy with respect to Negroes. Former President Buchanan believed that the president's Amnesty Proclamation of December 3, 1863, would exasperate the Confederates and prolong the war, and a Greensburg newspaper said that "under the specious pretense of proposing a plan for the restoration of the Union, it adopts a plan which is sure to defeat it."[3]

Naturally black immigration to the state was unpopular. When some black refugees arrived in Harrisburg in the summer of 1864, the August 2 issue of the Harrisburg *Patriot and Union* predicted that the newcomers would "lead lives of vagrancy and crime or become paupers upon the public bounty." Three months before, on March 31, 1864, this paper reprinted the following poem, which coincided with its editorial views.

> When this cruel war is over
> And our friends all crippled are
> And the nigs will be in clover
> While white trash can work and sweat.
> Blacks at ease—whites at labor
> Pretty picture, ain't it neighbor?

Even Unionists were less than hospitable to the Afro-Americans, and they too worried about the black influx. One newspaperman concluded that, since blacks were innately inferior to whites, the freedmen were not likely to be able to master the skills needed to compete with Pennsylvania laborers. Therefore, it was doubtful that many whites would lose their jobs to Negroes.[4]

Copperheads utilized fear of black strikebreakers to exploit racial prejudice. To the same end they spread stories about black soldiers pillaging Southern towns, killing white men and raping white women and girls.[5] Emphasis was also given to lurid stories involving miscegenation and prostitution, since these could be used to persuade Pennsylvanians that continuation of the war would promote racial amalgamation and moral decadence. Joshua Francis Fisher wrote that Washington had become "a scene of open debauchery," a town where all nongovernment buildings and homes were devoted to drinking, gambling, and prostitution. In these houses of ill repute in "the once proud capital of American freemen" and its suburbs, added the July 21, 1864, Johnstown *Democrat,* dwelled about 20,000 Negro women and their children. "They live in huts built by the government and at an expense of some thousands of dollars and subsist upon Government bount[ies] and prostitution." Horrible as this might have seemed to white Pennsylvanians, it was not so bad as what they were told was taking place at Port Royal. According to the Greensburg *Argus and Westmoreland Democrat,* the New England spinsters who had gone there to educate the former slaves were giving birth to mulatto children. "President Lincoln has used the money of the people to *prostitute these Yankee women with buck niggers,"* it alleged, "and we may now expect him to provide a grand Magdalen Asylum for them and their wooly paramours. Oh! the morality of this Republican Administration!" Lycoming County's Democratic organ printed similar stories.[6]

That the citizens of the United States would tolerate such activities and continue to support a stalemated war suggested to Copperheads that, "if there be such a disease as national insanity, the American people have it in its most fearful form." James Alexander Fulton believed that the willingness of the Northerners to wage war to overthrow the political and domestic institutions of their Southern brethren was a sign of the decline of

Christianity and morality in the country. Further proof of this
backsliding was evident to him in the lack of respect the people
were showing for the Constitution and the laws. "There is not in
Christendom a community more devoid of these essential require-
ments of freeman life," he wrote, "than are the people of the
United States." Thus "eternal justice" would punish the North for
trying to deprive the South of its "right to self-government" by
destroying its civil liberties, "which so exalted us among the
nations."[7]

Similar sentiments came from the pen of Joshua Francis Fisher,
who hoped that God would root out the errors and transgressions
of the North. "Teach us," he asked, "how we may regain the
affections and confidence of our revolted fellow citizens [rather]
than how we can conquer them in arms." He concluded by
warning that for his readers to condemn the sins of others was to
employ the very worst method of reforming their own.[8]

Of course Democrats believed that "fanatical" New England
abolitionists, who were as "unshakeable" in their purpose as men
"driven by a demonical propulsion," were responsible for leading
the nation into sin, and some suggested that if New England were
driven out of the United States, the Confederacy would voluntarily
seek readmission into the Union. Among the sins, claimed Fisher,
was the North's deliberate denial of adequate food and clothing to
Confederate prisoners of war. Neighbors told him that Yankee
prisoners were also suffering, but Fisher insisted that food was
scarce in Dixie and that Yankee captives often ate as well as did
Southerners.

It was a different story, however, when the Philadelphian spoke
about the Lincoln administration. He castigated the president for
allowing the plundering and burning of Southern villages and
farms and for mistreating Confederates. Not until the destruction
of Chambersburg would he admit that Southerners could be
equally adept at pillaging and then he rationalized that this was
done to show the North what it was like to suffer vandalism from
an enemy army. Although few others—if any—spoke out in
behalf of Southern prisoners, the Greensburg *Argus* joined Fisher

in condemning the barbarism of Yankee troops at Washington, North Carolina, and at Alexandria, Louisiana.[9]

Still another reason for increasing opposition to the war was a growing conviction in peace circles that the contest could never be won on the battlefield. True, Unionists spoke of army victories, but Copperheads argued that, if the reports of abolitionist newspapers and orators were accurate, the rebellion had been crushed on several occasions, the backbone of the Confederacy had been broken over fifty times, and the Southern army had all been killed or had starved to death. Even if the Confederates could be subdued—and not many of the peace men were willing to admit this—more than a million Yankee soldiers would be needed to force the slave states to submit to the laws. Such a Union could have no real permanency.[10]

Many war critics refused to concede that the South could be defeated and they declared that continuation of the struggle would completely bankrupt the nation and would eventually result in eternal separation. Therefore, the longer the hostilities went on, they said, the less desirable reunion would be, the more bankrupt the North would be, and the more widows and orphans the state would have. On the other hand, they insisted, peace would be a panacea to all of the nation's woes; it would end the killing, it would lower taxes, and it would even promote union sentiment in the South.[11]

Many leading Democrats including Charles and Edward Ingersoll openly declared that the North would lose the war. Even Pennsylvania Supreme Court Justice James Thompson feared that the country was "going to ruin." The judge told his nephew, George Randolph Snowden, that the South would eventually win its freedom and that "our now loyal states will be subdued into several confederacies."[12]

Unionists tired of hearing peace advocates denounce the war and uphold the South. When a veteran working in a Reading factory sharply criticized the conflict, he was informed that, if he wished to avoid physical injury to himself, he should leave the shop. Loyal men, he was told, could not work when such things were being said. The veteran failed to take this advice and subsequently was involved in a shooting affray in which one man was killed.[13] On January 1, 1864, the Harrisburg *Telegraph* warned those men who called the United States a military despotism that the nation could never become a dictatorship until it had enough room on its highways to hang all of the traitors deserving such punishment.

The controversy between peace advocates and Unionists was carried on in the churches, in the press, in Congress, and in the halls of the state legislature. Copperheads continually denounced those Northern clergymen who dared to defend slavery. In Sugar Loaf Township, Columbia County, a band of war critics interrupted the sermon of the Reverend E. P. Eyer and demanded to know whether he was a Democrat or an abolitionist. They informed him that, if he was the former, he could continue to preach, but if he was the latter, they intended to hang him. The minister found it necessary to escape through a window. Levi Tate, the editor of the Bloomsburg *Columbia Democrat,* told his readers on August 24, 1864, that any man "who pays a dollar to an Abolitionist political preacher might as well pay an incendiary to set fire to his own house."[14]

Many clergymen found it prudent not to discuss war issues before their congregations, but sometimes Copperheads so infuriated them that they could not keep silent. When a York minister was asked to baptize an infant named Beauregard, he angrily left the church, refusing to "prostitute the holy sacrament of baptism to any such vile purpose."[15]

As had been the case in 1863, supporters of the war in 1864 attempted to suppress peace journals and to arrest war critics. During the spring of 1864 mobs destroyed the office of the *Northumberland County Democrat* and threatened the editors of the Meadville *Crawford Democrat* and the Greensburg *Argus.* Peace men occasionally found it dangerous to voice their antiwar views. For example, one resident of Venango County was arrested for sending a letter in which he wrote, "Old Abe has made another draft for five thousand more men. Now will we suffer our men to be drafted out, or will we say no more men?" Another man, who lived in Lycoming County, was jailed solely because he was a Democrat. Authorities alleged that he promoted discontent amongst the soldiers, but after Senator Buckalew and Unionist Congressman James Hale demanded an investigation of the charges against the prisoner, he was quickly released. Officials claimed that the arrest "had been made through a misapprehension."[16]

Naturally peace Democrats implied that all of those who were jailed were innocent victims of tyrannical despotism. They urged the party faithful to protest arbitrary arrests, for "if the President can seize whom he pleases, all liberty is gone, and they may be the next victim."[17] Convinced that under Lincoln the United States was no better than Austro-Hungary or Poland, they feared that Americans would soon lose the right to dissent. In a poem published in the Philadelphia *Age* of September 23, 1864, they expressed their apprehension for the future:

A thousand memories of wrong, which freemen n'er forget
Are brooded o'er in Warren and the vaults of Lafayette.
The shield of law our fathers gave, their children's sole defense,
You've wrested on the "safety" plea, the tyrant's old pretense.
. . . .
By shades of Franklin, Jefferson, of Henry, Adams, Lee,
And sires that fought with Washington the battles of the free,
We will not be your willing slaves while one warm drop remains,
Unchilled by tyrant's menaces in dauntless freemen's veins.

Fear about the future course of the nation was not limited to ordinary citizens. On May 2, 1864, Congressman Charles Denison exclaimed, "There does not exist on earth a more despotic Government than that of Abraham Lincoln." The president, he alleged, had denied the people their constitutional right to bear arms and there was no telling what other liberties he would take from them next. Most Pennsylvanians in Congress probably thought these words were extreme, but five joined him in voting not to table Fernando Wood's motion requiring the president to appoint three commissioners to start negotiations with Richmond to end the "bloody, destructive, and inhumane war." The motion was tabled by a vote of 98 to 59.[18]

In 1864, several Pennsylvania congressmen, Sydenham Ancona, Alexander Coffroth, William Denison, William Miller, Philip Johnson, Samuel Randall, and John Stiles, and Senator Charles Buckalew signed an address in which they warned, "Let no one be deceived by the assertion that the arbitrary acts of the Administration indicate but a temporary policy." Although these men denounced the continuation of the war, the draft law, and the suspension of the writ of habeas corpus, they were especially worried about confiscation legislation and plans to end slavery.[19] John Stiles complained that, if Congress passed a constitutional amendment to free slaves, it would "cheat any soldier who went into this war believing it was not to interfere with the rights of the States but to preserve the unity of this Republic." Even Samuel Randall, a Philadelphia war Democrat, objected to the amendment. Not only would it give Southerners a new reason to fight for independence, he argued, but it would also insult many Northerners, who, like himself, believed that God did not intend that the blacks be the physical, mental, and social equal of whites. Charles Denison agreed that ending slavery would prolong the war and considered it foolish talk about bringing the Confederate States "back" into the Union. The old Union, the Constitution, and civil liberties had all been destroyed, he said, and Southerners believed that "they can but fare worse than to fight, and fight they do."[20]

Senator Edgar Cowan, Pennsylvania's Unionist senator, sometimes joined the Democrats in objecting to harsh treatment for the South. Cowan spoke out against confiscation bills and strongly opposed all proposals to enfranchise the blacks in the District of Columbia. Conceding that a few Negroes were qualified to vote, he nonetheless doubted that there would be anything gained by allowing a few "ignorant blacks" in the District of Columbia "to exercise, or I beg pardon, [to] ... abuse the elective franchise." To him such a policy would work against restoration of the Union.[21]

Democrats hailed his words, and Unionists denounced him for

being the only member of their party to vote against the repeal of "that foul abomination of barbarism, the Fugitive Slave Law." His action, one editor said, "was neither true to the Union nor to civilization."[22]

If Unionists had unkind words for Senator Cowan, they had even harsher ones for the sixteen Democratic members of the Pennsylvania Senate. Because a Unionist senator was a Confederate prisoner, there was an equal number of Democrats and Unionists in the state senate, and each party wanted its candidate for speaker to be elected. For months the senate was deadlocked, and not until the beginning of March 1864 were the senators able to perform their legislative duties. Unionists argued that Jefferson Davis and antiwar Democrats had purposely planned the deadlock to embarrass the Lincoln administration.[23]

Affairs were less hectic in the other branch of the legislature. Members of the house spent a great deal of time discussing a bill to compensate Pennsylvanians who had suffered losses during the Confederate invasion of 1863. Unionists proposed that no one receive any state money until he had taken a loyalty oath affirming that he had not helped the enemy. To Democrats, who insisted that there was little disloyalty in 1863, this provision seemed to be a means of rewarding only Unionists, and they asked that funds be available to all who could prove that they had lost property during the invasion. The legislature adjourned without taking final action on the bill. After the conclusion of the war, partisanship subsided, and in 1865, funds were appropriated to help compensate the citizens of Chambersburg for their losses in the Confederate raid on their city.[24]

Considerably more important was the question of soldier voting. The men in blue had been ineligible to cast ballots outside the commonwealth since the Pennsylvania Supreme Court had made its ruling on the matter in 1862. The absence of army ballots in 1862 had contributed to the Democratic victory in 1862 and had almost cost Curtin reelection in 1863. Unionists believed that the adoption of an amendment to the state constitution authorizing the soldiers to vote would insure them of future electoral triumphs. Moreover, if Democratic legislators refused to support such an amendment, their political rivals could call them disloyal and ungrateful to the Yanks for their sacrifice to preserve the Union.

Democrats were quick to realize the nature of the dilemma facing them. Naturally the war faction of the party voted with the Unionists, but most of the peace men feared that soldier ballots would be overwhelmingly pro-administration and could be decisive in close elections. Antiwar Democrats were certain that the Lincoln administration would prevent them from campaigning at army bases. Soldiers therefore would only see Unionist candidates and receive Republican election literature. If the president was willing to tolerate arbitrary arrests, peace men reasoned, was it not likely that he would threaten to jail those critical of his emancipation proclamation? Had not soldiers arrested Clement Vallandigham in 1863 for denouncing the war as a conflict being waged in behalf of the blacks and against the interests of the poor whites? Moreover, it was feared that Secretary of War Edwin Stanton would order the destruction of Democratic ballots. What safeguards would there be to prevent Stanton from burning Democratic tickets? Many remembered that he had sent thousands of Republican soldiers home to vote for Curtin in the 1863 gubernatorial contest; Democratic Billy Yanks, on the other hand, had been forced to remain in the field.

Given these fears peace Democrats ingeniously devised a number of reasons for opposing the proposed amendment. First, they claimed, its passage would result in the casting of fraudulent ballots. In 1861, votes from nonexistent soldiers had been counted and had even decided some contests, and there was no assurance that similar frauds would not again take place. Second, soldiers would be forced to vote as their officers ordered, they said, and the officers, seeking promotions, would insist that they support the Lincoln administration. Billy Yank, complained state senator William Wallace, is "a mere machine in the hands of his officers; he dare neither think nor act independently." Others agreed and insisted that to maintain proper discipline and morale, the army would be forced to discourage any open discussion of political issues, and soldiers would have to cast ballots with inadequate knowledge of the questions before the people.[25]

Unionists, who had slender majorities in both the senate and the house, responded that the Democrats' arguments were weak excuses designed to cover up the fact that soldier ballots were likely to be Unionist votes. Why, they asked, should men who had purchased substitutes be allowed to vote when soldiers, who were risking their lives to defeat the Confederacy, were unable to do so? There was no acceptable answer to the question, and the amendment was passed with comparatively little difficulty. Rather than be on record as opposing the measure, many Democrats absented themselves from the legislative halls when the vote was being taken. If soldiers could vote, they knew, it would be unlikely that peace forces would be able to control the legislature or the Pennsylvania delegation to Congress.

To become law the amendment had to be approved by popular vote; a special election was scheduled for August 2. Some Democratic journals opposed soldier voting because, they said, it would allow blacks in the army to cast ballots and this would soon lead to the enactment of Negro suffrage. "The Democracy," proclaimed the Harrisburg *Patriot and Union* of July 8, 1864, "do not fear the *white* soldiers' vote." Many party papers, however, said nothing at all about the amendment, which Unionists alleged was little better than outright opposition.[26]

Most voters apparently agreed with the Philadelphia *Inquirer* of July 29, 1864, that soldiers deserved two votes rather than one, for they overwhelmingly approved of the amendment. Almost 200,000 ballots were cast in favor of the measure, nearly double the 105,000 ballots opposing the amendment. The outcome of the election of August 2 helped to insure that Lincoln would carry the state in November.

The Unionist press was quick to note that the counties casting majorities against the amendment (Berks, Cambria, Centre, Clearfield, Clinton, Columbia, Elk, Fulton, Juniata, Lehigh, Monroe, Northampton, Pike, Sullivan, and Wayne) were the

Democratic strongholds of the state. Similarly, in Philadelphia only the voters of the fourth and seventeenth wards, which always went Democratic, refused to sanction soldier voting. This information, of course, was widely broadcast to help persuade loyal citizens that the Democracy was the party of treason.[27]

Though he had favored the amendment, John Covode feared that it might work to the advantage of Democrats. Soldiers, he thought, would "feel their power and the Administration will not give them all the[y] want." Democrats, on the other hand, he thought, would doubtless agree to all of their demands. Under such circumstances many of the men in blue would vote against Lincoln. "The Administration will have to toady to the Army," he warned, "or suffer loss[es]."[28] These fears later proved to be groundless, but in August Unionist leaders realized that the upcoming October and November elections would be close, and it was best not to ignore the wishes of any sizable block of voters.

NOTES

1. Pottsville *Miners' Journal,* June 4, 1864; Pittsburg[h] *Dispatch,* August 9, 1864; Paul Hartranft, *The History of Schuylkill County, Pennsylvania* (New York, 1881), pp. 64–65; Joseph Walker, *Hopewell Village* (Philadelphia, 1966), p. 64.

2. *Northampton County Democrat,* n.d., quoted in Philadelphia *Age,* December 17, 1863.

3. Lewis Coryell to Buchanan, January 30, 1864, Buchanan MSS; Buchanan to Coryell, December 21, 1863, Coryell MSS, HSP; Greensburg *Argus and Westmoreland Democrat,* n.d., quoted in Philadelphia *Age,* December 11, 1863. Hereafter this paper will be cited as the Greensburg *Argus.*

4. Harrisburg *Telegraph,* January 13, 1864.

5. Bishop John Hopkins to Peter McCall, April 2, 1864, McCall Papers, Cadwalader Collection, HSP; Fisher, *Cruelties,* pp. 28–35; Philadelphia *Age,* August 24, 1864.

6. Fisher, *Cruelties,* pp. 26–27; Greensburg *Argus,* February 24, 1864; Williamsport *Lycoming Gazette,* March 9, 1864.

7. Philadelphia *Age,* April 25, 1864; Kittanning *Mentor,* March 17, 1864.

8. Fisher, *Cruelties,* pp. 44–45.

9. Ibid., *passim;* Greensburg *Argus,* June 8, July 6, 1864; *Fisher Diary,* pp. 468, 486–87.

10. Harrisburg *Patriot and Union,* April 18, 1864; Erie *Observer,* April 30, 1864.

11. Kittanning *Mentor,* December 24, 1863; Greensburg *Argus,* May 25, June 29, 1864; Philadelphia *Age,* August 1, 1864; Fisher, *Cruelties,* p. 42.

12. *Fisher Diary,* pp. 471–72; Charles Ness, ed., "Home to Franklin: Excerpts from the

Civil War Diary of George Randolph Snowden," *Western Pennsylvania Historical Magazine* 54 (1971): 159.

13. Philadelphia *Evening Bulletin,* June 17, 1864.

14. William Schnure, "The Fishing Creek Confederacy," *Northumberland County Historical Society Proceedings* 18 (1950): p. 103; William Hummel, "The Military Occupation of Columbia County, Pennsylvania," *Pennsylvania Magazine of History and Biography* 80 (1956): p. 325; Thomas Meredith, "The Copperheads of Pennsylvania" (M.A. thesis, Lehigh University, 1947), p. 85.

15. Meredith, "Copperheads," p. 85; see also Fisher, *Cruelties, passim.*

16. Easton *Argus,* March 24, 1864; Uniontown *Genius of Liberty,* March 24, 1864; Muncy *Luminary,* April 19, 1864; Gettysburg *Compiler,* May 16, 1864; Franklin *Venango Spectator,* August 24, 1864.

17. Philadelphia *Age,* May 28, 1864.

18. *Congressional Globe,* Thirty-eighth Congress, 1st session, December 14, 1863, May 2, 1864, pp. 21, 2041.

19. Charles Buckalew and others, *Congressional Address* (Washington, 1864), *passim.*

20. *Congressional Globe,* Thirty-eighth Congress, 1st session, February 3, 24, April 20, May 2, June 15, 1864, pp. 475, 801–804, 1972, 2039–41, 2991; John Stiles to Lewis Coryell, February 15, 1864, Coryell MSS, HSP; Joel Silbey, *A Respectable Minority* (New York, 1977), p. 74.

21. *Congressional Globe,* Thirty-eighth Congress, 1st session, May 12, 1864, p. 2248; Appendix, June 27, 1864, pp. 133–37.

22. Muncy *Luminary,* July 5, 1864.

23. Eventually a Unionist was selected to replace Harry White, the senator who was a prisoner of war. Arnold Shankman, "John P. Penney, Harry White, and the 1864 Pennsylvania Senate Deadlock," *Western Pennsylvania Historical Magazine* 55 (1972): 77–86.

24. *L.R.,* February 10, 18, 24, 1864, pp. 173, 212–15, 251–58.

25. Ibid., March 16, 18, 1864, pp. 425, 470; Harrisburg *Patriot and Union,* March 21, 1864; speech of Wallace quoted in Uniontown *Genius of Liberty,* April 21, 1864.

26. Johnstown *Democrat,* July 27, 1864; Chambersburg *Franklin Repository,* July 27, 1864; Harrisburg *Telegraph,* August 3, 1864.

27. Philadelphia *Evening Bulletin,* August 3–8, September 23, 1864.

28. John Covode to Uriah Painter, August 26, 1864, Painter MSS, HSP.

9

"Suspend Old Abe—By the Neck If Necessary"

"All Rebels desire the election of McClellan."*

"We must have an armistice & a National Convention. But we want you to be our leader. Ninety nine Democrats in a hundred in this County [Berks County] are now peace men & in *the same proportion* they want you for their candidate."**

The Copperheads of Pennsylvania were without peer in their ability to denounce Abraham Lincoln. To them no epithet was too severe or too damning, and among other things, they called the president stupid, deceptive, cold-blooded, ignorant, dishonest, deceitful, heartless, inept, tyrannical, vacillating, hypocritical, craven, timid, weak-minded, frivolous, and bloodthirsty. To peace men Lincoln was a murderer, a jester, the modern Attila, and hell's Pandora's box.[1] Among the numerous deprecatory false-hoods spread about him was the following tale, which appeared in the Johnstown *Democrat* of August 24, 1864: "When but a lad in Hardin County, Ky., his *reputed* father, old Tom Lincoln, a bummer of the first water, actually drove him from his presence because of his notoriously bad character after which he was forced to take up abode with his mother's *friend,* a man called Enlow."

*Williamsport *West Branch Bulletin,* October 29, 1864.
**J. D. Davis to McClellan, July 22, 1864, McClellan MSS.

The thought of Lincoln's being reelected haunted peace men, who believed that four more years under "the demented occupant of the White House . . . [that] ape of royalty," would be a catastrophe. "His defeat or his death," warned John Laird, editor of Greensburg's antiwar organ, the *Argus,* on August 10, 1864, "is an indispensable condition to an honorable peace." The Ebensburg *Democrat and Sentinel* agreed, adding that a Lincoln victory in November would give the United States the very worst government on earth and would lead to the eventual disintegration of what was left of the nation.[2] Furthermore, predicted the Erie *Observer* of July 23, 1864, the war would continue, the conscription of all able-bodied men would be enforced "with the most remorseless vigor," substitutes would be unavailable to any but millionaires, and taxes would be raised to such heights that the farmers would be unable to pay them.

The list of the president's alleged crimes was so long that some must have wondered whether anything good had taken place during his administration. According to his Pennsylvania critics, he had violated nearly every article of the Constitution and had attempted its total destruction, he had made the army superior to civil authorities, he had banished some Americans from the country and had imprisoned others merely for expressing their opinions on politics, he had substituted greenbacks for gold and silver, he had raised taxes, he had passed a national conscription act, he had wasted unparalleled sums of money, and he had created a federal debt equal to over three-fourths of the nation's wealth. Moreover, he had freed the slaves and transformed them into vagabonds and thereby strengthened the Confederacy's will to fight.

"If the rebels, for firing at the flag, deserve to be devastated by war," asked the February 6, 1864, Philadelphia *Age,* "what punishment should be visited upon the President for firing into the Constitution?" To antiwar men the answer to this question was defeat at the polls, for bad as Lincoln had been in the past and was at the present, they feared that he would be even worse in the future.

Already, noted the *Jefferson County Union,* so many had been killed in Lincoln's war that if the dead were placed next to each other, their bodies would encircle the state, or, if placed on top of one another, they would make a 200-foot pile on a ten-acre plot of land. If the blood of these men had been accumulated, the paper declared, it would weigh 75,000 tons. Most depressing of all, the termination of the conflict was not in sight, and Lincoln's reelection would be a mandate to continue the war to end slavery. When would it all end?[3]

The June 17, 1864, Bellefonte *Democratic Watchman* offered its answer to the question:

> [Not] until the craving appetite of abolitionism is satisfied, [not] until the red demon is gorged; [not] until puritan fanatics wreak a terrible revenge upon a brave and hospitable people; [not] until shoddy is filled with greenbacks and glory; [not] until despotism triumphs completely, and debt and ruin make the once-free American a slave forever.

For a brief while, Democrats were hopeful that Lincoln would not be renominated. On May 31, a group of dissident Unionists meeting in Cleveland nominated General John Fremont for president, and when the general wrote his letter of acceptance on June 4, he was harshly critical of the president. Lincoln's administration, he alleged, had been marked at home by a disregard of constitutional rights and by its abandonment of the rights of asylum. Although the general was considerably more opposed to slavery than Lincoln and although the president was unanimously renominated by Unionists meeting in Baltimore on June 7, Democrats gleefully seized upon the letter as evidence that Lincoln was tyrannical, inefficient, extravagant, and cruel. James Alexander Fulton of the Kittanning *Mentor* alleged that the letter was "the testimony of our enemies that what we said of this wicked, corrupt, and ruinous administration was true." Similarly, when the Wade-Davis Manifesto strongly criticized Lincoln's use of the pocket veto to kill the Radicals' plan of reconstruction, the Philadelphia *Age* called the protest an attack upon dictatorial usurpation.[4]

What bothered Copperheads more than his pocket veto of radical legislation was his refusal actively to seek peace through Confederate commissioners in Canada. In July 1864, William Cornell Jewett of Colorado, an eccentric self-appointed peace-maker, notified Horace Greeley that rebel agents in Canada, Jacob Thompson, Clement Clay, and J. P. Holcombe, had been given the power to negotiate a peace with the United States. At first the New York editor, who was a pacifist as well as an abolitionist, asked that Lincoln summon the men to Washington, but later he agreed to go with John Hay to Niagara Falls to meet with the Southerners. The three Confederates claimed that they had not been given instructions to negotiate a settlement, but they accept-ed a letter Lincoln had sent to Canada with Hay. This was the President's famous "To Whom It May Concern" letter:

Executive Mansion
Washington, July 18, 1864

To whom it may concern:—

Any proposition which embraces the restoration of peace, the integrity of the whole Union, and the abandonment of slavery, and which comes by and with an authority that can control the armies now at war with the United States will be received and considered by the Executive Government of the United States and will be met by liberal terms on substantial and collateral points, and the bearer or bearers thereof shall have safe conduct both ways,

Abraham Lincoln

After receipt of this message, negotiations fell apart.[5]

The reaction of peace men to Lincoln's letter was uniformly hostile. At the August 1 meeting of the Clearfield County Demo-cratic Central Club a resolution was passed which called the message revolutionary and subversive and which added that, by writing it, Lincoln had put himself above the people and had therefore "forfeited all claim to our confidence, respect and obedience." Charles Ingersoll insisted that the three Southerners were confidential employees of the Confederacy and would have worked to negotiate a settlement mutually honorable and advantageous to both parties had Lincoln received them rather than insulted them.[6]

Newspaper editorials were strongly critical. The Reading *Gazette and Democrat* of July 30, 1864, concluded that, although the Southerners desired peace, Lincoln was so unwilling to entertain any peace propositions retaining slavery that there was no "hope of peace by negotiation." Eleven days later the Philadelphia *Age* denounced "the fiat of our flippant, cunning undignified despot" that there would be no end to the war which was destroying American liberty, lives, and property. "Mr. Lincoln will have no peace," it declared, "even if the integrity of the Union is tendered as a basis." On September 15, 1864, the Easton *Argus* stated that, if the voters were willing to endorse the activities of a man who was prosecuting the war primarily to end slavery, they had fallen very low "in vice and degradation."

The sad state of national affairs persuaded the August 17, 1864, Johnstown *Democrat* that the government could no longer claim that it was seeking to restore constitutional authority or to "reunite the fragments of a once glorious, powerful, happy, free, and prosperous Union." Lincoln's letter, added the paper, provided the "evidence" that the true purpose of the bloody and cruel war was to allow the fanatics of New England to "liberate the negro and rivet their chains upon white freemen." Similar sentiments were expressed in several other Democratic journals.

Another peace effort was undertaken by Jeremiah Black, who, for a brief while, had been Buchanan's secretary of state. Before leaving for Canada in August to see Jacob Thompson, he had contacted Edwin Stanton and was under the impression that the secretary of war approved of his mission. Thompson probably overestimated the significance of Black's visit and the former secretary of state did little to deflate this exaggerated view of his importance. According to Thompson, who had served in Buchanan's cabinet with Black and Stanton, the South wanted peace but feared that this could only be had if it agreed to the confiscation of its land, the execution or banishment of its leaders, and the emancipation of its slaves.

Black reported this to Stanton and suggested that peace might be had if the Confederates were to be assured that they would be able to retain control over their domestic institutions. The former secretary of state was willing to favor an armistice if it was needed to effect the reunion of the North and South and if it was requisite to the making of an agreement that both sides would abide by the Constitution. Stanton believed that Black had greatly—and perhaps deliberately—exceeded his instructions and angrily disassociated himself from the matter.[7] To antiwar Democrats this episode was but further proof that Lincoln and his cabinet wanted peace by subjugation rather than an honorable negotiated settlement of the war.

The Democracy had long before concluded that only a Democratic president could successfully conclude the fighting, and they heralded the upcoming Chicago convention as a meeting of the grand jury of the nation. Although a few Democrats in the state supported Jeremiah Black, Franklin Pierce, George W. Woodward, or Horatio Seymour for president, the overwhelming majority of the party faithful favored General George B. McClellan, who was a native of Philadelphia. Even such outspoken antiwar journals as the Johnstown *Democrat,* the Kittanning *Mentor,* and the Easton *Argus* proudly endorsed "Little Mac" as their favorite candidate to lead the party to victory, restore the Union, and end the war.

Indebted to the general for his last-minute letter in behalf of Woodward, Copperheads persuaded themselves that only he could defeat Lincoln and that, once inaugurated, he could be made receptive to their views about the war. Besides, they believed he could win a large number of soldier votes. It was no surprise, therefore, that at the Democratic state convention in Philadelphia in March, the delegates enthusiastically passed a resolution expressing their preference for McClellan as the party's presidential nominee.[8] Only one native of the state had ever been president, and Pennsylvanians were eager to augment that number.

But if there seemed to be a consensus about the candidate, there was no such unanimity about the party platform. Non-Copperheads such as James Buchanan wanted it to contain a resolution favoring the prosecution of the war, fearing that a peace plank was likely to lead to the recognition of the Confederacy. Furthermore, he believed, the South would reject reunion with the North even if guaranteed the restoration of its rights. Others in Pennsylvania agreed with former President Fillmore, who argued that attempting to maintain the Union by force of arms would lead not to peace but rather to a military despotism and the exhaustion of the nation's resources.[9]

Antiwar Democrats hoped that McClellan would take note of the meetings in Bedford, Chester, Clearfield, and Crawford counties which called for an immediate cessation to hostilities, a resumption of commercial intercourse between the sections, and a convention of the states to negotiate terms of reunion. Few found it incongruous that these conventions which opposed "the wicked, cruel, and inhumane" war were willing to endorse a general for president.[10]

Unionists surveyed the scene with dismay. George Fahenstock thought that "the entire Democratic Party" was in league with the rebels and wanted to proclaim peace at any price. He greatly feared for the future of the nation.[11] Many other Unionists doubtless shared his sentiments.

McClellan's strength with many peace men was that he was an unknown quantity. That he had once favored the war and that he hated Lincoln were obvious, but some thought that after the president replaced him, he had become disgusted with the war and favorable to a peaceable solution of intersectional difficulties. A few antiwar Democrats, however, believed that the general should end his silence and make known any desire he might have to appoint peace commissioners to settle the grievances between the United States and the Confederacy. Otherwise, they said, they were not sure they could continue to support him. John Bell Robinson wrote McClellan and offered his endorsement but warned that most Pennsylvania Democrats wanted a candidate in favor of constitutional liberty and would only vote for a man who favored "an armistice and commissioners of peace."[12]

Critics of the war even tried to exploit the burning of Chambersburg on July 30, 1864, to prove to McClellan and others that the war was far from being concluded. That the rebels could invade the state in the summer of 1864, ravage the countryside, and destroy a city unable to pay a sizable ransom was evidence that the Confederacy was still strong. Such forays would continue, warned the Bellefonte *Democratic Watchman* of August 12, 1864, until Northerners agreed to end the hostilities. "When we stop burning Southern towns and villages," wrote editor Peter Gray Meek, "our own will be perfectly secure. When we cease demolishing private residences in the Confederate States, our own will not be molested." If the farmers wished to gather their crops in peace and security, he concluded, they should urge Lincoln to withdraw all Union troops from the South.

Unionists tried to counter this propaganda with their own polemics, which warned that this type of peace would promote disunion, for once an armistice was declared, the South would have no reason to seek the restoration of the Union. Outwardly they mocked the Democrats and suggested that such "sterling" Democrats as Charles Ingersoll or William B. Reed be nominated for president, but inwardly they were worried. One Unionist, A. D. Vandling, confessed that the success of his party and its cause looked "dark" from his standpoint, and the astute Simon Cameron, who was in charge of the party's campaign in Pennsylvania, observed, "The *tone* of this state is not right and all efforts of all good men will be needed to win." George Fahenstock was fearful that "blood may flow before long in the streets of Northern cities."[13]

Not all clouds were gray though. Some Democratic farmers in Franklin County who had suffered during the Confederate raid had second thoughts about peace. Moreover, some war Democrats were becoming so disillusioned with the state party organization, which was increasingly falling into the hands of the peace faction, that they were more comfortable with Unionists than with Democrats. More than a few changed their political affiliation.

Probably the most prominent of the new supporters of Lincoln was John Cessna of Bedford County, a Douglas Democrat and the speaker of the state house of representatives in 1863, who addressed war rallies in Philadelphia, Harrisburg, and Lancaster. The new convert to the Unionist party denounced Copperheads as traitors and claimed that some Democrats were so used to getting on their knees and offering the slaveholders whatever they wanted that they found it impossible to celebrate Union victories.[14]

Since these words came from a former leader of the Democracy, they could not be ignored. Democrats denounced Cessna as a renegade and an opportunist who lacked sense "or common honesty." They claimed that he had left the party solely because he had been denied its gubernatorial nomination in 1863 and because he hoped to rise to high office with the Unionists.[15]

Another war Democrat, William Y. Lyon of Reading publicly—and caustically—informed the Democracy of Berks County that he resented their having nominated him for president of the county party organization. "The meeting was made up mostly of Huberites," he complained, "and I can have nothing to do with such cattle and will not be their candidate." Five weeks later William Hiester, also of Reading, left the Democracy because he could not endorse its position on the war.[16]

Whether such defections would insure a Unionist victory was dependent upon the identity of the Democratic candidates and the nature of the Democratic platform. Thus all eyes were on Chicago, where the Democracy assembled for their national convention on August 29. The work of the delegates was gratifying to most Pennsylvania Democrats opposed to the war. McClellan was nominated for president; George Pendleton, a peace congressman from Ohio, was selected as his running mate; and an acceptable platform was adopted.

Especially pleasing to peace Democrats was the fourth resolution of the Chicago platform, which declared that the "experiment" of war was a failure and called for a cessation of hostilities to restore peace "on the basis of the Federal Union of the States."

One thing, however, was disturbing; there was talk that McClellan might refuse the nomination or might repudiate the party platform. A resident of Susquehanna County wrote the general and warned that most of his Democratic neighbors sincerely believed that the war was unjustified "and have already declared against the Chicago nominee saying they cannot vote at the November election." Nonetheless, the writer implied that, if McClellan called for a national convention, he might yet receive their support.[17]

On the other hand, war Democrats were glum. To them the candidate was as acceptable as the platform was unsatisfactory. Peter Abel of Philadelphia spoke for a large number of McClellan admirers in that city who were strongly opposed to the peace plank. Abel wrote the general on September 7, expressing the belief that McClellan could successfully prosecute the war and restore the Union as it was if he were elected and voicing the hope that he would repudiate the resolution which called the war a failure. Daniel Carroll of Union Mills Township was even more explicit. He informed McClellan, "We cannot endorse the Chicago Platform—come fourth [sic] on a platform Baised [sic] on your owne [sic] previous carere [sic] and we will Elect you." James Buchanan tried to convince a Copperhead friend that peace "would cost too dear at the expense of the Union." To him, it was unbearable to think of recognizing the Confederacy.[18]

McClellan probably needed no persuasion. In any event, when he released his letter of acceptance on September 8, he declared that the reestablishment of the Union in all of its integrity would be an indispensable condition in any settlement of the war. Yet such a "settlement," he said, need not mean continued fighting if the South would agree to the restoration of the Union under the Constitution.

War men were pleased. A resident of Chambersburg exulted, "To every word, syllable, and sentence of your letter, we in this section of Penna, give a hearty response . . . and we desire no peace other than you ask for." Robert Wright of Philadelphia liked the letter but thought that McClellan had not gone far enough; he suggested that the general endorse the use of black soldiers and call for compensated emancipation.[19]

Very different letters were being sent to the Democratic candidate by Pennsylvania's peace men. One farmer who did not like "to fight for the *nigger* agreed to vote for the General and against "Massa Leancorn," but he expected McClellan to stop the "horrible war." A former Whig, he had voted for "Leancorn" in 1860 because he had wanted a change "& we got a change & a mighty bad one." Another correspondent, William Garvin, wanted McClellan to express misgivings about the constitutionality of the conscription laws. Claiming that his letter of acceptance had "fallen like a wet blanket upon our leaders," he attempted to persuade the general that the North had "neither a constitutional nor a moral right to force a government on the Southern States against their will." He would regret a division of the states, he wrote, but if the South could not be peaceably brought back to the Union, "I pray God they never may be brought back. I want no subjugated States tied to us by the force of arms."[20] Both men were displeased with McClellan's letter; however, it was significant that they were willing to vote for him.

In Ohio, Copperhead leaders such as Alexander Long, Clement Vallandigham, and Samuel Medary refused to support the party nominee after reading his prowar letter, but there was no comparable activity in Pennsylvania. On August 29, 1864, the day that the Chicago convention began its work, Franklin Weirick wrote: *"If this war is to be prosecuted beyond the year 1864, we much prefer that Abraham Lincoln shall have the privilege and pleasure of doing so. Before we consent to support a man who is in favor of this war, we shall prefer to consign our establishment to the flames."* Yet he later hoisted McClellan's name on the masthead of the Selinsgrove *Times* and insisted that, if elected, the general would end the draft.[21]

Other Copperhead journals also endorsed McClellan and professed to see no inconsistency in the language of his letter and the text of the Chicago platform. The editor of the Lancaster *Intelligencer* confessed that the two statements differed "somewhat in phraseology," but he argued that both were for peace and compromise. Similarly, J. Lawrence Getz of the more moderate Reading *Gazette and Democrat* insisted that "the two documents do *not* conflict in any important particulars."[22]

Why then would Copperheads support a man who had repudiated their peace plank? First and foremost, they thought that McClellan, a native of the state, could win. James Tredwell wrote from Somerset, "While I can name thirty Republicans who will vote for McClellan, I don't know of a Democrat who will vote for *Abrahamas honestus.*" Despite the rantings of Franklin Weirick and Lewis Coryell that Lincoln was preferable to a war Democrat, hatred of the president and his party was so strong that few wanted four more years of what they called "abolitionist" rule. To nominate a third candidate who would favor an armistice would only insure Lincoln's victory, and this Pennsylvania peace men could not do. They had not forgotten that in their hour of need, despite his own personal misgivings, McClellan had endorsed Justice Woodward. Thus it was only fitting that the judge and his friends tell the voters to support the general and Pendleton.

Also the Democracy was hungry for spoils. Under the Buchanan administration, a fair number of Pennsylvania Democrats had been rewarded with important political offices, and many longed to be on the government payroll again. In every sizable town, there would be jobs in the post office, and many fancied themselves as postmasters or letter carriers. If elected, they thought, a grateful McClellan would reward them for their help. If he was defeated, only Unionists would benefit.

Of great importance to the mass of Democrats was the widespread belief, based more on hope than on fact, that McClellan was bound to obey the platform. According to this argument, his letter of acceptance had been worded so as to lure prowar voters from Lincoln. However, once in office, McClellan would do as they wished. George Wharton considered the nomination to be a "temporary cloud" over the sky. In a letter he sent to a Philadelphia rally, he wrote that the Chicago platform was the political creed of the Democracy. "It must necessarily be the rule of practice of everyone who accepts a nomination under it." Jehu Glancy Jones, who was an intimate friend of peace men, told them that McClellan was the only man who "could solve the problems for us & that they should trust in [him]."[23]

Ignoring McClellan's past violations of the constitutional rights of citizens in Maryland, Democrats declared that the Bill of Rights could only be restored if the general won. Similarly, they said that McClellan would be able to stop the centralization of power Lincoln had usurped from them. Elect McClellan, they cried, and there would be no more arbitrary arrests, no more banishments, no more suppression of newspapers, and no more unconstitutional laws. It was no accident, therefore, that one of the most popular displays at the massive Democratic rally held in Philadelphia on September 17 was a nearly repaired house. The home bore the inscription: "The House Our Fathers Built: State Rights, Free Speech, Free Press, Founded by Washington, 1787, Damaged by Lincoln, 1861, Restored by McClellan, 1865."[24]

Of particular importance to Copperheads was the persuasive argument that McClellan could bring peace to the troubled land. Historians have often minimized the differences between the general and the president, and they have concluded that McClellan would have conducted the military aspect of the war with as much vigor as Lincoln. However, they have generally ignored one factor which seemed to be critical to peace men: at no time during the campaign did McClellan endorse the Emancipation Proclamation or indicate that the abolition of slavery would be a condition of restoring the Union. Therefore, when he spoke about continuing the war until an honorable peace which restored the Union could be negotiated, he was not necessarily talking about depriving the South of its domestic institutions. "Mr. Lincoln," acidly commented the Uniontown *Genius of Liberty* on September 19, 1864, "has said distinctly that we can have no peace without the abolition of slavery—that he will not even receive peace commissioners unless they notify him in advance that the South will abandon slavery. Therefore the war must go on until slavery is abolished." McClellan, on the other hand, would work to promote peace; for him it was not "a war for abolition."

Unwilling to concede that the war had brought about too many changes to turn back the clock to 1860, the peace men insisted that it would be possible under a McClellan administration to "have the Constitution as it is and the Union as it was." This belief perhaps more than anything else explains why even the most vociferous of Pennsylvania Copperheads were willing to overlook McClellan's acceptance letter and call for his election.

Many voters in the Keystone State believed that, if Southerners could keep their slaves, they would agree to rejoin the United States. The repudiation of Lincoln's odious "To whom it may concern" letter, they thought, would lead to the growth of union sentiment in the South. But this could only happen if McClellan defeated Lincoln.

"General McClellan will bring into the Presidential chair a will to have peace," said the antiwar Greensburg *Argus* of September 14, 1864, "and a disposition to make it possible by withdrawing the abolition conditions which now stand in the way of the Union." On October 28, 1864, the Bellefonte *Democratic Watchman,* one of the most outspoken of all pro-peace newspapers in the North, reiterated this point of view:

> If our people want to be cursed with four more years of war—with its conscription, its blood, its debt, its taxes, its desolation and death, let them support Abraham Lincoln. But if they would have a peaceable settlement of our difficulties, a recon-struction of the Union upon honorable terms, and an honest, competent and patriotic administration to administer the af-fairs of our Government, they will vote for George B. McClellan.

Over and over again Democrats urged Copperheads to vote for McClellan and warned them that a Lincoln victory would close the door to negotiations with the enemy and insure the continuation of the fighting. "American freemen," pleaded the editors of the Philadelphia *Age* on September 23, 1864, "you who desire the old Union back again will vote for the Hero of Antietam. You who care more for the negro than the Union will vote for Abraham Lincoln."

McClellan was smart enough not to say anything that would cost him the racist vote. Probably he shared the Copperheads' belief in black inferiority and he did have a great admiration for Southerners. If elected, he might have been willing to try to restore the Union with slavery intact, but he might have discovered that this point alone would not persuade the Confederates to end the rebellion.

A final reason for peace men to support McClellan was frequently mentioned in Unionist papers: the Democratic vice-presidential candidate was George Hunt Pendleton, a war critic. If McClellan should be elected and die, resign, be impeached, or become incapacitated, a Copperhead would become president, and he would be likely to propose an armistice. Naturally no one expected McClellan to die, but two vice-presidents had already become chief executive of the nation because of death. There is no real evidence that some people voted for McClellan solely because Pendleton was his running mate, but neither is there any proof that this factor was not important in persuading some antiwar Pennsylvanians to vote Democratic in November.[25]

The Democracy did not spend all of its time trying to prove to Copperheads that McClellan was an acceptable candidate; there were other issues as well. Most prominent of these was the tremendous cost of the war and the accompanying evils of inflation and high taxation. Voters were told that the national debt was so high that it could never be repaid. Moreover, this was said to be but a small fraction of the real cost of the war. According to the September 7, 1864, Franklin *Venango Spectator* the conflict had cost the nation in excess of fifteen billion dollars:

Democratic newspapers warned farmers that to finance several more years of war Lincoln was planning to increase their taxes by 400 percent and to mortgage their farms to the rich men of Europe. Furthermore, citizens would be obliged to pay duties for coffee, tea, and sugar, and to pay an income tax so that European and American investors could collect interest on their tax-free government bonds. "Oh, God!" exclaimed the editors of the Philadelphia *Age,* "that bread should be so dear and flesh and blood so cheap."[26]

The *Spectator's* Estimate of War Expenses
(all amounts in millions of dollars)

Item	Cost
Cost of army and navy	3,000
Expense of state and local bounties	450
Value of the labor lost because of killings and maimings	2,000
Value of the labor lost to employers because of men joining army	8,000
Loss of property on the seas	300
Loss of profits from commerce	700
Property destroyed because of war	200
Pensions to wounded veterans and widows for life	400
	15,050

Another issue stressed by Democrats was that of racism. Lincoln was repeatedly represented as the pawn of abolitionists bent on establishing racial equality; McClellan, on the other hand, was called the white man's candidate. The Harrisburg *Patriot and Union* of October 4, 1864, alleged that Unionist factory owners were firing their white employees and hiring black workers in their place. To reelect the man whom the Johnstown *Democrat* contemptuously called "Abe, the Bloody King of the Ebony Crown" would be to vindicate the abolitionist contention that the overthrow of slavery was necessary to effect reunion. The Greensburg *Argus* voiced its arguments in verse:

> The "proclamation" is the law
> For it—let all their weapons draw,
> And ram it down the rebel's maw
> Digest it if they may.
> . . . .
> The Constitution is effete
> The word will soon be obsolete
> And we'll have niggerdom complete.
> Without that paper flam.[27]

News that there would be a draft to supply the army with 500,000 more men made conscription an important election issue. One college student consoled a friend and urged him to cast his vote in the coming election "against the conscript & tyrannical administration." The student warned that if Old Abe were re-elected, the Union would be forever gone, and he proposed that a day of fasting and prayer be held so that God "would not permit us to be cursed with another four years of Abe's Administration."[28]

The Altoona *Tribune* of September 24, 1864, published and denounced a letter which characterized the new draft as but another call for sacrifice "for the emancipation of the dark race" and which stated, "Oh! Lord! Is it not awful to think of so many men being killed and crippled to satisfy a few fanatics?" If the *Tribune* considered such a letter to be treasonable, it was nonetheless tame when compared with the July 27, 1864, Johnstown *Democrat,* which, like many other issues of the paper, made frequent denunciations of "Abe the Widowmaker" in its editorials and editorial cartoons. According to the *Democrat:* "Lincoln has issued a proclamation appointing the 1st Thursday in August as a day of humiliation and prayer, also a proclamation for 500,000 more men and boys to be slaughtered, which will be an additional cause for humiliation, prayers, and tears. Let the war be stopped and Old Abe [be] dismissed," he concluded, "and there will be no necessity for the appointment of days of humiliation."

On August 17, 1864, after editor John Laird of the Greensburg *Argus* heard that local citizens were circulating petitions to be sent to Lincoln calling on him to suspend the draft, he urged them: "Go a step further, brethren, and suspend Old Abe—by the neck if necessary to stop the accursed slaughter of our citizens." Ironically there was no real reason to expect that McClellan would abolish the draft, yet the Greensburg *Argus*—and the Johnstown *Democrat*—proudly endorsed him.

Naturally there were the perennial complaints during the campaign about arbitrary arrests and other violations of the Constitution, but to give these arguments new force, Democrats insisted that the outcome of the election would decide the destiny of American civilization. Just as Woodward's defenders had insisted that the 1863 election might be the last opportunity to elect a decent governor and save the commonwealth from disaster, so did

McClellan's friends warn that, if he were defeated, the country would be plunged into ruin. "If the votes of the people confirm [for] four years more the power of Lincoln," warned one prominent Philadelphian, "we will cease to be free."[29]

Reelect old Abe, thundered the October 7, 1864, Bellefonte *Democratic Watchman,* and "THE RIGHT OF SUFFRAGE WILL BE PROHIBITED and like the serfs of Russia you will be compelled to bow the knee to an Emperor or King." The issue was clear to peace men; either the days of Lincoln's presidency were numbered or the days of the nation's future as a democracy were few indeed.

Democrats expected victory and to assure that result they staged large and impressive rallies throughout the state. In Philadelphia, the Keystone Club, the successor to the Central Democratic Club, imported such well-known speakers as Horatio Seymour, Emerson Etheridge, and vice-presidential hopeful George Pendleton and employed such local luminaries as Charles Ingersoll, George Wharton, Jeremiah Black, William B. Reed, Richard Vaux, Joel Cook, and General Robert Patterson to address their rallies. Their massive parades featured fireworks, bands, and transparencies, and these attracted large crowds. James Ross Anderson, a Unionist, confessed that the October 29 Democratic gathering was one of the largest demonstrations he had ever seen. "The procession was composed of 40,000 men, 5 abreast, & was 3 hrs. and 20 minutes in passing," he wrote. "This exceeded anything I ever beheld."[30] The Democracy staged similar rallies throughout the commonwealth.

As had been true in 1862 and 1863, these gatherings were occasionally marred by violence. At the October 29 rally in Philadelphia an innocent bystander and seventeen others were injured when Democrats tangled with jeering Unionist spectators. Just after the last speaker had addressed a Pottsville Democratic demonstration on September 19, twenty cavalrymen suddenly appeared, dismounted, and menacingly waved their swords at the crowd. In the fighting that ensued six Democrats were wounded, among them a veteran.[31]

Although the Democratic campaign was most impressive, Unionists, working under the direction of the astute Simon Cameron, conducted an even more vigorous and enthusiastic canvass. Since no major state offices were before the electorate, the Curtin and Cameron factions of the party agreed to forget their differences temporarily and work for the success of Lincoln and their twenty-four congressional candidates.

To be sure, Unionists realized that it was a difficult task that was before them. McClellan, one of the most popular men in the commonwealth, was certain to appeal to large segments of the electorate, but Lincoln men were convinced that the Democracy's platform was a godsend that would alienate enough voters to provide their party with a margin of victory. Therefore the Unionists tried to convince the public that the Chicago platform was a humiliating surrender to Richmond and that no voter favoring the preservation of the nation's integrity would endorse it.[32] Benjamin Bannan of the Pottsville *Miners' Journal,* for example, wrote on September 10, 1864, that the peace plank was ridiculous since Yankee forces were in all of the so-called Confederate states and this fact belied the claim that the war was a failure.

Despite their bravado, Unionists were worried; for a while they hoped that McClellan either would refuse the nomination and force the Democrats to choose a peace candidate or would enthusiastically endorse the platform and call for an armistice. To their chagrin the general did neither of these, and they had to content themselves with arguing that the platform was binding on the candidate and emphasizing the sentence in his acceptance letter in which he said that he believed his views were those of the convention that had nominated him. In 1856, according to the Harrisburg *Telegraph* of September 23, 1864, James Buchanan had said, "I am no longer James Buchanan. I am the Cincinnati Platform." Similarly, added the *Telegraph,* McClellan was no longer free to be himself, but instead had to embody the Chicago platform. On the other hand, throughout the campaign the Philadelphia *Evening Bulletin* frequently chided McClellan for trying to make his views those of the men who had nominated him.

On October 8, the *Evening Bulletin* reprinted a poem that pointed out the problems facing the general:

> Alas! alas! McClellan
> A craven crew you lead.
> "Peace" glistens on their banners
> While yet our soldiers bleed.
> They basely cry "surrender"
> 'Ere the Union is restored.
> They kiss the feet of traitors
> And throw away the sword.

After the text of McClellan's letter was made public, Unionists no longer felt bound to treat him with respect. They declared that his victory would promote Southern independence, foreign intervention in the war, desertion in the army, and eternal separation. The editors of the Muncy *Luminary* and the Lewistown *Gazette* wondered why McClellan continued to receive the pay of a major general though he was rendering no service to his country and insisted that, if he were an honest man, he would resign. Others argued that, if elected, he would be the tool of extreme peace men and disloyal secret societies. A few claimed that he would call for reunion with slavery intact and would agree to have the United States assume the Confederate debt.[33]

As much as Pennsylvanians wanted an end to the war, they sought an honorable peace. Repeatedly Unionists declared that a McClellan victory would only bring a hollow truce. "For a mess of pottage Esau sold his birthright," noted the editors of the Lewisburg *Chronicle* on November 1, 1864. "Let us not foolishly and blindly for the chance of a temporary peace endanger all we have gained." Either the North would be forced to agree to a humiliating surrender that would lead to eternal separation or the Union would be restored in such a fashion that the South would dominate the government and oppress the North. In both cases, they said, it would become painfully obvious that all sacrifices for the Union had been for a short time. Reelect Lincoln and there would be victory, an end to slavery, and a restored Union free of Southern domination.[34]

Toward the end of the campaign Unionist papers printed sworn statements from soldiers who were allegedly released from rebel prisons after promising to vote for McClellan. This supposedly proved that the general was Jefferson Davis's candidate. In truth, however, few—if any—Northern prisoners were sent to their homes to cast Democratic ballots.

So many charges and countercharges were made that the electorate tired of the campaign. Voters shunned Unionist speakers who spoke of a harsh reconstruction and of giving blacks civil rights, and they ignored Democratic extremists who wanted Pennsylvania to join the Confederacy. Probably many felt as Edgar Cowan, who complained that both parties were equally "bad" and feared that the nation was "politically wicked . . . corrupt—malignant—obstinate."[35]

Since it was thought that the home vote would be close, Democrats and Unionists eagerly courted soldier votes. In 1863, the Democracy had been tied to a candidate associated with the disfranchisement of the men in blue; things were different in 1864. McClellan had been an extremely popular general, and many had been quite upset when Lincoln replaced him. Early in 1864 one Pennsylvania soldier confessed to his friend Daniel Musser that, if his support of McClellan would make him a Copperhead, he would rather accept such a title than to be one of the abolitionist "nigger fuggers." Private H. A. Tiffany also thought that there was far "too much nigger in the present Administration." A third Yank, William McCandless, shocked his superiors when he declined a promotion to the rank of brigadier general of volunteers until the government agreed to "readopt the original intention of prosecuting the war for the restoration of the Union."[36]

The text of the Chicago platform and the nomination of Pendleton were extremely unpopular with the soldiers, but some Yanks continued to insist that Lincoln's reelection would prolong the war for four more years since he would not "eaven [sic] listen to any terms of peace without the niger [sic] in it." When Unionists stated that of the thousands of Pennsylvanians stationed at Camp Reynolds only ten would vote for McClellan, ten Democrats representing only a few companies pledged their support for "Little Mac" and insisted that hundreds more would do the same.[37]

Privately Democrats worried about the army vote. Christopher Ward, state campaign director, confessed that the new law gave him "infinite trouble [and] vexation" and made his "position one of great labor." William Bigler agreed that the most difficult task before the Democracy was to persuade soldiers that it was not disloyal to vote for McClellan; he also feared fraudulent returns.[38]

The army election law was indeed quite cumbersome, and after the elections members of both parties called for its repeal. Under its provisions the governor was to appoint at least one commissioner to carry ballots to each regiment of soldiers and to oversee the election. Unfortunately commissioners were not empowered to prevent the casting of fraudulent ballots or to correct other violations of the law. Each regiment was required to record the votes of its members in duplicate poll books and to use a different series of books for each county from which there were electoral returns. To avoid election frauds and criticism of the law Governor Curtin appointed a number of Democratic commissioners, but this did not satisfy the Democracy.[39]

As the October elections approached, Unionists, confident of victory, mocked their rivals for calling the war a failure. "Peace Democrats are just as mistaken when they say we cannot conquer and repossess our own country," exclaimed William D. Kelley, "as they were in supposing that Grant and Sherman and Sheridan would not move our columns onward or Farragut bring his guns into play."[40]

It would hardly be an exaggeration to state that the slender Unionist plurality in October was a result of the timely fall of Atlanta and other Yankee successes. The final vote was close—so close in fact that not until a week after the election was it apparent that the Democrats had been defeated by 391 votes on the home vote. Soldier ballots, however, had been strongly Unionist and had decided many close contests. Unionists gained four seats in Congress, three in the state senate, and twelve in the state house of representatives, and even such a popular Democrat as William Bigler, who ran for Congress, was among the defeated candidates.[41]

Tales of frauds committed by both parties filled the newspapers. Democrats in Clearfield County brought at least one deserter to vote for Bigler. In Bedford, Cambria, and Susquehanna counties Unionist soldiers were at the polls to catch deserters, but their presence intimidated many other potential antiwar Democratic voters. One man falsely accused of being a deserter was killed as he tried to escape from three soldiers and one civilian who were marching him to jail.[42]

Voting irregularities were most common in military camps. Shortly before the election Simon Cameron sent over one hundred men to army posts to campaign for the Unionists; this was done with Governor Curtin's knowledge. On election day several regiments and army hospitals reported that they had no poll books or insufficient ballots for all of the men eligible to vote. Unionist officers warned that a similar situation in November would cost Lincoln thousands of ballots.[43]

Democrats indignantly noted that in some instances only Unionist voting tickets were available to soldiers, and they blamed the governor and Secretary of the Commonwealth Eli Slifer for this irregularity. Peace journals reported that soldiers were rewarded with ale for voting Unionist and that some Democratic ballots were later recorded as being cast for Unionist candidates.[44]

Even when there were no charges of irregularities, officers complained that the soldier voting law was so complicated that it took days to tabulate the returns. Recording the election results from a regiment with soldiers from twenty or more counties was no easy task, and one Yank complained that he was "nearly three days with half a dozen clerks, counting off and preparing proper duplicate returns" for one regiment. He added: "The officers of the last election shudder in view of the labors of the next and will avoid them if they can. Is there no remedy?"[45]

Since they lost the home vote by fewer than 3,000 ballots in October, Democrats expected victory in November. On November 7, the day before the election, one of McClellan's closest friends assured him that he would carry the state "unless fraud is used—but there is no doubt there will be [some] fraud." Democrats circulated a letter from Pendleton dated October 18, which endorsed the "constitutional" goals of the war, and this pacified some Democrats but hardly enough to offset the effects of recent army victories. Hendrick B. Wright urged the general to tour the state, warning that, if he did not, it might be *"doubtful* how it would go," but McClellan foolishly ignored this advice.[46]

The Democracy had correctly predicted that "Little Mac" would win a higher percentage of soldier ballots than had their congressional candidates one month before. Unfortunately they did not realize that most soldiers would support "Old Abe" and would actively urge their friends to vote for Lincoln and the "subjugation of all traitors [and] the freedom of all classes of mankind."[47] Since a majority of the men in blue favored Lincoln, Unionists encouraged soldiers to vote. They arranged for army furloughs so that

Yanks could persuade neighbors to vote for Lincoln, and they made sure that all regiments and army hospitals had ample polling books and ballots.

Table 8

1864 Pennsylvania Presidential Election

County	Lincoln Home Vote	Lincoln Soldier Vote	McClellan Home Vote	McClellan Soldier Vote
Adams	2,362	250	2,886	130
Allegheny	19,427	2,092	11,588	826
Armstrong	3,165	361	3,039	202
Beaver	2,993	244	2,200	104
Bedford	1,954	382	2,585	167
Berks	6,197	513	12,929	337
Blair	2,827	465	2,496	190
Bradford	6,200	685	2,819	188
Bucks	6,196	240	7,235	100

Table 8 (cont.)
1864 Pennsylvania Presidential Election

County	Lincoln Home Vote	Lincoln Soldier Vote	McClellan Home Vote	McClellan Soldier Vote
Butler	3,064	411	2,823	124
Cambria	1,856	388	2,886	150
Cameron	307	28	226	6
Carbon	1,612	169	2,180	71
Centre	2,410	407	3,256	143
Chester	8,076	370	5,828	159
Clarion	1,655	125	2,704	129
Clearfield	1,371	135	2,762	39
Clinton	1,458	208	2,012	123
Columbia	1,739	175	3,185	182
Crawford	5,904	537	4,428	98
Cumberland	3,243	361	4,013	343
Dauphin	4,927	617	3,826	394
Delaware	3,445	219	2,056	85
Elk	296	52	821	14
Erie	6,387	524	3,619	103
Fayette	2,848	373	3,840	286
Franklin	3,516	346	3,562	259
Fulton	605	89	869	37
Forest	80	5	62	0
Greene	1,433	150	2,963	113
Huntingdon	2,865	456	2,256	221
Indiana	3,764	556	1,959	220
Jefferson	1,614	209	1,756	112
Juniata	1,276	161	1,644	109
Lancaster	13,165	1,004	7,987	461
Lawrence	3,152	256	1,324	65
Lebanon	8,581	199	2,689	90
Lehigh	3,681	227	5,780	140
Luzerne	6,646	999	9,541	504
Lycoming	3,024	377	3,952	255
McKean	733	34	642	10
Mercer	3,929	291	3,479	90
Mifflin	1,430	213	1,519	199
Monroe	581	104	2,608	90
Montgomery	6,504	368	7,772	171
Montour	993	132	1,458	38
Northampton	3,498	228	6,812	132
Northumberland	2,686	229	3,486	122
Perry	2,048	388	2,148	298
Philadelphia	51,551	4,240	42,046	1,986

Table 8 (cont.)

1864 Pennsylvania Presidential Election

County	Lincoln Home Vote	Lincoln Soldier Vote	McClellan Home Vote	McClellan Soldier Vote
Pike	237	23	1,151	29
Potter	1,167	223	640	40
Schuylkill	7,166	685	9,245	295
Somerset	2,478	310	1,631	88
Snyder	1,521	153	1,339	38
Sullivan	330	39	647	23
Susquehanna	3,846	357	2,895	64
Tioga	4,105	538	1,494	90
Union	1,718	227	1,283	69
Venango	3,573	276	3,240	101
Warren	2,309	232	1,448	57
Washington	4,526	425	4,419	160
Wayne	2,003	271	2,872	117
Westmoreland	4,084	566	5,683	294
Wyoming	1,179	158	1,322	80
York	4,888	680	8,111	389
Total	269,670	26,712	263,967	12,349
Lincoln	296,382			
McClellan	276,316			

Source: Tribune Almanac for 1865, p. 54.

Finally election day arrived. Again the results were so close that it took a few days to determine which candidate had won. When returns were finally tabulated, it was apparent that soldier votes were largely responsible for Lincoln's narrow victory. The president had received about two-thirds of the 39,000 army ballots, which gave him a 20,000 majority of the state's total vote. McClellan, however, had carried thirty-five of the commonwealth's sixty-six counties.[48] (See Table 8.)

Democrats declared that McClellan had lost the state only because of myriad election frauds. Though these claims were exaggerated, they did have some foundation. There were flagrant voting irregularities in Luzerne and Columbia counties, where scores of Democrats were subjected to arbitrary arrests. Democrats also insisted that thousands of the 99,700 votes cast in

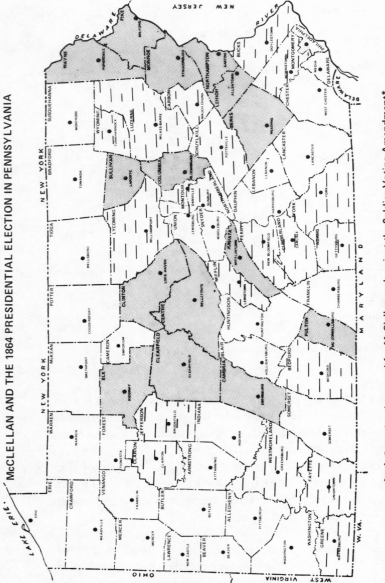

McCLELLAN AND THE 1864 PRESIDENTIAL ELECTION IN PENNSYLVANIA

▨ Counties that voted for McClellan and against the Soldier Voting Amendment*

[=] Counties that voted for McClellan and for the Soldier Voting Amendment

*McClellan carried every county won by Woodward in 1863, plus Jefferson, Mifflin, and Perry Counties. McClellan won a majority of the civilian vote in Franklin County, but soldier ballots were so overwhelmingly Republican that in the end Lincoln carried the county.

Philadelphia were bogus, and the unusually large vote in that city seemed to support their allegations. Democrats, however, had also committed frauds in several counties.[49]

One Democratic editor had predicted that McClellan would win the army vote if there was no cheating at the polls. He was wrong, for Lincoln was, in the words of Emmanuel Dougherty, "alected by fare means," but unquestionably there were voting irregularities in the army. The most flagrant of these involved the arrest of Jerre McKibben, a Democratic commissioner. Stanton, who disliked McKibben, had him jailed for allegedly defrauding soldiers of their votes. The prisoner convinced Eli Slifer of his innocence, and the secretary of the commonwealth and Alexander McClure had to go to Washington to secure his release. These and other irregularities impelled the legislature to investigate the October and November elections; the investigation revealed that both parties had violated the law.[50]

As the Unionists were congratulating themselves over their victory, Democrats consoled themselves as best they could. Some urged the party faithful to bide their time in anticipation of future battles for constitutional liberty, but other peace men were too dejected to believe that there was much hope for the country. According to the pessimists, on November 8, 1864, "the American people perpetrated the darkest, blackest crime that has been perpetrated by any nation or people for eighteen hundred years. . . . The eagle of Liberty shrieked and fled forever from the God forsaken land."[51] The Lewisburg *Argus* of November 19, 1864, warned Democrats to "prepare to escape the frightful conflagration of Divine wrath and self-inflicted woe and misery which will soon burst upon and envelope the land." What the Copperheads failed to realize was that the war was finally coming to an end.

NOTES

1. Johnstown *Democrat,* April 20, 1864; Ebensburg *Democrat and Sentinel,* July 27, 1864; Selinsgrove *Times,* December 24, 1863, quoted in *L.R.,* April 30, 1864, p. 962.

2. Ebensburg *Democrat and Sentinel,* July 27, August 3, 1864.

3. *Jefferson County Union,* n.d., quoted in Franklin *Venango Spectator,* August 31, 1864; see also Uniontown *Genius of Liberty,* September 29, 1864.

4. Ibid., June 15, 1864; Kittanning *Mentor,* June 16, 1864; Philadelphia *Age,* August 5, 1864.

5. James G. Randall and Richard N. Current, *Lincoln the President* (New York, 1954), 4: 158–62, hereafter cited as *Lincoln.*

6. Philadelphia *Age,* September 23, 1864; Charles Ingersoll, *Civil War Speeches* (Philadelphia?, 1865?), pp. 383–89.

7. Black to Stanton, August 24, September 3, 1864, Black MSS; Edward Kirkland, *The Peacemakers of 1864* (New York, 1927), pp. 118–24.

8. Philadelphia *Evening Bulletin,* March 25, 1864; New York *World,* March 26, 1864. An interesting account of the Democrats in the 1864 election can be found in Joel Silbey, *A Respectable Minority* (New York, 1977), chapter 5.

9. *Works of Buchanan,* 11 vols., ed. John B. Moore (Philadelphia, 1910), 11: 358, 370; Frank Severance, ed., *The Millard Fillmore Papers* (Buffalo, 1907), 2: 431–32; *To the Voting Millions of the United States* (Washington, 1864), pp. 7–8.

10. Bedford *Gazette,* May 6, 1864; Harrisburg *Patriot and Union,* August 12, 13, 1864; Greensburg *Argus,* August 24, 1864.

11. George Wolff Fahenstock Diary, August 18, 1864, HSP. This entry was written while Fahenstock was in Baltimore.

12. John Bell Robinson to McClellan, July ?, 1864, McClellan MSS.

13. Philadelphia *Evening Bulletin,* July 26, August 18, 1864; Vandling to Slifer, July 2, 1864, Slifer-Dill MSS; Cameron to Wayne McVeagh, August 21, 1864, McVeagh MSS, HSP; Fahenstock Diary, August 18, 1864, HSP; [anonymous], *Chronicle of the Union League of Philadelphia* (Philadelphia, 1902), p. 118.

14. Philadelphia *Evening Bulletin,* July 28, September 12, 1864; Harrisburg *Telegraph,* September 26, 1864.

15. Ebensburg *Democrat and Sentinel,* August 17, 1864; Uniontown *Genius of Liberty,* September 15, 1864; Greensburg *Argus,* September 21, 1864.

16. Philadelphia *Evening Bulletin,* August 8, September 14, 1864.

17. Hiram White to McClellan, September 7, 1864, McClellan MSS.

18. Abel to McClellan, September 7, 1864; Carroll to McClellan, September 7, 1864, ibid.; Buchanan to Lewis Coryell, September 6, 1864, Coryell MSS.

19. William Cook to McClellan, Septmeber 15, 1864; Wright to McClellan, October 13, 1864, McClellan MSS.

20. Isaac Metzler to McClellan, September 26, 1864; Garvin to McClellan, n.d., but between September 9 and November 8, 1864, ibid., Series 2, Box 20.

21. Vallandigham did later support McClellan. Selinsgrove *Times,* August 29, 1864, quoted in Coudersport *Potter County Journal,* September 28, 1864; William Russ, "Franklin Weirick: 'Copperhead' of Central Pennsylvania," *Pennsylvania History* 5 (1938): 251.

22. Both papers were quoted in Clearfield *Raftman's Journal,* October 5, 1864.

23. Tredwell to Jeremiah Black, September 19, 1864, Black MSS; Coryell to Buchanan, September 22, 1864, Buchanan MSS; Jones to McClellan, September 9, 1864, McClellan MSS; Philadelphia *Age,* September 19, 1864.

24. Erwin Bradley, *The Triumph of Militant Republicanism* (Philadelphia, 1964), p. 205; Philadelphia *Age,* September 1, 19, 1864.

25. Philadelphia *Sunday Dispatch,* September 4, 1864; Muncy *Luminary,* November 8, 1864.

26. Philadelphia *Age,* September 20, 29, 1864; Ebensburg *Democrat and Sentinel,* October 12, 1864; Easton *Argus,* November 3, 1864; Uniontown *Genius of Liberty,* September 29, 1864.

27. Johnstown *Democrat,* October 26, 1864; Greensburg *Argus,* October 26, 1864; Philadelphia *Age,* n.d., quoted in Uniontown *Genius of Liberty,* November 3, 1864.

28. W. H. Logan to William Cairnes, October 6, 25, 1864, Cairnes MSS; see also Lancaster *Intelligencer,* n.d., quoted in Uniontown *Genius of Liberty,* October 27, 1864.

29. The Philadelphian was Charles Ingersoll. Philadelphia *Age,* September 3, 1864.

30. Reed's support of McClellan was lukewarm. Reed to Edward McPherson, December 17, 1864, McPherson MSS, LC; Christopher Ward to Manton Marble, September 12, 1864, Marble MSS, LC; Anderson to Sister, October 30, 1864, Anderson MSS, Pennsylvania Historical and Museum Commission.

31. Meadville *Crawford Democrat,* September 27, 1864; Philadelphia *Evening Bulletin,* November 2–5, 1864.

32. Elizabeth to Sidney George Fisher, September 3, 1864, Fisher MSS, HSP.

33. Muncy *Luminary,* October 4, 1864; Lewistown *Gazette,* October 5, 1864; Philadelphia *North American,* November 7, 1864.

34. *A Democratic Peace Offered for the Acceptance of Pennsylvania Voters* (Philadelphia, 1864), pp. 3–13; Philadelphia *North American,* September 26, November 7, 1864.

35. Cowan to Jeremiah Black, September 12, 1864, Black MSS.

36. Cyrus Bearnenderfer? to Daniel Musser, February 20, 1864, Musser MSS, Pennsylvania Historical and Museum Commission; Tiffany quoted in Johnstown *Democrat,* August 10, 1864; McCandless cited in Franklin *Venango Spectator,* August 31, 1864.

37. Jacob Weidensall to Parents, September 27, 1864, Weidensall MSS; Meadville *Crawford Democrat,* October 4, 1864; see also the anonymous letter from a soldier in the 85th Pennsylvania Volunteers quoted in Uniontown *Genius of Liberty,* September 22, 1864.

38. Ward to Manton Marble, September 30, 1864, Marble MSS, LC; Bigler to Ward, September 20, 1864, Bigler MSS.

39. Pottsville *Miners' Journal,* September 10, 1864; Philadelphia *Evening Bulletin,* September 28, 1864; Curtin to Slifer, October 3, 1864, Slifer-Dill MSS; Alexander McClure, *Old Time Notes of Pennsylvania* (Philadelphia, 1905), 2: 128–30.

40. *Replies of the Hon. William D. Kelley to George Northrup, Esq. in the Joint Debates in the Fourth Congressional District* (Philadelphia, 1864), p. 26.

41. *The Tribune Almanac for 1865* (New York, 1865), p. 54; Josiah Benton, *Voting in the Field* (Boston, 1915), pp. 201–202; Pittsburgh *Gazette,* October 21, 1864.

42. Clearfield *Raftman's Journal,* October 12, 1864; Ebensburg *Democrat and Sentinel,* October 26, 1864; Montrose *Democrat,* October 27, 1864.

43. Francis Johnson to Curtin, October 11, 1864; Charles Kennedy to Curtin, October 18, 1864, Slifer-Dill MSS.

44. Meadville *Crawford Democrat,* November 8, 1864; Greensburg *Argus,* November 9, 1864.

45. Robert Cooper to Slifer, October 18, 1864, Slifer-Dill MSS.

46. Samuel L. M. Barlow to Samuel S. Cox, October 15, 1864, Cox MSS, Brown University; Wright to McClellan, October 25, 1864; William B. Franklin to McClellan, November 7, 1864, McClellan MSS; Easton *Sentinel,* October 27, 1864.

47. Zeriah Monks to Hattie Rohrer, October 9, 1864, Monks MSS, Emory University.

48. Benton, *Voting in the Field*, p. 202; Bradley, *Militant Republicanism*, p. 207n.

49. Meadville *Crawford Democrat*, December 5, 1864; Clearfield *Raftman's Journal*, November 16, 1864.

50. Dougherty to Mrs. C. Musser, November 8, 1864, Musser MSS, Pennsylvania Historical and Museum Commission; Jere McKibben to Slifer, November 12, 24, 1864, Slifer-Dill MSS; *L.R.*, Appendix for 1865, pp. i–v.

51. Greensburg *Argus*, November 16, 1864.

10

"I Yield to No Man in Sympathy for the South"

"I fully embrace the doctrine of secession."*

"The overthrow of Abolitionism or the recognition of the Confederacy is the only possible chance there is of putting an end to this horrible war. . . . Separation must come, and the sooner we make up our minds to accept it, the better it will be for all concerned."**

Even before the reelection of Lincoln some Copperheads were convinced that it was too late to restore the old Union. Harry Ingersoll and his wife, Sally, left for London in May 1864, preferring to live in England rather than to remain in the North. Their friend Joshua Francis Fisher had been so disheartened with the course of the war that he no longer took an active interest in politics. Family problems and an unwillingness to accept the changes brought about by the conflict made him unhappy and prematurely old. Formerly an outgoing man, he now contented himself with preparing a genealogy of his family. In Kittanning, James Alexander Fulton gave up the operation of the *Mentor* on July 28, 1864, stating that he "would rather be right than popular," and shortly thereafter he moved his family to Dover, Delaware.[1]

---

*Excerpt from a speech of Edward Ingersoll, April 13, 1865, quoted in Philadelphia *Evening Bulletin,* April 21, 1865.
**Bellefonte *Democratic Watchman,* February 3, 1865.

Disillusionment with the future of the nation grew after McClellan's defeat. James Campbell was so upset with the thought of four more years of Lincoln that he announced the sale of his paper, the Johnstown *Democrat*. Fearing that the Lincoln administration was "determined to crush beneath its heel every journalist who shall dare to impugn the motives or question the wisdom of [its] ... conduct," he declared on November 16 that he was "not disposed to suffer martyrdom." On December 21, after having sold his paper to H.D. Woodruff, he left Johnstown to seek his fortune in the Pennsylvania oil fields. Woodruff was only slightly less opposed to the war than his predecessor, but he had few good things to say about Lincoln.

Another editor, J. Grundy Winegarden of the Lewisburg *Argus*, declared on November 19 that he was temporarily shutting down operations to improve the typographical design of his paper, but he was "unable to give the exact date upon which we shall be able to resume publication." Later he decided to move West, prompting one Unionist editor to sneer, "One would suppose that his natural course would be South."[2]

Other antiwar spokesmen refused to be silenced. Peter Gray Meek of the Bellefonte *Democratic Watchman* absolved himself of any guilt for the misfortunes brought about by the war. Unable to admit that any series of military successes could restore the Union, he called for the making of a peace recognizing Southern independence. He was constantly assuring his readers that the economic collapse of the North was imminent, and he dismissed all peace rumors as propaganda designed to pacify the people and make them willing to supply new victims for the draft. "Let those who are rejoicing over the news of the ... [victories of the] past few days remember that they have rejoiced over the same kind of news everytime more victims were wanted for the slaughter pens," he wrote, "but we remember the past and that tells us of the future." Meek's recommendation was that the Democrats give neither more men nor more money to continue what he called a war of subjugation.[3]

On March 2, 1865, an army sergeant arrested Meek for counseling resistance to the draft and took him to Harrisburg, where he was put into a crowded jail cell. As soon as news of his incarceration was made public, several prominent Democrats visited prison officials and demanded that he be released or be charged with having committed some crime. Three days after his imprisonment, panicky officials released Meek and sent him home. Obviously having enjoyed his martyrdom, the young editor returned to Bellefonte humming "Home Again, Home Again." If Unionists thought that his stay in jail would cause him to moderate the tone of his editorials, they were to be disappointed.[4]

John Laird of the Greensburg *Argus* was another who refused to endorse any aspect of the war. His accounts of the activities of the "bungling butcher Grant, the marauder Sherman, and the incendiary Sheridan" differed little from those reported in Confederate journals. For example, he alleged that Sheridan's troops needlessly destroyed 30 homes, 31 mills, and 100 miles of fences. Unwilling to join those who considered such devastation to be a victory for the North, he caustically commented, "Let them [the antislavery men running the government] rub their hands and rejoice; their master, the devil is also rejoicing." Like Meek, he called the draft a "death lottery" and he urged Democrats to refuse to fight the "negro war." Furthermore, he warned that unless Lincoln made a peace with the South "on the basis of the supremacy of the Constitution," the British would sign a treaty of alliance with the Confederates.[5]

Meek and Laird were not the only ones to fear foreign intervention. Around the time of Lincoln's inauguration, the Ebensburg *Democrat and Sentinel* alleged that the British and French had tired of the blockade and were ready to make an alliance with the rebels. This would mean either war with France or England, it feared, or a humiliating "backing down" on the part of Lincoln. Even the Philadelphia *Age* professed to believe that the war would "never end" without foreign intervention and therefore it dismissed all talk of the collapse of the Confederacy.[6]

Peace Democrats persuaded themselves that the only impediment preventing the restoration of the Union was President

Lincoln's stubborn insistence that the South agree to the abolition of slavery. All but the antislavery zealots, argued the Philadelphia *Age,* wanted an end to the spilling of blood and the death of soldiers. No longer were there any attractions from "the rainbow glory formed from rank showers of blood and the red lights of blazing homes," but the abolitionist fanatics still refused to let the North have the peace it so desperately needed. "Oh! give the nation peace!" pleaded the Bedford *Gazette.* "Humanity bids you [to] end this bloody strife. . . . Civilization stands aghast at the carnage which ye have wrought and blushes at the murderous barbarism which desolates her fairest dwelling place."[7]

Particularly upsetting to Democrats was the failure of the Hampton Roads Conference. Armed with a pass from Lincoln, Francis P. Blair, Sr., met with Jefferson Davis in Richmond on January 12, 1865, and told him that, if the Confederates drove Maximilian out of Mexico, Unionist forces would probably assist them in that undertaking. Such an action, he said, would expand the United States into Central America and would win praise for Davis from both Northerners and Southerners. Blair envisaged this Mexican venture as a means for ending the war, and Davis agreed to a meeting of representatives of the United States and the Confederacy to decide how to bring peace to the two warring nations. Lincoln also welcomed such a conference to restore peace "to our common country."

A rendezvous was scheduled at Hampton Roads on February 3. Davis sent Vice-President Alexander H. Stephens, Robert M. T. Hunter, and John A. Campbell to represent the Confederacy; Lincoln and Seward headed the Union delegation. Because Lincoln refused to discuss any subject but the restoration of the Union, the Mexican invasion was all but forgotten by the delegates. At one point the president vaguely implied that, if the South would return to the Union, the passage of the proposed constitutional amendment abolishing slavery might be postponed, but he would not disavow the Emancipation Proclamation. Lincoln promised to be lenient in his interpretation of the confiscation laws and to grant amnesty to all who had engaged in the rebellion. In fact, he even promised to treat the Southern states as though they had never left the Union and to ask Congress to offer compensation to slaveowners based on the value of their Negroes in 1860. But under no circumstances would he agree to a cessation of hostilities until the South abandoned its resistance and disbanded all troops hostile to the government of the United States. To the Confederates these terms were as unacceptable as they would have been to Thaddeus Stevens and negotiations broke off.[8]

Naturally each side tried to exploit the other's intransigence for propaganda purposes and for boosting the morale of its own citizens. Confederate papers argued that no settlement could end the war unless it recognized Southern independence. The Unionist press of the North claimed that it would be foolish to do other than what Lincoln proposed. To give in to the Southerners would put "an indelible stain on our national escutcheon." "Much as we desire peace," proclaimed the Philadelphia *North American* of February 1, 1865, "we prefer war to dishonor."

Peace men were quite dismayed with the result of the conference. To them it represented further proof that under no circumstances would the Lincoln administration end the war unless the South renounced slavery. To the president and his cohorts, they said, abolition was more important than reunion.[9] According to the Bedford *Gazette* of February 17, 1865, the importance of the meeting could best be summarized in verse:

> reform?"
>   To settle the nation's hash.
> Up jumped the 'tarnal nigger
> And knocked it all to smash.

For years the Copperheads had declared that the Emancipation Proclamation was null and void because it was unconstitutional. In 1865, the peace men were aghast that Congress sought to remedy the situation by passing a constitutional amendment abolishing slavery. This, they believed, would make reunion impossible. How could there be concord and harmony, asked the Philadelphia *Age* on January 3, 1865, if "like the locusts of Egypt, the spirit of New England is to spread all over the states to devastate and destroy the rights and property of the people under the pretense of reform?"

Thus it was only natural that antiwar journals would have bitter words for Joseph Baily, Alexander Coffroth, and Archibald McAllister, the only members of the state's Democratic congressional delegation to vote in favor of the constitutional amendment abolishing slavery. But human bondage in America was fated to die, and recognizing this fact, both houses of the state legislature adopted the proposed constitutional amendment on February 3, 1865.[10]

Just as slavery was doomed, so was the Confederacy. Nonetheless, Copperheads stubbornly refused to admit that the Southerners could be defeated. To the York *Gazette* of January 31, 1864, talk of getting "the Southern Confederacy on its knees before Mr. Lincoln, begging for peace" was mere foolishness, and it predicted that those entertaining such delusions would be sadly disappointed. Using dubious logic, the West Chester *Jeffersonian* attempted to prove statistically that the South was invincible. Editor John Hodgson estimated that Confederate deaths totaled 106,000 per year, but he argued that this figure was more than offset by the yearly population increase of 212,500 whites. Thus, he insisted, despite the war, each year the rebels were getting stronger than they had been before. Moreover, he concluded, the South would be able to draft nearly 400,000 men in 1865, and this would enable the Confederates to continue the war for a long time.[11]

To the very end of the conflict peace men declared that the Union victories were inconsequential. As late as March reports circulated in their journals that the Confederates had recaptured Columbia, South Carolina. Even after the fall of Richmond, the Ebensburg *Democrat and Sentinel* announced that the disappearance of the Southern government would not "of itself produce peace." Peter Gray Meek also thought that Lee's surrender did not mean the end of the war, and he insisted that, even if peace did result, it could have been had years before without the shedding of so much blood.[12]

Some jeremiahs claimed that, although the present hostilities were ending, there would be another rebellion within twenty years. As far back as February 9, 1865, H. D. Woodruff of the Johnstown *Democrat* asked his readers:

> Suppose there is peace, what good will it do? Will it cement the broken cistern or mend the golden bowl? It is true that peace is better than war, but peace will not restore the pros-perity of the country or bring us good times again. Peace may end the war, but it will not cancel the [huge national] debt.

When it became apparent that the fighting was about over, the Philadelphia *Age* turned its attention from calling for a national convention to trying to mitigate any punishment the Radicals intended for the South. Applauding the conciliatory speeches of Senator Cowan, the *Age* warned that it would be un-American to subjugate the Southerners. If the doctrine of secession was heresy, it declared, the revolted states had never left the Union; therefore it was ridiculous to speak of them as territories. Similarly, once armed resistance ceased, there would be no further need for destruction or confiscation of property in Dixie, disfranchisement of Confederates, hangings of rebel leaders, or military occupation of the South. Since Lincoln also wanted to minimize the rigors of reconstruction—albeit not so much as the *Age* did—the paper found itself praising the president for the first time, but never did it fully appreciate his efforts to reunite the country as painlessly as possible.[13]

Before the nation could celebrate the end of four years of civil war, a madman assassinated Lincoln. The president's sudden and violent death disturbed many Copperhead leaders. Men who had previously said nothing good about the Illinois statesman now mourned his passing, emphasized his leniency toward the van-quished Southerners, and strongly condemned his assassin, who had once spent some time in Venango County engaged in the oil business. "The atrocious deed was so awful," insisted the Easton *Argus*, "that it would shock the heart of any individual not entirely insensible to the finer feelings of humanity." To the Johnstown *Democrat* the killing of Lincoln was "one of the most wicked and damnable episodes in the history of man's depravity . . . [and] a tocsin of awful warning."[14] The editors of the Philadelphia *Age*, who feared that angry mobs might destroy their offices at night because of their antiwar views, called the assassination "the greatest misfortune that could befall the country." Though he refused to border his editorial page with heavy black lines, John Hodgson of the West Chester *Jeffersonian* took great pains to denounce the murder of Lincoln as a great calamity.[15]

Regardless of whether there was hypocrisy mixed with true mourning for the passing of a great man, it was clear that Lincoln's death forced many Copperheads to reevaluate the qualities of the man whom they had not long before called an ape and a dictator. Not a few deplored the assassination because they feared that Johnson would be a more willing tool of the Radicals than Lincoln.

A few editors, however, indicated to their readers that they were not unduly upset about the murder of Lincoln. Although deploring assassinations, Franklin Weirick stated that his opinion of Lincoln was unchanged and that the president's death could not cover up his faults. The Bellefonte *Democratic Watchman* bore no black border in memory of Lincoln. The editor professed to be sorry that the murder had taken place but concluded that there was "no cause for despair. He [Lincoln] began the great work of conciliation; let his successor continue it and all may yet be well."[16]

Philadelphia Copperheads found it prudent to mourn Lincoln's death. When John Bear, a Unionist orator, discovered that one of his neighbors had not put crepe on his windows, he visited the man's home and asked if he intended to drape his house. On being told that the neighbor had no crepe, Bear, according to his account, responded to the man and his wife thusly:

I told them that if it [their home] was not draped in one hour, I would not leave one brick on top of another, for, said I, your party has killed our President and you are glad of it, but you shall seem to mourn by draping your house, or I will have a posse of men here in one hour to tear it down, and then I walked away.

Within minutes the neighbors draped their home. Those who, like Pierce Butler, refused to place crepe around their dwellings were careful not to speak openly about political matters lest they be arrested. This was no idle threat, for one Philadelphian foolish enough to say that Lincoln's death was a good thing had to be jailed to protect him from an angry crowd.[17]

Naturally there were others who also lacked the good taste to keep quiet. One anonymous man, probably from Philadelphia, expressed delight "that the despot Lincoln had been gathered to his fathers." His only regret was that "the villain had not met such a fate years ago at his first inauguration." Believing, however, "that it is never too late to do good," he praised the "Deliverer" both for wrenching away Lincoln's sceptre and for providing an example "to strike terror to the hearts of such gaunt-like demons as Abraham Lincoln no. 2."[18]

Such sentiments were extreme, but they had their counterparts elsewhere in the commonwealth. In Perry County a group of Democrats celebrated Lincoln's death by staging a bonfire; surprisingly enough, their Unionist neighbors did not disrupt their rally. When a man in Pittsburgh expressed joy at Lincoln's death, a woman threw a bowl of milk at him. In another part of the city a worker in a tannery found himself in a filthy vat after saying that Lincoln's assassination was long overdue. Two men in McKeesport were arrested when they expressed joy that the Illinois statesman was finally dead. Others daring to echo these sentiments were hurled from moving trains or threatened with lynchings.[19] All citizens were expected to join in the national mourning or to keep their views private.

Evidence that, regardless of his prominence, no one could defame Lincoln and escape retaliation came after Edgard Ingersoll made a foolish speech in New York. Normally more reticent in expressing his views than was his brother, Charles, Edward had addressed the Anti-Abolition State Rights Society on April 13, the night before Booth shot the president. After toasting American laborers with the words "From the curse of a great public debt may American institutions deliver them," he vigorously defended the concept of state rights. Not only did he argue that workers should refuse to help repay the national debt, but he also declared:

> I yield to no man in sympathy for the South, a gallant people struggling nobly for their liberty against as sordid and vile a tyranny as ever proposed the degradation of our race—nay, I go further and with Jefferson, Madison, and Livingston, I fully embrace the doctrine of secession as an American doctrine without the element of which American institutions cannot permanently live.[20]

Unionists were furious, and but for the fact that Ingersoll rented a house from a "loyal" man, his home would probably have been reduced to shambles. The Philadelphia *Evening Bulletin* was so enraged that it launched a personal campaign against him. Calling him an enemy of the people, it published extracts of the New York speech on April 21, and asked, "Shall such a traitor be allowed to dwell among us in Philadelphia?"

Apparently the answer was no. Ingersoll's neighbors in Germantown made known their intention to make him "disclaim his disloyal sentiments or quit the neighborhood"; his bank ordered him to close his account; and the Philadelphia district attorney threatened to prosecute him for treason. No longer dared he to walk the streets without a pistol or without subjecting himself to vicious slurs.[21]

While en route to his office on April 27, 1865, he quarreled with a veteran, who insisted that he apologize for his remarks in New York. Ingersoll, a stubborn man, tried to strike the former soldier with his cane and then waved his pistol menacingly. Police seized him, carted him to jail and required a $2,000 bond for his release.

When Charles Ingersoll, Edward's brother, came to jail with the money, a mob, including several police officers, ruthlessly beat him. None of Charles's attackers was arrested, and the city council refused to allocate a $500 reward for information leading to the arrest and conviction of the men involved in the assault.[22]

On April 29, 1865, Edward Ingersoll was secretly released from prison, and on the advice of friends he left the city for an unknown destination. Tempers had cooled down considerably when he returned a few days later, but he was forced to resign from the prestigious Philadelphia Club and his law practice suffered greatly for a rather long time.[23]

Philadelphia Copperheads looked upon the episode with considerable disgust, knowning that, had they dared to celebrate Lincoln's death or endorse the right of a state to secede, the mob would have attacked them too.

For many Pennsylvania peace men the surrender at Appomattox was a personal Waterloo. Not only did it shatter their political pretensions, but it also made them look to their neighbors like foolish prophets of doom. Moreover, the end of the war effected many of the things they had feared: the abolition of slavery, the punishment of the South for leaving the Union, the repudiation of the doctrine of secession, the centralization of power in Washington, and the granting of civil rights to blacks. Furthermore, an increasing number of voters began to believe the Republican claims that Democrats had brought about the war and had sympathized with the rebels during the conflict. Soon the state that had once been considered the keystone of northern Democracy became a citadel of Republicanism.

What was the extent of Pennsylvania Copperheadism? Although a few peace men did willingly assist Southerners and hoped that Pennsylvania would join the Confederacy even after the fighting had started, the overwhelming majority were loyal to the old Union. Despite some misgivings about the nature of the war, nearly all Pennsylvania Democrats supported the administration until the summer of 1862. Then, when it became apparent that the war was not about to terminate, that civil liberties might be suspended, and that emancipation was imminent, significant numbers of men began to ally themselves with the peace factions of the Democracy. It is not possible to estimate precisely the strength of antiwar feeling; voting for a Copperhead candidate does not necessarily mean that one is himself a Copperhead. Similarly some peace men doubtless lived in areas in which there was no antiwar candidate for whom to cast ballots. Nonetheless educated estimates can be made. A reading of contemporary documents, letters, and newspapers and a study of election statistics indicates that in the fall of 1862 at least a third of all Pennsylvania Democrats were hostile to the war. Few outside of Philadelphia were for "peace at any price"; probably only ten percent of the Democrats, about one-twentieth of the state electorate, held such extreme views then.

In 1863, however, the number of Copperheads nearly doubled, and the peace factions were able to nominate George W. Woodward for governor. Woodward was at least as extreme in his views as Clement Vallandigham, but he received a larger percentage of votes than the Ohioan. Even when one excludes the votes of Ohio soldiers, who, unlike Pennsylvania's Billy Yanks, were able to vote in 1863, the result is the same. Woodward was more popular with the electorate of Pennsylvania than Vallandigham was with the non-soldier voters of Ohio.[24]

Contemporary evidence suggests that, as late as the spring of 1864, about half of the Pennsylvania Democracy, nearly a fourth of the state's electorate, favored summoning a convention of the states to propose a nonmilitary solution to the war. This was not the same thing as favoring a Southern victory, for peace Democrats genuinely believed that reunion could best be achieved by declaring an armistice and abrogating Lincoln's Emancipation Proclamation. The ranks of the "peace at any price" men grew in 1863 and 1864, but again they were a minority of the Copperheads. It is doubtful that this extreme element ever numbered more than a tenth of the commonwealth's voters.

Union military victories during the 1864 presidential campaign did much to persuade war critics that the South could be defeated.

These battle triumphs were the decisive factor in the Unionist electoral successes in October and November. Nonetheless, General George B. McClellan, who ostensibly ran for president on a peace platform, carried a majority of the counties in the commonwealth. The general's defeat, however, was the death knell of Copperheadism. Like rats deserting a sinking ship, Democrats hastily fled from the peace factions of the party. Two months after Lincoln's reelection probably less than ten percent of the state's Democracy still called for a nonmilitary solution to the war.

What then was the importance of Pennsylvania Copperheadism? It is true that some wanted an armistice or a military stalemate, but they wanted it because they believed that cessation of hostilities would facilitate the reunion of the two warring sections under "the Constitution as it is and the Union as it was." At a time when men were prone to disregard civil liberties and castigate all dissenters as traitors, Pennsylvania Copperheads stood up and reminded the nation that the Constitution applied both in time of war and in time of peace. For their actions they suffered personal attacks, imprisonment, loss of friends, and the failure of business; but had they acquiesced in the violations of constitutional rights, a very dangerous precedent would have been established.

Too many Civil War scholars have tended to regard Copperheads as unpatriotic draft dodgers or treasonable fanatics. Others, taking the view that peace sentiment was strong only in the border states, the Middle West, and New York have overlooked Pennsylvania's Copperheads entirely.[25] But Keystone peace Democrats were both a reality and a considerable force in the state. An understanding of who they were, why they existed, and what they did is essential to a proper understanding of the Civil War.[26]

NOTES

1. R. Sturgis Ingersoll, *Sketch of the Ingersoll Family of Philadelphia* (Philadelphia, 1966), p. 12; Sophia Cadwalader, comp., *Recollections of Joshua Francis Fisher* (n.p., 1929), pp. ix-x; Kittanning *Mentor*, July 28, 1864; Fulton, "Western Pennsylvania," p. 96.

220   THE PENNSYLVANIA ANTIWAR MOVEMENT

2. Lewisburg *Argus*, November 19, 1864; Sunbury *American*, December 17, 1864, quoted in William Schnure, "The Fishingcreek Confederacy of Columbia County," *Northumberland County Historical Society Proceedings* 18 (1950): 98.

3. Bellefonte *Democratic Watchman*, January 6, 20, February 3, 24, 1865.

4. *Ibid.*, March 3-17, 1865; Bellefonte *Central Press*, March 3-31, 1865.

5. Greensburg *Argus*, December 14, 1864 - January 5, 1865; Bedford *Inquirer*, April 21, 1865.

6. Ebensburg *Democrat and Sentinel*, January 18, February 8, 1865; Philadelphia *Age*, March 3, 1865.

7. Bedford *Gazette*, November 18, 1864; Philadelphia *Age*, January 7, 1865.

8. James G. Randall and Richard N. Current, *Lincoln the President* (New York, 1954), 4: 325-27; Edward Kirkland, *The Peacemakers of 1864* (New York, 1927), pp. 92, 230-50.

9. Philadelphia *Age*, February 3, 1865; Gettysburg *Compiler*, February 13, 1865; Greensburg *Argus*, February 15, 1865.

10. Greensburg *Argus*, February 15, 22, 1865; *Congressional Globe*, Thirty-eighth Congress, 2nd session, January 31, 1865, pp. 523-24; Edward McPherson, *The Political History of the United States of America During the Great Rebellion*, 2nd ed. (Washington, 1865), p. 597.

11. *Jeffersonian*, n.d., quoted in Greensburg *Argus*, December 21, 1864.

12. Meadville *Crawford Democrat*, March 7, 1865; Ebensburg *Democrat and Sentinel*, April 12, 1865; Bellefonte *Democratic Watchman*, April 14, 1865.

13. Philadelphia *Age*, January 7, April 1, 10, 1865; *Congressional Globe*, Thirty-eighth Congress, 2nd session, January 24, February 2, 16, 1865, pp. 383-86, 560, 845.

14. Johnstown *Democrat*, April 19, 1865; Easton *Argus*, April 20, 1865; Ernest Miller, *John Wilkes, Oilman* (New York, 1947), pp. 27-33.

15. Adam Glossbrenner and William Welsch to Mayor Alexander Henry, April 15, 1865, Henry MSS, HSP; Philadelphia *Age*, April 15, 1865; West Chester *Jeffersonian*, n.d., quoted in Greensburg *Argus*, May 17, 1865; Ray Abrams, "The *Jeffersonian:* Copperhead Newspaper *Pennsylvania Magazine of History and Biography* 48 (1933): 281-82.

16. Bellefonte *Democratic Watchman*, April 21, 1865; William Russ, "Franklin Weirick 'Copperhead' of Central Pennsylvania," *Pennsylvania History* 5 (1938): 253.

17. John Bear, *The Life and Travels of John Bear* (Baltimore, 1873), p. 224; Philadelphia *Evening Bulletin*, April 18, 1865; *Fisher Diary*, pp. 493-96.

18. "One who knows and rejoices" to Mayor Henry, April 17, 1865, Henry MSS, HSP.

19. Harrisburg *Telegraph*, April 16, 1865; Clearfield *Raftman's Journal*, April 19, 1864; Pittsburg[h] *Dispatch*, n.d., quoted in Philadelphia *Evening Bulletin*, April 22, 1865; Arthur Bolze, "Perry County, Pennsylvania in the Civil War" (master's thesis, Pennsylvania State University, 1937), p. 43.

20. Philadelphia *Evening Bulletin*, April 21, 26, 1865; Lancaster *Examiner and Herald*, May 3, 1865.

21. Philadelphia *Evening Bulletin*, April 21-27, 1865; John Marshall, *American Bastile* (Philadelphia, 1873), p. 135.

22. *Fisher Diary*, pp. 492-96; Philadelphia *Age*, April 26, 1865; Philadelphia *Sunday Dispatch*, April 30, 1865.

23. Philadelphia *Public Ledger*, May 5, 1865; R. Sturgis Ingersoll, *Ingersoll Family*, p. 13.

24. Table 7 lists the results of the 1863 Pennsylvania gubernatorial election. The 1863

vote for governor by counties in Ohio can be found in Arnold Shankman, "Soldier Votes and Clement L. Vallandigham in the 1863 Ohio Gubernatorial Election," *Ohio History* 82 (1973): 102–104.

25. See, for example, Frank L. Klement, *The Copperheads in the Middle West* (Chicago, 1960); Wood Gray, *The Hidden Civil War: The Story of the Copperheads* (New York, 1942); and George Fort Milton, *Abraham Lincoln and the Fifth Column* (New York, 1942).

26. As Joel Silbey observes, "Until there is a close examination of the unsuccessful army, a significant gap will remain in our scholarship concerning the American political system in the Civil War era." He also notes that the Democrats were able "forcefully" to challenge the Lincoln administration's efforts to abolish slavery by "whatever means necessary." Silbey concludes that the Democracy "did not readily acquiesce in or celebrate the government's efforts even to win the war." *A Respectable Minority* (New York, 1977), pp. ix, xi, xiv.

Bibliographical Essay

Manuscript Collections

Although most Copperheads destroyed their personal papers for the Civil War years, a sufficient number of significant collections is available to provide a sound basis for a study of antiwar sentiment in Pennsylvania. Only the most important of these will be listed below.

Jeremiah Black never considered himself to be a Copperhead, but he was highly critical of the Lincoln administration's conduct of the war. In his papers are letters from George W. Woodward, Edgar Cowan, William B. Reed, James Buchanan, and Charles Buckalew. The papers of John Jordan Crittenden contain several letters from Pennsylvanians opposed to keeping the South in the Union against her will. Though neither George B. McClellan nor Manton Marble was a peace Democrat, they corresponded with George W. Woodward, William B. Reed, Charles Ingersoll, and Christopher Ward. Particularly useful were letters of antiwar farmers to McClellan in 1864, urging him to end the "bloody" conflict. All of these collections are in the Library of Congress (LC); the Black MSS are available on microfilm.

The papers of Simon Cameron include letters from Abraham Lincoln, Francis W. Hughes, Charlemagne Tower, and Edgar Cowan. They provide much information about Pennsylvania politics during the war, but Cameron evidently destroyed all letters that he considered damaging to his character. There are Cameron letters both in LC and in the Dauphin County Historical Society in Harrisburg. Those at Harrisburg are available on microfilm from the Pennsylvania Historical and Museum Commission (PHMC).

The papers of Cameron's rival, Governor Andrew Gregg Curtin, were apparently burned or lost, but Eli Slifer, Secretary of the Commonwealth during the Curtin administration, preserved a number of letters sent to the governor. Microfilm copies of the original letters, which are at Dickinson College, can be found at PHMC and the Historical Society of Pennsylvania (HSP).

In addition to copies of the Slifer-Dill MSS, HSP has a number of other important manuscript holdings. Among these are the papers of William Bigler and Lewis Coryell, two Copperhead leaders, and James Buchanan, a war Democrat. Correspondents of Bigler and Coryell included Francis W. Hughes, George W. Woodward, and Jeremiah Black. The most valuable items in the Buchanan papers are letters from William B. Reed, Jeremiah Black, Lewis Coryell, and George W. Woodward. Other valuable collections at HSP are the papers of Alexander Henry, mayor of Philadelphia; Uriah Painter, reporter for the Philadelphia *Inquirer,* friend of John Covode, and Unionist spokesman; Wayne McVeagh, another Unionist political figure; the Cadwalader and McCall Family Collections, papers of two of the most influential families in Philadelphia; and the diaries of George Wolff Fahenstock, a Philadelphia Unionist and a civic and business leader.

At PMHC are papers for James Stephen Africa, a Democratic editor in Huntingdon; Daniel Musser, a Democrat who corresponded with several Pennsylvania soldiers; and James Alexander Fulton, the editor of the antiwar Kittannning *Mentor.* Unfortunately the Fulton papers contain no items dated after 1861.

Several university libraries have manuscript collections that were helpful in the preparation of this study. At Emory University (EU) are the papers of Robert Gourdin, who corresponded with William B. Reed. EU also has a microfilm copy of the letters from a Pennsylvania soldier, Zeriah Monks, to his family and friends. At Wilkes College are the Charles Buckalew MSS. This collection, which numbers about a hundred pieces, includes letters from George W. Woodward, Warren J. Woodward, and William B. Reed. At George Williams College are the Weidensall Family Papers. Though Jacob and Robert Weidensall supported the war, they were sometimes critical of the Lincoln administration.

Two privately owned collections of papers were quite useful. Charles Taylor, brother of famed writer and lecturer Bayard Taylor, was a Unionist soldier killed at Gettysburg. Letters he received from his family offer insights about life on the home front and reveal the contempt of Unionists for Copperheads. The Taylor correspondence is in the possession of Charles F. Hobson, editor of the Papers of John Marshall. A few of the letters have been published in Charles Hobson and Arnold

Shankman, eds., "Colonel of the Bucktails: Civil War Letters of Charles Frederick Taylor," *Pennsylvania Magazine of History and Biography* 97 (1973): 333–61. Another valuable collection is the series of letters exchanged by William Cairnes and W. H. Logan, two college students critical of Lincoln. These items are in the possession of Mrs. Roy Keene of Christiana, Pennsylvania.

The National Archives contains a wealth of information about draft problems in Pennsylvania during the Civil War and about Pennsylvanians arrested for disloyalty. The problems provost marshals and draft enrollers encountered are well described in the hundreds of volumes that are included in the records of the Provost Marshal General's Bureau for Pennsylvania. These are part of the War Department's Records, Record Group 110 (RG 110). Information about disloyalty can be found in the Proceedings Relating to Prisoners, 1862, RG 59.

Newspapers

Contemporary newspapers were the single most valuable source of information. Not only did they report local news, but they also printed letters, political and government documents, and the proceedings of local political meetings. Many of the letters and documents they published are no longer extant. The best guide to Pennsylvania newspapers available within the commonwealth is Ruth Salisbury, ed., *Pennsylvania Newspapers, a Bibliography and Union List* (Pittsburgh, 1969). Unfortunately this list does not include information about newspapers available outside of the Keystone State. This bibliography will list the locations of some particularly valuable papers; a significant number of these are available on microfilm. In many cases only broken files could be located.

The most useful antiwar journals for which issues could be found are the Philadelphia *Age* (LC, HSP); Johnstown *Democrat* (EU); Bellefonte *Democratic Watchman* (Pennsylvania State University [PSU]); Greensburg *Argus and Westmoreland Democrat* (PHMC); Ebensburg *Democrat and Sentinel* (PMHC); Tunkhannock *North Branch Democrat* (PMHC); Kittanning *Mentor* (EU); Easton *Argus* (EU); West Chester *Jeffersonian* (Western Reserve Historical Society); Bedford *Gazette* (PMHC); *Christian Observer and Presbyterian Witness* (Presbyterian Historical Society of America); *Palmetto Flag* (HSP); Franklin *Venango Spectator* (Franklin Public Library); Carlisle *American Volunteer* (Pennsylvania State Library); Gettysburg *Compiler* (EU); Philadelphia *Pennsylvanian* (LC, HSP); and Chambersburg *Valley Spirit* (LC).

The following Democratic newspapers are also quite helpful: Harrisburg *Patriot and Union* (University of Pittsburgh); Pittsburgh *Post* (EU); York *Gazette* (PSU); New York *World* (EU); Montrose *Democrat* (PMHC); and Uniontown *Genius of Liberty* (EU).

Several Unionist journals provide information unavailable elsewhere. These include the Philadelphia *Evening Bulletin* (EU); Philadelphia *Inquirer;* Philadelphia *North American and United States Gazette* (LC); Philadelphia *Sunday Dispatch* (LC); Pittsburgh *Gazette* (EU); Pittsburg[h] *Dispatch* (EU); Harrisburgh *Telegraph* (PMHC); Pottsville *Miners' Journal* (PSU); Chambersburg *Franklin Repository* (EU); and Clearfield *Raftman's Journal* (PMHC).

The most important independent journal is the Philadelphia *Public Ledger* (EU). Also valuable for this study is the Confederate organ in London, *The Index* (EU).

Printed Primary Sources

Since only a few Pennsylvania congressmen left any personal papers, it is necessary to consult the appropriate volume of the *Congressional Globe* (Washington, 1860–65) for information about their attitudes and activities. Similarly the very best source of information on state politics is George Bergner, comp., *The Legislative Record, Containing the Debates and Proceedings of the Pennsylvania Legislature for the Sessions of 1860–65* (Harrisburg, 1860–65). A veritable gold mine of information is the 128-volume *War of the Rebellion: A Compilation of the Official Records of the Union and Confederate Armies* (Washington, 1880–1901).

A number of letters, books, and speeches of Pennsylvania Democrats have been published. One very important work is Charles Ingersoll, *Civil War Speeches* (Philadelphia?, 1865?); another is his *Brief View of Constitutional Powers, Showing that the Union Consisted of Independent States United* (Philadelphia, 1864). James Buchanan's letters and speeches have not yet been published in an adequate edition, but the eleven-volume *Works of Buchanan,* edited by John Bassett Moore (Philadelphia, 1910), is still useful.

Seven years before the outbreak of the war Jacob Dewees wrote an interesting book, *The Great Future of America and Africa, an Essay Showing Our Whole Duty to the Black Man Consistent with Our Own Safety and Glory* (Philadelphia, 1854), which proposed that money collected from the sale of public lands be used to colonize blacks in Africa. In 1862, Dewees, a Copperhead, wrote *To the People of Pennsylvania* (Pottsville, 1862), which shows the importance of racism in the state elections of that year.

Though not a Pennsylvanian, Samuel Francis DuPont spent much time in Philadelphia. *Samuel Francis DuPont: A Selection from His Civil War Letters,* 3 vols. (Ithaca, N.Y., 1969), ed. John D. Hayes, contains some comments on antiwar activities in Pennsylvania.

Nicholas B. Wainwright's superbly edited *A Philadelphia Perspective: The Diary of Sidney George Fisher* (Philadelphia, 1967) is one of the most valuable sources on pro-peace sentiment yet published. Though he sometimes was given to exaggeration, Fisher, a Unionist, was perceptive. Moreover, he was related to the Ingersolls, Joshua Francis Fisher, and several other Copperheads, and he was acquainted with Pierce Butler. Butler's daughter, Sarah, kept a fascinating diary in 1861 that has only recently been published. See Fanny Kemble Wister, "Sarah Butler Wister's Civil War Diary," *The Pennsylvania Magazine of History and Biography* 102 (1979): 271–327.

Biographical data about William B. Reed appears in his *A Paper Containing a Statement and Vindication of Certain Political Opinions* (Philadelphia, 1862) and his *The Last Appeal* (Philadelphia, 1860). Information about George McHenry can be found in his *The Position and Duty of Pennsylvania* (London, 1863) and his *The African Race in America* (London, 1861). William Winder wrote of his prison experiences in his *Secrets of the American Bastile* (Philadelphia, 1863). Useful material about Alexander McClure and many of his contemporaries is included in his *Old Time Notes of Pennsylvania*, 2 vols. (Philadelphia, 1905) and his *Abraham Lincoln and Men of War Times* (Philadelphia, 1892).

Two interesting pamphlets by Joshua Francis Fisher are *Concessions and Compromises* (Philadelphia, 1860) and *The Cruelties of the War by a Churchman* (Philadelphia, 1864).

Newspaper editorials can be found in Henry Lea, *The Record of the Democratic Party, 1860–1865* (Philadelphia?, 1865) and in Howard Perkins, ed., *Northern Editorials on Secession,* 2 vols. (New York, 1942).

Secondary Sources: Books

The outstanding study of Civil War Copperheadism is Frank L. Klement, *The Copperheads in the Middle West* (Chicago, 1960). His study, however, is not concerned with peace sentiment east of Ohio. Similarly, Wood Gray, *The Hidden Civil War: The Story of the Copperheads* (New York, 1942) and George Fort Milton, *Abraham Lincoln and the Fifth Column* (New York, 1942) also slight Pennsylvania war critics. Of limited value is Elbert J. Benton's badly dated *The Movement for Peace Without a Victory During the Civil War* (Cleveland, 1918). A recent study of war Democrats is Christopher Dell, *Lincoln and the War Democrats* (Rutherford, N.J., 1975).

Mention should be made of several state studies which discuss the Copperhead movement. Historians have given more attention to peace sentiment in Ohio and Indiana than for any other Midwestern states.

The most valuable works on the antiwar movement in Ohio are Frank L. Klement, *The Limits of Dissent: Clement Vallandigham and the Civil War* (Lexington, 1970); Eugene Roseboom, *History of the State of Ohio,* vol. 4, *The Civil War Era* (Columbus, 1944); Robert Harper, *The Ohio Press in the Civil War* (Columbus, 1962); George Porter, *Ohio Politics During the Civil War Period* (New York, 1911); Kenneth Wheeler, ed., *For the Union: Ohio Leaders in the Civil War* (Columbus, 1968); and David Lindsay, *"Sunset" Cox* (Detroit, 1959). For Indiana the three most important books are G. R. Tredway, *Democratic Opposition to the Lincoln Administration in Indiana* (Indianapolis, 1973); Kenneth Stampp, *Indiana Politics During the Civil War* (Indianapolis, 1949); and Emma Lou Thornbrough, *Indiana in the Civil War Era* (Indianapolis, 1965).

For information on other Midwestern Copperhead movements consult Frank L. Klement, *Wisconsin and the Civil War* (Madison, Wisc. 1962); David Lendt, *Demise of the Democracy: The Copperhead Press in Iowa* (Ames, Ia., 1973); William Parrish, *Turbulent Partnership: Missouri and the Union, 1861-1865* (Columbia, Mo., 1963); and Arthur Cole, *The Centennial History of Illinois,* vol. 3, *The Era of the Civil War* (Springfield, Ill., 1919).

Scholars have written only a few books on peace sentiment in other sections of the North. Those interested in Copperheadism should consult Richard Curry, *A House Divided: A Study of Statehood Politics and the Copperhead Movement in West Virginia* (Pittsburgh, 1964); John Niven, *Connecticut for the Union* (New Haven, Conn., 1965); Basil Lee, *Discontent in New York City, 1861-65* (Washington, 1943); Stanley Brummer, *Political History of New York State During the Period of the Civil War* (New York, 1911); Samuel Pleasants, *Fernando Wood of New York* (New York, 1948); E. Merton Coulter, *The Civil War and Readjustment in Kentucky* (Chapel Hill, N.C., 1926); Charles Clark, *Politics in Maryland During the Civil War* (Chestertown, Md., 1952); Harold Hancock, *Delaware During the Civil War* (Wilmington, Del., 1961). Attention should also be given to Adrian Cook's fascinating *The Army of the Streets: The New York City Draft Riots of 1863* (Lexington, Ky., 1974).

Political events in Civil War Pennsylvania are treated in two recent volumes, Erwin Bradley, *The Triumph of Militant Republicanism: A Study of Pennsylvania and Presidential Politics, 1860-1872* (Philadelphia, 1964), and William Dussinberre, *Civil War Issues in Philadelphia, 1856-1865* (Philadelphia, 1965). Though both books are helpful, neither makes full use of the material available on pro-peace sentiment. Of slight value is Frank Taylor, *Philadelphia in the Civil War* (Philadelphia, 1913).

Other books which deal in part with Pennsylvania and the Civil War are William Wright, *The Secession Movement in the Middle Atlantic States* (Rutherford, N.J., 1973); Robert Harper, *Lincoln and the Press* (New York, 1951), and William B. Hesseltine, *Lincoln and the War Governors* (New York, 1948). A valuable general study of conscription is Eugene Murdock, *One Million Men: The Civil War Draft in the North* (Madison, Wisc., 1971). A useful study of Pennsylvania before the Civil War is John Coleman, *The Disruption of the Pennsylvania Democracy, 1848-1860* (Harrisburg, Pa., 1975).

The problems political prisoners encountered are treated in James G. Randall, *Constitutional Problems Under Lincoln* rev. ed. (Urbana, 1964); John Marshall, *American Bastile* (Philadelphia, 1873); and John Freeze, *A History of Columbia County, Pennsylvania* (Bloomsburg, Pa., 1883).

Several biographical studies provide information about prominent Pennsylvania politicians. George W. Woodward's career is the subject of George Kulp, *Sketch of the Life and Character of George W. Woodward* (Wilkes-Barre, Pa., 1875) and of George A. Woodward, *Biography of George Washington Woodward* (n.p., 1924). On Andrew Curtin see William Egle, ed., *Andrew Gregg Curtin* (Philadelphia, 1895). Simon Cameron is sympathetically presented in Erwin Bradley, *Simon Cameron* (Philadelphia, 1966). Phillip Auchampaugh, *Robert Tyler* (Duluth, 1934), covers Tyler's pre–Civil War career. A scholarly study of Jeremiah Black is William Brigance, *Jeremiah Sullivan Black* (Philadelphia, 1934). On James Harvey see Daniel Crofts, "James E. Harvey and the Secession Crisis," *Pennsylvania Magazine of History and Biography* 103 (1979): 177–95.

Four other studies of value are Dennis Clark, *The Irish in Philadelphia* (Philadelphia, 1973); Michael Feldberg, *The Philadelphia Riots of 1844* (Westport, Conn., 1975); William Gudelunas and William Shade, *Before the Molly Maguires: The Emergence of the Ethno-Religious Factor in the Politics of the Lower Anthracite Region, 1844-1872* (New York, 1976); and Robert Alotta, *Stop the Evil: A Civil War History of Desertion and Murder* (San Rafael, Calif., 1978).

Appearing in print after this book was accepted for publication was one of the most important books yet written on Civil War politics. Insofar as possible I have incorporated information from Joel Silbey's *A Respectable Minority: The Democratic Party in the Civil War Era* (New York, 1977) in this book. Silbey uses different terminology than I do when discussing factions in the Democracy.

Secondary Sources: Articles

For Copperhead historiography consult Richard Curry, "The Union

As It Was: A Critique of Recent Interpretations of the Copperheads," *Civil War History* 13 (1967): 25–39; Frank L. Klement, "Civil War Politics, Nationalism, and Postwar Myths," *The Historian* 38 (1976): 419–38; Eric J. Cardinal, "Disloyalty or Dissent: The Case of the Copperheads," *The Midwest Quarterly* 19 (1977): 24–35; Robert Abzug, "The Copperheads," *Indiana Magazine of History* 66 (1970): 40–55.

An outstanding treatment of Philadelphia Copperhead leaders is Nicholas Wainwright, "The Loyal Opposition in Civil War Philadelphia," *Pennsylvania Magazine of History and Biography* 88 (1964): 294–315. Ray Abrams, "Copperhead Newspapers and the Negro," *Journal of Negro History* 20 (1935): 131–52, examines the negrophobia of the Philadelphia *Age* and other newspapers. The Pennsylvania Senate deadlock of 1864 is discussed in Arnold Shankman, "John Penney, Harry White, and the 1864 Pennsylvania Senate Deadlock," *Western Pennsylvania Historical Magazine* 55 (1972): 77–86. The arrest of Albert Boileau is the subject of Arnold Shankman, "Freedom of the Press: The Case of Albert Boileau," *Pennsylvania History* 42 (1975): 305–15.

Several biographical articles are useful. John Hodgson is the subject of Ray Abrams, "The *Jeffersonian:* Copperhead Newspaper," *Pennsylvania Magazine of History and Biography* 48 (1933): 260–83. For information on Amasa Converse, see Arnold Shankman, "Converse, *The Christian Observer,* and Civil War Censorship," *The Journal of Presbyterian History* 52 (1974): 227–44. A good study of Charles Ingersoll is Irwin Greenberg, "Charles Ingersoll: The Aristocrat as Copperhead," *Pennsylvania Magazine of History and Biography* 93 (1969): 190–217. The only study of Francis W. Hughes is Arnold Shankman, "Francis W. Hughes and the 1862 Pennsylvania Election," ibid., 95 (1971): 383–93. The career of Franklin Weirick is well covered in William Russ, "Franklin Weirick: 'Copperhead' of Central Pennsylvania," *Pennsylvania History* 5 (1938): 245–56. On William B. Reed one might consult Arnold Shankman, "William B. Reed and the Civil War," ibid., 39 (1972): 455–68. The most recent study of Andrew Curtin is Rebecca Albright, "The Civil War Career of Andrew Gregg Curtin," *Western Pennsylvania Historical Magazine* 47 (1964): 323–41, 48 (1965): 19–42, 151–74. The writer's essay on George Woodward can be found in James Robertson and Richard McMurry, *Rank and File: Civil War Essays in Honor of Bell Irvin Wiley* (San Rafael, Calif., 1976) pp. 93–111. A valuable article on Jeremiah Black is John T. Hubbell, "Jeremiah Sullivan Black and the Great Secession Winter," *Western Pennsylvania Historical Magazine* 57 (1974): 255–74.

Among the other scholarly articles of value are two studies of the Fishingcreek Confederacy of Columbia County. These are William Schnure, "The Fishing Creek Confederacy," *Northumberland County*

Historical Society Proceedings 18 (1950): 94–115, and William Hummel, "The Military Occupation of Columbia County, Pennsylvania," *Pennsylvania Magazine of History and Biography* 80 (1956): 320–38. Virtually all of chapter 7 of this book appeared in Arnold Shankman, "Draft Resistance in Civil War Pennsylvania," ibid., 101 (1977): 190–204.

Unpublished Studies

Two master's theses have been written about the Copperhead movement in Pennsylvania. Much outdated is Stella White, "Opposition to the Civil War in Pennsyslvania" (Pennsylvania State University, 1920); more satisfactory is Thomas Meredith, "The Copperheads of Pennsylvania" (Lehigh University, 1947), which is based upon published sources and a limited number of newspapers and manuscript collections. Pennsylvania politics during the start of the war are well covered in Stanton Davis's doctoral dissertation, "Pennsylvania Politics, 1860–63" (Western Reserve University, 1935).

Several biographical studies shed light on the Pennsylvania antiwar movement. The career of Alexander Kelly McClure is adequately portrayed in William Russell, "A Biography of Alexander K. McClure" (Ph.d. diss., University of Wisconsin, 1963). "Hendrick Bradley Wright: A Study in Leadership" is a well-researched dissertation on Wright by Daniel Curran (Fordham University, 1962). A good treatment of Simon Cameron is Brooks M. Kelley, "A Machine is Born: Simon Cameron and Pennsylvania" (Ph.d. diss., University of Chicago, 1961). The writer was not able to make much use of William Hummel's dissertation, "Charles R. Buckalew: Democratic Statesman in a Republican Era" (University of Pittsburgh, 1963).

An excellent discussion of the draft in Pennsylvania is William Itter, "Conscription in Pennsylvania During the Civil War" (Ph.d. diss., University of Southern California, 1941). Another useful dissertation was Edward Everett, "Pennsylvania's Mobilization for War, 1860–61" (University of Pittsburgh, 1954).

May McHenry, "Military Invasion of Columbia County and the 'Fishingcreek Confederacy'" (Bloomsburg, 1938) is a brief and biased treatment of this unfortunate event in Pennsylvania history. An extremely valuable memoir of the Civil War is James Alexander Fulton, "It Happened in Western Pennsylvania, 1822–65," ed. Cecil Fulton (Dover, Del., 1962). A microfilm of this transcript is at the Pennsylvania Historical and Museum Commission.

Index

Abel, Peter, 185

Adams, Thomas, 157

Afro-Americans: call for repeal of personal liberty laws protecting blacks, 40, 42–46; disfranchisement of, 24; efforts to bar immigration of, 113; hostility towards, 24–25, 40, 82, 97–100, 113, 132, 163–65; riots against, 24

Agnew, Daniel, 152

Ancona, Sydenham, 84, 142, 149, 170

Antiwar Sentiment, 70–71; as expressed in 1861, 75–76, 109–11; condemned by Unionists, 64–65, 69, 86, 117–18; concealed because of fear, 64–65, 69; expressed by soldiers, 116–17; hostility to war in 1864, 165–68; hostility to coercing South, 40, 42–57; in 1865, 208–12; manifests itself in 1862, 82–84, 89–90, 98, 101; opposition to suspension of writ of habeas corpus, 88–89; peace efforts of Jeremiah Black, 180–81; peace efforts of Horace Greeley, 178–79; peace meetings in 1861, 77; peace meetings in 1862–63, 108–9. *See also* Copperhead; Treason

Apple, John, 92

Arrests for disloyalty, 70–75, 87–88, 92–94, 111–14, 145, 147–51, 153–54, 208–9

Babbitt, Elijah, 58

Baily, Joseph, 212

Baker, Lafayette C., 87

Bannan, Benjamin, 194

Barr, James, 98

Barrett, Ormond, 87

Barzizi, Decimus and Ultimus, 119

Bayard, James, 65

Bear, John, 214–15

Bergner, George, 87

Bertolet, Abraham, murdered, 146

Biddle, Charles John, 17, 85, 113; elected to Congress, 83; opposes conscription act, 143; organizes militia to repel Confederates, 119, 126–27; unhappy with result of 1863 election, 137

Biddle, George, 108

Bigler, Samuel, 148

Bigler, William, 17, 59, 158, 197; defeated for Congress, 198; favoring Crittenden Compromise, 47–48, 58, 99; praises Cresson Compromise, 30; proposes convention of states to end war, 90; supports Morrill Tariff, 58

Bingham, Thomas, 131

Binney, Horace, 88–89

Black, Jeremiah Sullivan, 17, 130, 193; peace mission to Canada, 180–81; urged to avoid coercion of South, 53

Blacks. *See* Afro-Americans

Blair, Cassandra, 119

Blair, Samuel, 58

231